The Glannon Guide
to Constitutional Law:
Governmental Structure and Powers

The Glannon Guide to Constitutional Law: Governmental Structure and Powers

Learning Constitutional Law Through Multiple-Choice Questions and Analysis

Second Edition

Brannon Padgett Denning
Professor of Law
Cumberland School of Law
Samford University

Wolters Kluwer
Law & Business

Published by Wolters Kluwer Law & Business in New York.

Wolters Kluwer Law & Business serves customers worldwide with
CCH, Aspen Publishers, and Kluwer Law International products.
(www.wolterskluwerlb.com)

To contact Customer Service, e-mail customer.service@wolterskluwer.com,
call 1-800-234-1660, fax 1-800-901-9075, or mail correspondence to:

> Wolters Kluwer Law & Business
> Attn: Order Department
> PO Box 990
> Frederick, MD 21705

Printed in the United States of America.

1 2 3 4 5 6 7 8 9 0

ISBN 978-1-4548-1664-5

Library of Congress Cataloging-in-Publication Data

Denning, Brannon P.
  The Glannon guide to constitutional law : governmental structure and powers,
learning constitutional law through multiple-choice questions and analysis / Brannon
Padgett Denning, Professor of Law, Cumberland School of Law, Samford
University. —Second edition.
    pages cm
  Includes index.
  ISBN 978-1-4548-1664-5
1. Constitutional law—United States—Problems, exercises, etc.   2. Judicial
power—United States—Problems, exercises, etc.   3. Separation of
powers—United States—Problems, exercises, etc.   I. Title.
  KF4550.Z9D45 2013
  342.730076—dc23

                                                       2012049073

Certified Chain of Custody
Product Line Contains At Least
20% Certified Forest Content
www.sfiprogram.org
SFI-00756

About Wolters Kluwer Law & Business

Wolters Kluwer Law & Business is a leading global provider of intelligent information and digital solutions for legal and business professionals in key specialty areas, and respected educational resources for professors and law students. Wolters Kluwer Law & Business connects legal and business professionals as well as those in the education market with timely, specialized authoritative content and information-enabled solutions to support success through productivity, accuracy and mobility.

Serving customers worldwide, Wolters Kluwer Law & Business products include those under the Aspen Publishers, CCH, Kluwer Law International, Loislaw, Best Case, ftwilliam. com and MediRegs family of products.

CCH products have been a trusted resource since 1913, and are highly regarded resources for legal, securities, antitrust and trade regulation, government contracting, banking, pension, payroll, employment and labor, and healthcare reimbursement and compliance professionals.

Aspen Publishers products provide essential information to attorneys, business professionals and law students. Written by preeminent authorities, the product line offers analytical and practical information in a range of specialty practice areas from securities law and intellectual property to mergers and acquisitions and pension/benefits. Aspen's trusted legal education resources provide professors and students with high-quality, up-to-date and effective resources for successful instruction and study in all areas of the law.

Kluwer Law International products provide the global business community with reliable international legal information in English. Legal practitioners, corporate counsel and business executives around the world rely on Kluwer Law journals, looseleafs, books, and electronic products for comprehensive information in many areas of international legal practice.

Loislaw is a comprehensive online legal research product providing legal content to law firm practitioners of various specializations. Loislaw provides attorneys with the ability to quickly and efficiently find the necessary legal information they need, when and where they need it, by facilitating access to primary law as well as state-specific law, records, forms and treatises.

Best Case Solutions is the leading bankruptcy software product to the bankruptcy industry. It provides software and workflow tools to flawlessly streamline petition preparation and the electronic filing process, while timely incorporating ever-changing court requirements.

ftwilliam.com offers employee benefits professionals the highest quality plan documents (retirement, welfare and non-qualified) and government forms (5500/PBGC, 1099 and IRS) software at highly competitive prices.

MediRegs products provide integrated health care compliance content and software solutions for professionals in healthcare, higher education and life sciences, including professionals in accounting, law and consulting.

Wolters Kluwer Law & Business, a division of Wolters Kluwer, is headquartered in New York. Wolters Kluwer is a market-leading global information services company focused on professionals.

Still for E.I.D.

Contents

Acknowledgments for the Second Edition

I want to thank all the students who have found this volume useful and have taken the time to write to tell me so. I hope that it continues to be of use to law students. Again, I want to thank my Dean, John Carroll, and the Cumberland School of Law both for financial assistance, and for allowing me the time to finish the updates to the second edition. My research assistant, Robbie McNaughton, Cumberland, Class of 2013, eased my labors considerably, as did my assistant Donna Klowsowsky; I am grateful to both for their help. Thanks, too, to Alli and Gram whose love and support are constants.

Acknowledgments

This project would not have been possible without Carolyn Czick's recommendation of me to Lynn Churchill, who then issued an invitation to submit a proposal. I thank both of them, and Joe Glannon, the creator of the series, for this opportunity. Christine Hannan has been an outstanding editor and has made the production of this volume run smoothly; Teresa Horton provided excellent copyediting.

I am equally grateful to a series of colleagues who provided invaluable feedback on drafts of this volume: Michael P. Allen, Stetson University College of Law; Cindy G. Buys, Southern Illinois University School of Law; John Min Kang, St. Thomas University School of Law; Laura E. Little, Temple University Beasley School of Law; Calvin R. Massey, University of California Hastings College of the Law; Robert G. Natelson, The University of Montana School of Law; Mark C. Rahdert, Temple University Beasley School of Law; Ruthann Robson, CUNY School of Law; Jon M. Van Dyke, University of Hawaii at Manoa William S. Richardson School of Law; and Rebecca E. Zietlow, The University of Toledo College of Law. Special thanks are due to my former Cumberland colleague Marcia M. McCormick, now at St. Louis University School of Law, and Jeff Hirsch at the University of Tennessee College of Law, both of whom went above and beyond the call of duty in reviewing the manuscript. Of course, none of these are responsible for errors or omissions that remain. The Cumberland School of Law and my wonderful dean, John L. Carroll, supported this work financially through the award of a summer research grant. I thank Alli and Gram for their support and their patience as I raced to meet deadlines. Finally, I thank all my past and present students at the Cumberland School of Law and, before that, at the Southern Illinois University School of Law. It was because I learned so much from them that I am able to create this tool for use by future students of constitutional law.

The Glannon Guide
to Constitutional Law:
Governmental Structure and
Powers

1

A Very Short Introduction

The purpose of this book is to familiarize the reader with the doctrines that the U.S. Supreme Court uses to enforce provisions of the U.S. Constitution most commonly covered in a one- or two-semester law school course in constitutional law. It is not a book about constitutional interpretation or the role of other branches (or the role of other parts of the *judiciary*) in creating and enforcing constitutional law; nor is it a work of constitutional history. It does none of those things because such topics are rarely covered in the typical law school constitutional law class. Such topics are certainly not covered by the Multistate Bar Exam's constitutional law questions. For better or worse, the typical law school course equates "constitutional law" with "the work product of the U.S. Supreme Court," and so does this book. *In Important to make sure klarman agrees.*

Because "constitutional law" encompasses so much material, this is the first of two volumes. This volume, like the first-semester constitutional law class, covers the scope of and limits on the powers of the three branches, as *SoP* well as other structural topics like constitutional limits on state power to *Federalism* regulate interstate commerce, separation of powers controversies, and the like. The second volume covers civil rights and civil liberties, including the First and Fourteenth Amendments, among others. Both volumes emphasize current doctrine and its application by the Court, although some description of doctrinal evolution will be included where necessary to provide context.

I intend each volume to function as an "interactive treatise." There will be narrative portions covering particular doctrinal areas that discuss the major cases making up that doctrine. Unlike ordinary hornbooks and treatises, the *Glannon Guides,* like this one, provide opportunities throughout the narrative to test your comprehension of what you just read using multiple-choice questions and detailed answers that explain not only why one answer is the better one, but also why the other choices were inadequate.

The volume includes a number of different kinds of questions, and the intent is that they get more difficult as you progress through a chapter. Some questions will simply test *comprehension*—did you understand what you just read, and can you correctly identify the black-letter law? Others involve *application,* testing whether you can apply the black-letter law to facts very similar to ones in the narrative. Still others involve advanced application, and ask you to apply the black-letter law to facts *different* from the facts discussed in the section. Finally there are *capstone* questions that force you to grapple with open questions, new facts, multiple related doctrinal areas, or some combination of these. These capstone questions appear in the final chapter, "Closing Closers."

Before discussing how best to use the book, let me preempt some skepticism about the ability to test comprehension of constitutional law through the use of multiple-choice questions. The skepticism isn't unwarranted—Joe Glannon himself was skeptical about the feasibility of a *Glannon Guide* for constitutional law. If you've taken a few constitutional law classes, you might have come away convinced that the subject is too malleable, too indefinite to test "objectively." Not to be too instrumental about it, but the drafters of the Multistate Bar Exam certainly don't think that constitutional law defies objective assessment! Rank instrumentalism aside, even if constitutional law—with all its open-textured-ness—is "best" assessed using essay exams, I firmly believe that the multiple-choice questions in these two volumes will provide useful, fast feedback on basic concepts in constitutional law. They furnish a means, not always available in law school, to track your progress and test your comprehension. Multiple-choice questions make it hard to fool yourself—if you choose A and the answer is B, you can't really pretend that you *really* chose B.

As far as using this volume, it should go without saying that it is not intended to be a substitute for conscientious class preparation, faithful class attendance, and diligent study. I think that the best use of this *Glannon Guide* would be as both a periodic self-test and as pre-exam review. For the former, you might use it after covering material that you found particularly difficult or confusing (e.g., the power of Congress to alter the jurisdiction of the federal courts) to test basic comprehension and application. Alternatively, you might use it at the conclusion of a major segment of the course (e.g., separation of powers). If you use it for these periodic reviews, I urge you to use the *Glannon Guide* last. Read your casebook, aided perhaps by a hornbook such as Erwin Chemerinsky's *Constitutional Law: Principles and Policies.* Use this volume to review the major points, then test your comprehension with the questions. Reading the same material in several different forms, and at different levels of detail, will make it more likely to stick in your mind. Using the questions can then identify gaps in your understanding and allow you to study more efficiently.

As for end-of-semester review, my intent is for the narrative material to be presented succinctly enough that it could be read through to reinforce important concepts and aid in outlining. In addition, the Closing Closers pose more

Use Ed's study technique

detailed and difficult questions that will help you identify where your comprehension is weakest.

However you use this *Glannon Guide,* I sincerely hope that you find it helpful. If you have comments, criticisms, or suggestions, please e-mail me at bpdennin@samford.edu.

2

Judicial Power and the Constitution

[handwritten: 3 BIG TOPICS FOR THIS CHAPTER.]

A.   Overview

[handwritten: As always]

Most constitutional law courses begin by looking at the origin of the Court's power of *judicial review*—the power of courts to review actions of other branches of the federal government, and those of state and local governments, for constitutionality—and that is where this chapter begins as well. It opens with an examination of the origins of the Court's power to review federal and state acts for compliance with the Constitution, and briefly discusses the scope of the Court's power to interpret the Constitution relative to that of the other branches. The rest of the chapter is devoted to *limits* on judicial review, including not only those in the Constitution itself, but also those devised by the Court. Specifically, we examine the various justiciability doctrines, the most important of which are standing and the so-called political question doctrine. Finally, we'll look at the power of Congress to alter the jurisdiction of lower federal courts and the U.S. Supreme Court, as well as the limits that the Eleventh Amendment places on the jurisdiction of the federal courts.

[handwritten left margin: (1) Court's ability to review federal & state acts for constitutionality.]

[handwritten bottom left: (2) Scope of court's power to interpret the constitution relative to other branches. → Do other branches have that power? → Is it diff than court's power to interpret other laws?]

[handwritten bottom right: (3) Limits on judicial review → Some from the Constitution → Some from the court itself]

B.   The Origin and Scope of Judicial Review

1.   Introduction

A3 silent on judicial review but creates the fed. courts?

It comes as a surprise to many students that Article III of the Constitution — the article dealing with the structure and jurisdiction of the federal judiciary — is silent on the power of judicial review. For a time, scholars debated judicial review's legitimacy given this constitutional silence; the current consensus is that there were plenty of examples of judicial review by state courts at the time of the Framing and that the practice was not unknown to those who drafted the Constitution in Philadelphia during the summer of 1787. In fact, com-ments by various delegates during the debates over the Constitution strongly suggest that they expected the courts to exercise some form of independent constitutional review as a check on the other two branches and on the states. Other scholars argue that it was well understood that judicial review was included in the term "judicial power" mentioned in Article III, § 1 ("The judicial Power of the United States, shall be vested in one Supreme Court, and in such inferior Courts as the Congress may from time to time ordain and establish").

· Framers expected the Courts to exercise independent Constitutional review (comment from Framers @ the time)

Although the propriety of courts passing on the work product of coor-dinate branches — at both the state and federal level — remained contested through the late eighteenth and early nineteenth centuries, it was firmly established by the mid-nineteenth century. Whatever else might be said about judicial review, however, this much is true: Chief Justice John Marshall did not *invent* judicial review in the famous case of *Marbury v. Madison,* 5 U.S. 137 (1803). In fact, *Marbury* was not even the first instance of the Court's exercising judicial review. In an earlier case, *Hylton v. United States,* 3 U.S. 171 (1796), several of the Justices seemed to assume that the Court had the power to review acts of Congress for constitutionality; and in *Ware v. Hylton,* 3 U.S. 199 (1796), the Court invalidated a state law that conflicted with the treaty ending the American Revolution. *Marbury* is nevertheless considered foundational, probably because of the detailed argument in favor of judicial review that contrasts with the rather offhand manner with which the power was asserted (or assumed) in the earlier cases. Therefore, it is with *Marbury* that we begin.

2.   Judicial review of federal legislation

Marbury arose in a highly charged political context. In 1800, the Federalists (those who tended to favor a strong national government and national eco-nomic policies) were swept out of office by "Republicans," whose followers were allied with Thomas Jefferson and James Madison (who feared a strong central government and tended to favor state institutions over federal). At the time the new administration did not take power until March,[1] so there was a lame-duck session of Congress that convened in early 1801. Among other things, the lame-duck Congress created a number of new judgeships, including several justices of the peace. The President made nominations to these positions and the Senate confirmed the nominees, but there was a rush to get the new judges' commissions signed and delivered before the new administration took over.

Several commissions were not delivered, including that of William Marbury. He filed suit in the Supreme Court seeking a writ of mandamus directing Jefferson's Secretary of State, James Madison, to deliver the commission to which, he argued, he was legally entitled, because he had been confirmed by the Senate and his commission had been signed by former President Adams. Jefferson and Madison's position was that, like a deed of gift, the commission had to be delivered to be valid, and they weren't about to deliver any of Adams's commissions.

According to Chief Justice Marshall in *Marbury v. Madison,* 5 U.S. 137 (1803), Marbury's case presented three questions, which he addressed in the following order:

> 1st. Has the applicant a right to the commission he demands?
> 2dly. If he has a right, and that right has been violated, do the laws of his country afford him a remedy?
> 3dly. If they do afford him a remedy, is it a mandamus issuing from this court?

5 U.S. at 154. Marshall concluded that Marbury was indeed entitled to his commission; that the signing of the commission created vested property rights in the position.

Because he was legally entitled to his office, and the responsible officer refused to deliver it, Marshall then concluded that a writ of mandamus — an order to a government official compelling that official to perform an act the officer is legally obligated to perform — was the appropriate remedy. *Id.* In doing so, the Chief Justice made a distinction between those acts — say, making the nomination in the first place — that are within the discretion of officials and for which the law will provide no remedy, and those involving the rights of individuals that the official "cannot at his discretion sport away...." *Id.* In other words, if, during a night of heavy drinking, Adams promised to nominate Marbury as a justice of the peace, then reneged after he sobered up, Marbury would have no legal recourse against Adams. But here, Madison had no discretion when it came to Marbury's commission, given Marshall's conclusion that Marbury's rights to the position vested when the commission was signed and the seal of the United States affixed. *Id.* at 162.

---

1. The Twentieth Amendment, ratified in 1933, established the new Inauguration Day as January 20, and specified that "the terms of Senators and Representatives [end] at noon on the 3d day of January...." U.S. Const. amend XX.

The question remained, though, whether the Court had the power to issue the writ. Section 13 of the Judiciary Act of 1789 seemed[2] to give the Court the ability to issue such writs under its original jurisdiction. The problem was that unlike the provision in Article III granting Congress the ability to make "regulations and exceptions" to the Court's appellate jurisdiction, the Court's original jurisdiction, which didn't mention the issuing of writs of mandamus, contained no such proviso. Thus, Marshall had to address what the Court's responsibility was when an ordinary statute, such as the Judiciary Act of 1789, conflicted with a provision of the Constitution. That question, he wrote, "is a question deeply interesting to the United States; but, happily, not of an intricacy proportioned to its interest." *Id.* at 176. "It is a proposition too plain to be contested, that the constitution controls any legislative act repugnant to it; or, that the legislature may alter the constitution by an ordinary act." *Id.* at 177. Either the Constitution is higher law, or it is alterable at will by the legislature, he maintained.

Assuming that the Constitution *is* superior to mere legislative enactments, who decides when there is a conflict? Marshall answered that "[i]t is emphatically the province and duty of the judicial department to say what the law is. . . . If two laws conflict with each other, the courts must decide on the operation of each." *Id.* In addition to Article III's grant of the "judicial power" to the Court, Chief Justice Marshall justified this role for the courts by referring to the written nature of the Constitution; the Supremacy Clause of Article VI, which makes the Constitution and all laws "pursuant thereto" the supreme law of the land; and the oath that judges take to uphold the Constitution. *Id.* at 178–180.

Later Courts claimed power not only to "say what the law is," but to authoritatively interpret the Constitution and to bind all other governmental actors with that interpretation. *Cooper v. Aaron,* 358 U.S. 1 (1958). In *Cooper,* the Court rejected claims by the State of Arkansas that it was not bound by *Brown v. Board of Education,* 347 U.S. 483 (1954), which held that state-enforced segregation was unconstitutional, because Arkansas was not a party to the *Brown* suit. The Court wrote that "the federal judiciary is supreme in the exposition of the law of the Constitution" and that, as a result, the Court's interpretation was binding on all states, even those not sued in *Brown.* 358 U.S. at 18.

3.   *Judicial review of state legislation*

Martin v. Hunter's Lessee, 14 U.S. 304 (1816), can be thought of as a companion case to *Marbury.* The latter established judicial review as between coequal branches of the federal government — think of it as establishing "horizontal" judicial review. *Martin,* on the other hand, vindicated the power of Congress to create mechanisms for "vertical" judicial review — that is, creating mechanisms

---

2.   It isn't clear that § 13 actually did this; scholars continue to disagree about Marshall's interpretation of this provision.

for the Supreme Court to review the decisions of state courts (at least in the cases enumerated in § 25 of the 1789 Judiciary Act).

Martin was the culmination of land litigation of Dickensian complexity that began in the late eighteenth century in Virginia state court, and was ultimately appealed to the U.S. Supreme Court. Essentially, the contest was between Denny Martin, the successor to the land's original (British) owner, Lord Fairfax, and another person (Hunter) who had acquired title after Virginia seized the land, as commonly happened with land and other property owned by British subjects during and after the Revolution. An important provision of the Treaty of Paris, which ended the Revolution, was the restoration of the rights of British subjects to property that had been taken. When the Supreme Court first held for Martin in 1813, the Virginia Supreme Court refused to enter judgment, claiming that § 25 of the 1789 Judiciary Act, which gave the U.S. Supreme Court power to review certain state court judgments, and which had been invoked to review state high court decisions a number of times before *Martin,* was unconstitutional. Thus the Court heard the case a second time; Justice Joseph Story wrote the Court's opinion because Chief Justice Marshall—who usually spoke for the Court during his tenure as Chief Justice—and Marshall's brother sought part of the land in question. Even by the somewhat relaxed attitudes of the nineteenth century regarding conflicts of interest, the Chief Justice thought it appropriate to recuse himself.

Virginia's argument against § 25's constitutionality proceeded along two tracks. First, the state argued that Article III said nothing about the judicial power of the United States extending to state courts, and that Congress's attempt to extend it to those courts was unconstitutional. Second, it maintained that any such review was inconsistent with Virginia's status as a sovereign state, which stood on an equal footing with the United States; and that any appellate review of its high courts implied subordination and inferiority, which was inconsistent with the state's sovereign status. While not quite denying that the Constitution or federal law wasn't supreme or that uniformity wasn't an appropriate goal, Virginia claimed that the burden was on Congress, through a removal statute, to provide for the movement of federal questions from state into federal courts so that they might ultimately be decided, by the Supreme Court, in a uniform fashion.

For his part, Justice Story's opinion for the Court had three responses. It was true, he conceded, that Article III did not mention state courts, but that omission was irrelevant. Article III extended the judicial power of the United States to the *cases* specified therein, giving inferior federal courts original jurisdiction over them and the U.S. Supreme Court appellate jurisdiction over those issues. Moreover, he emphasized that the power extended to "*all* cases" regardless of where they originated. *Id.* at 338. He also used history to describe why this arrangement made sense: Had Congress decided *not* to create inferior federal courts, and it could *not* exercise appellate review over questions arising in state courts, then the Court would have nothing to do except preside over its tiny original docket. That, Story wrote, was not what the Framers intended. *Id.* at 340.

Second, the Court held that Virginia's concern with its sovereign status and the independence of its judiciary suggested a fundamental misunderstanding of the nature of Union created by the Constitution. Article VI, he noted, explicitly subordinates state law and state constitutions to the U.S. Constitution and to federal laws passed pursuant to the Constitution. Congress hadn't subordinated anyone to anything in § 25, the Constitution had. *Id.* at 325–326.

Finally, the Court noted how important federal uniformity was, not only in the interpretation and application of federal statutes and treaties, but also in the interpretation of the Constitution. Story noted the irony in holding that Congress could provide for removal of questions from state courts altogether. Under § 25, state courts retained jurisdiction of cases; only at the end, and only under certain circumstances, did the Court exercise judicial review. But Virginia seemed to be inviting Congress to step in and deprive state courts of any and all jurisdiction over federal questions. Which course, he asked rhetorically, implies inferiority and subordination more? *Id.* at 348–349; *see also Cohens v. Virginia,* 19 U.S. 264 (1821) (upholding the Court's ability to review *criminal* convictions for constitutionality under § 25).

It should be noted that the Court had, without objection, exercised appellate jurisdiction a number of times before *Martin.* Southern states began to challenge the scope of federal power in the early nineteenth century, and would continue to do so until after the Civil War. The reason was slavery. Southern states began to get very nervous about the claims that the federal government was making for the scope of its powers and feared that it was only a matter of time before the issue of abolishing slavery came up. There had been a tacit agreement to let the matter lie after the Constitution was ratified, but groups were beginning to emerge who threatened to upset that understanding. These objections to federal power, and claims about the Constitution being merely a "compact" among sovereign states, similar to the Articles, began to proliferate at this time and would come to dominate Southern political discourse by the middle of the nineteenth century.

Questions about the proper allocation of power between state and federal governments — federalism, in other words — have been called "the oldest questions in constitutional law." *Martin v. Hunter's Lessee* gives you an idea why. The ink was barely dry on the Constitution before questions over the proper roles of the state and federal governments under it began to arise. There was also the question of who would decide them. As was true in *Marbury,* the clear winner emerging from *Martin* was the Supreme Court itself.

QUESTION 1. Veto-gate. President Pauli has promised Ed Executive that she will veto a regulatory bill that has just passed Congress limiting the pay of publicly traded corporations' executives. The bill was born of the public — and Congress's — dismay at the large disparities between what the top earners made at various publicly traded corporations and what those at the bottom took home. To his dismay, however, the President soon reverses course and signs the bill, later claiming that she was persuaded that the curb was, indeed, needed. Furious because his own pay is due to be decimated, Ed files suit in federal district court seeking judicial review of the President's veto. A reviewing court is likely to:

 A. Grant judicial review, because of the President's promise to Ed.
B. Deny review because the decision whether to veto a bill or not is within the President's discretion.
C. Deny judicial review because acts of the President are not subject to judicial review.
D. Deny judicial review because courts will not review controversies involving politics.

ANALYSIS. This tested how well you understood the proposition for which *Marbury* stood. Recall the discussion about Chief Justice Marshall drawing a distinction between cases involving rights vested by law in an individual, for which a court could provide remedy if those rights were violated; and those decisions for which only a "political" remedy was available, because they were committed to the discretion of elected officials? That distinction is key to this question. The Constitution gives the President the discretion to veto or to sign a piece of legislation (subject to the veto being overridden by the requisite vote in both houses of Congress). Therefore, whatever private promise the President made has little bearing on her ability to exercise her veto according to the discretion committed by the Constitution. Therefore **A** cannot be the correct answer. Further, **C** is not the correct answer because it is an incorrect statement of law: Although certain acts are committed by the Constitution to the President's discretion, held *Marbury,* it does not follow that *all* are — indeed, the Court regularly reviews (and invalidates as unconstitutional) acts of Presidents. **D** is also incorrect; it is an overreading of *Marbury.* Many constitutional controversies in which the Court exercises judicial review involve politics of one sort or another. It is not the *political* nature of the controversy that *Marbury* says renders it unfit for judicial review; rather, it is whether the power exercised is one committed to the "political discretion" of another actor that matters. Article II gives the President the power to veto a bill or sign it at her pleasure, private promises to the contrary notwithstanding. Therefore **B** is the best answer. As Chief Justice Marshall put it, "By the constitution of the United States, the President is invested with certain important political powers, in the exercise of which he is to use his own discretion and is accountable only to his country in his political character, and to his own conscience."

C.   Limits on Judicial Review

1.   *Introduction*

In this section, we take up the *limits* on judicial review imposed by the text of the Constitution or that have been created by the Court as a matter of self-restraint. Many of the limits arise from the Constitution's language restricting the judicial power to "cases and controversies," which has given rise to what might collectively be referred to as "justiciability" doctrines the Court uses to ensure that the disputes it hears are live disputes between litigants with real interests at stake. Another justiciability doctrine—the "political question" doctrine—has its origins in the distinction Chief Justice Marshall drew in *Marbury* between those disputes for which a legal remedy may be had and those for which one must look to the political branches for relief. Finally, we'll look at the ability of Congress to alter the jurisdiction of lower courts and the Supreme Court, and at the limits on federal jurisdiction imposed by the Eleventh Amendment.

First, though, it's worth noting potential limits on judicial review that don't often generate Supreme Court cases. Judges and Justices are nominated by the President and must be confirmed by a majority vote in the Senate. U.S. Const. art. II, § 2, cl. 2. Presidents have tried to use the power to nominate to change the direction of the Court by appointing Justices whom they hope will subscribe to a particular judicial philosophy; conversely, some nominees have run into trouble in the Senate owing to fears that a nominee will tip the balance too far in one direction or another. It is safe to say, though, that owing to the relative rarity of Supreme Court vacancies, using nominees to "check" the Court is a highly uncertain proposition.

Further, Justices may be impeached and removed from office. Although theoretically a check, efforts to impeach and remove Federalist Justices during the Jefferson Administration came to naught; Jefferson himself referred to the threat of impeachment as no more than a "mere scarecrow." Despite occasional calls to impeach judges and Justices for unpopular rulings, norms of judicial independence seem firmly entrenched against the use of impeachment and removal to retaliate for unpopular decisions.

The Constitution—and the Court's construction of it—may be altered by amending the Constitution through the processes set forth in Article V. Four of the Constitution's 27 amendments were ratified to reverse Supreme Court cases.[3] Nevertheless, such events are notable for their infrequency. The supermajority requirements of Article V (two thirds of both houses have to propose an amendment and be ratified by three fourths of either state

---

3. The Eleventh Amendment reversed *Chisholm v. Georgia,* 2 U.S. 419 (1793); the Fourteenth reversed *Dred Scott v. Sanford,* 60 U.S. 393 (1857); the Sixteenth Amendment reversed *Pollock v. Farmers' Loan & Trust Co.,* 157 U.S. 429 (1895); and the Twenty-Sixth reversed *Oregon v. Mitchell,* 400 U.S. 112 (1970).

legislatures or specially called conventions) ensure this. For example, the Equal Rights Amendment, despite having its deadline for ratification extended, eventually failed to receive the necessary ratifying votes in the states. Although the provision has never been used, if two thirds of states request it, a constitutional convention must be called to consider amendments.

The next several subsections will address judicially created limitations on judicial review collectively known as "justiciability" doctrines. Some of these, as we shall see, the Court regards as being compelled by the Constitution itself; others, however, are sometimes termed *prudential,* and are rooted in the Court's own assessment of its institutional competence to adjudicate some controversies relative to that of other branches.

2. *Bar on advisory opinions*

The Court has declined to give advisory opinions on the constitutionality of pending legislation or proposed governmental action, as some state supreme courts and a number of foreign constitutional courts do. In 1793, during the Washington Administration, the Secretary of State, Thomas Jefferson, referred a set of questions regarding American neutrality in the renewed conflict between Great Britain and France to the Supreme Court for answer. Chief Justice Jay declined, arguing that separation of powers and the institutional role of the Court as the court of last resort "afford[ed] strong arguments against the propriety of our extra-judicially deciding the questions alluded to, especially as the power given by the Constitution to the President, of calling on the heads of departments for opinions, seems to have been *purposely* as well as expressly united to the *Executive* department." Calvin Massey, *American Constitutional Law: Powers and Liberties* 67 (3d ed. 2009) (reprinting the correspondence between Jefferson and Jay).

3. *Standing and related doctrines*

The cluster of justiciability doctrines that includes standing, mootness, and ripeness are some of the most important, and most confusing, limitations on judicial review, and on judicial power generally. Together, they represent the Court's understanding of limits imposed on it by Article III itself, as well as those imposed by its own sense of the judiciary's proper role. To risk oversimplification, "standing" doctrines ensure that courts hear only those cases brought by the "right" plaintiffs—those that have real interests at stake. "Mootness" and "ripeness," moreover, help courts ensure that those plaintiffs bring their cases at the right time. In a sense, all of these doctrines reinforce the Court's insistence that it not issue advisory opinions by ensuring that the controversies it hears are live disputes between parties who have real stakes in the outcome.

a. Standing. As already noted, Article III restricts the judicial power to "cases and controversies," which the Court has come to understand means actual, not hypothetical, disputes brought by adversarial, not collusive, parties with real interests at stake. The assumption is that in our adversarial system, parties with real interests will be motivated to vigorously prosecute their case, make their best arguments, and thus assist the courts in making the right decision on the basis of the best available information. As the Court's standing jurisprudence has developed over the years, it is composed of an "irreducible constitutional minimum" derived from the Constitution and "prudential" standing doctrines that are not constitutionally compelled and thus may be altered by legislation. We cover both branches of standing in this section, but it's worth noting at the outset that the line between these two branches is uncertain and often highly contested.

Standing's constitutional core. According to the Court, standing's irreducible constitutional minimum requires (1) plaintiffs to have suffered injury-in-fact that (2) was caused by the actions of the defendant and not some third party; and (3) that a decision favorable to the plaintiff will redress that harm. *Lujan v. Defenders of Wildlife,* 504 U.S. 555, 560–561 (1992); *Valley Forge Christian College v. Americans United for Separation of Church and State,* 454 U.S. 464, 472 (1982). Each of these three requirements has acquired its own gloss over the years.

As the Court held in *Lujan v. Defenders of Wildlife,* injury-in-fact requires that the injury be "concrete and particularized"—meaning that it must affect the plaintiff in a "personal and direct way." 504 U.S. at 560. The injury does *not* have to be economic or be an injury to common-law, statutory, or constitutional rights. One can claim injury to an aesthetic interest if the other requirements are met, but the injury has to be one suffered personally by the plaintiff. *See, e.g., Sierra Club v. Morton,* 405 U.S. 727 (1972) (aesthetic injury cognizable). In *Allen v. Wright,* 468 U.S. 737 (1984), the Court rejected the claims of parents of Memphis schoolchildren who argued that the IRS's grant of tax-exempt status to schools with racially discriminatory policies deprived their children of the opportunity to attend integrated public schools. The Court held that the injury described by the parents was abstract—plaintiffs didn't allege that their children were the specific victims of the harm caused by private schools with discriminatory admissions policies and thus they lacked the personal injury sufficient to maintain standing. 468 U.S. at 755–756.

Further, the injury must be "actual and imminent, not 'conjectural' or 'hypothetical.'" 504 U.S. at 560. That is, the injury must have happened or be fairly certain to happen soon. The Court rejected a bid to enjoin the Los Angeles Police Department from using a particular type of chokehold in a case brought by a motorist who had been subjected to it during a traffic stop. According to the Court, the allegation that, having been choked once before, the plaintiff was likely to be choked again lacked the "imminence" necessary for standing to seek the injunction. *Los Angeles v. Lyons,* 461 U.S. 94 (1983). Similarly, the Court denied standing in *Lujan* to plaintiffs who wished to challenge the Department of Interior's interpretation of a provision of the Endangered Species Act that prevented its application overseas. Although the plaintiffs testified that they had traveled abroad to view endangered species in the past, none testified to any firm plans to do so in the future. Without any definite plans to travel in the future, the injury was too speculative to sustain standing. 504 U.S. at 564.

The Court also regularly denies standing to plaintiffs whose injury can be characterized as a "generalized grievance" or as a type of "psychic injury" caused by the knowledge that governmental officials aren't following the law. Thus it has denied standing to citizens who sought to enforce the Constitution's "incompatibility clause" prohibiting members of Congress from simultaneously being "officers of the United States."[4] *Schlesinger v. Reservists Committee to Stop the War,* 418 U.S. 208 (1974) (no standing to challenge ability of members of Congress to hold reserve commissions in the military under the incompatibility clause); *see also United States v. Richardson,* 418 U.S. 166 (1974) (denying standing to challenge, as a violation of the "public accounting" clause of Article I, § 9, the policy of not disclosing the budget of the CIA).[5]

Closely related are cases that regularly deny standing to taxpayers objecting to various uses to which government has put tax revenue. *See, e.g., Frothingham v. Mellon,* 262 U.S. 447 (1923) (rejecting standing of plaintiff objecting to federal program seeking to reduce infant mortality and that of mothers as beyond the enumerated powers of Congress).

In 1968, however, the Court found that taxpayers alleging that federal financial aid to religious schools violated the Establishment Clause had standing to challenge the constitutionality of the program. *Flast v. Cohen,* 392 U.S. 83 (1968). The Court distinguished *Frothingham* on the basis that the Establishment Clause represented a specific limit on federal power, as opposed to the claim in *Frothingham* that the program exceeded Congress's enumerated powers. *Id.* at 105–106. The Court has refused to extend *Flast* in *Valley Forge,* which interpreted *Flast* narrowly, 454 U.S. at 479–480, and a plurality of the Court seemed to narrow it further in *Hein v. Freedom From Religion Foundation,* 551 U.S. 587, 604 (2007).

Hein limited *Flast* to cases in which plaintiffs are challenging "exercises of congressional power based on the taxing and spending clause" under specific constitutional limits to those congressional powers, such as the Establishment Clause. The plaintiffs in *Hein* were challenging executive branch expenditures of monies appropriated to it by Congress, as opposed to direct expenditures by Congress itself. The Court further narrowed *Flast* in *Arizona Christian School Tuition Organization v. Winn,* 131 S. Ct. 1436 (2010). In *Winn,* taxpayers challenged a tax credit granting donors to "student tuition organizations" that provided scholarships to private schools a credit of up to $500 against state income taxes. 131 S. Ct. at 1440. Because donors to STOs for religious schools

---

4. U.S. Const. art. I, § 6, cl. 2.
5. U.S. Const. art. I, § 9, cl. 7 ("No Money shall be drawn from the Treasury, but in Consequence of Appropriations made by Law; and a regular Statement and Account of the Receipts and Expenditures of all public Money shall be published form time to time.").

were eligible for the tax credit, the taxpayers alleged the state program violated the Establishment Clause. *Id.* The Court denied the plaintiffs standing, refusing to apply the *Flast* exception, and denying that a *tax* expenditure was equivalent to a cash outlay by the state. "A dissenter whose tax dollars are 'extracted and spent,'" Justice Kennedy wrote, "knows that he has in some small measure been made to contribute to an establishment in violation of conscience. . . . When the government declines to impose a tax, by contrast, there is no such connection between dissenting taxpayer and alleged establishment. Any financial injury remains speculative." *Id.* at 1447. For four dissenters, Justice Kagan criticized the majority decision, arguing that because "[a]ppropriations and tax subsidies are interchangeable," the Court "offer[ed] a roadmap . . . to any government that wishes to insulate its financing of religious activity from legal challenge." *Id.* at 1462 (Kagan, J., dissenting). *See also DaimlerChrysler Corp. v. Cuno,* 547 U.S. 332 (2006) (rejecting state and municipal taxpayers' standing in a constitutional challenge to certain state economic development incentives).

As one scholar has noted "[i]n practice, causation and redressability are the Gemini twins of standing. They are so often linked that they are sometimes fused together in discussion as a single 'nexus' requirement." Calvin Massey, *American Constitutional Law: Powers and Liberties* 79 (3d ed. 2009). Both require plaintiffs to allege facts that the defendants — and not some third party not involved in the litigation — are responsible for the harm suffered and that it will be alleviated ("redressed") by the litigation. The plaintiffs in both *Allen v. Wright* and *Warth v. Seldin* saw their claims founder on this requirement. In the former, the Court found no evidence that the inability of the plaintiffs' children to attend an integrated public school was fairly traceable to the IRS. 468 U.S. at 758. In *Warth,* it was also unclear that but for the zoning laws of Penfield, New York, there would be low-income housing and, perforce, economic diversity in the town. 422 U.S. at 504. In both cases, the real harm was caused by private parties whose actions might not be influenced by changes in government policy sought by the plaintiffs.

The *Lujan* plaintiffs' claim also foundered on redressability concerns. The American aid that the plaintiffs were challenging made up a limited percentage of the overseas projects that were said to harm certain endangered species, and there was no proof that, but for the U.S. money, the projects would not go forward. More likely the money would be replaced from some other source. 504 U.S. at 571. In *Warth,* similarly, there was no proof that low-income housing would follow ineluctably from the invalidation of the residential zoning rules in Penfield. 422 U.S. at 506.

Before leaving constitutional standing, some mention should be made of the Court's recent decision in *Massachusetts v. Environmental Protection Agency,* 549 U.S. 497 (2007), in which the Court held that the State of Massachusetts had standing to challenge the EPA's decision not to regulate emissions of certain greenhouse gases, including carbon dioxide, alleged to contribute to global warming. The EPA, citing *Lujan,* sought to deny the state standing, arguing that the complaint failed to plead injury-in-fact, causation, and redressability. The Court rejected the EPA's arguments.

First, the Court distinguished the private individuals in *Lujan* from the State. "We stress here," the Court wrote, "the special position and interest of Massachusetts. It is of considerable relevance that the party seeking review here is a State and not, as it was in *Lujan,* a private individual. . . . " 549 U.S. at 518. The Court argued that Massachusetts had an "independent interest" in, inter alia, a "well-founded desire to preserve its sovereign territory today . . . . " *Id.*

The Court then called the harms associated with climate change "serious and well recognized" and that insofar as the State stood to lose miles of coastline if rising sea levels associated with climate change continued, the harms were actual, as opposed to hypothetical or conjectural. *Id.* at 519. (Though, as others have pointed out, the injury is not quite "imminent.") It continued to find that automobiles in the United States were significant emitters of carbon dioxide and that the lack of any reduction in those emissions could be traced to the EPA's refusal to regulate carbon dioxide. *Id.* at 524. Finally, the Court found that even incremental reductions in greenhouse gas emissions were sufficient to satisfy the redressability prong. *Id.*

What is unclear after *Massachusetts* is whether this represents a retreat by the Court from its rigorous application of constitutional standing requirements for *all* plaintiffs, or is simply a special set of rules for states. *Hein,* decided that same term, suggests the latter. *See also Summers v. Earth Island Institute,* 555 U.S. 488, 499-500 (2009) (rejecting argument that requirement of imminent harm be replaced with "realistic threat" of future harm standard).

Prudential standing. The Court has also articulated standing rules that follow from the Court's self-imposed restraints rather than from the constitutional strictures in Article III. Unlike those constitutional standing rules, the prudential rules may be altered by Congress. This section discusses the two main prudential standing rules: third-party standing rules barring the assertion by one plaintiff of another's interest and the so-called zone of interest requirement.

In general, a plaintiff must assert her own rights, not those of a third party. *See, e.g., Warth,* 422 U.S. at 499 (noting that a plaintiff "generally must assert his own legal rights and interests, and cannot rest his claim to relief on the legal rights or interests of third parties"). The Court has, however, created some exceptions to this rule. (1) The third party is unable to assert her rights and there is reason to believe the plaintiff will assert the rights of that third party adequately. In *Eisenstadt v. Baird,* 405 U.S. 438, 446 (1972), for example, a pharmacist prosecuted for selling contraceptives to unmarried persons was allowed to assert the rights of those persons to purchase contraceptives, because unmarried persons were not subject to criminal liability. (2) There is a special relationship between the plaintiff and a third party, as between a parent and a child, for example. *But see Elk Grove Unified School District v. Newdow,*

542 U.S. 1 (2004) (denying standing to noncustodial parent to challenge use of "under God" in Pledge of Allegiance). (3) In some cases, plaintiffs are permitted to challenge laws as constitutionally overbroad—that is, the law may be constitutional as applied to the plaintiff, but would be unconstitutional in other applications. (Ordinarily, a plaintiff would only be able to argue that a statute is unconstitutional as applied to *him*, not that other applications would be unconstitutional.) According to Erwin Chemerinsky, "[t]he overbreadth doctrine appears limited to First Amendment cases[,] reflect[ing] a fear that an overbroad law will chill protected speech and that safeguarding expression justifies allowing third-party standing." Erwin Chemerinsky, *Constitutional Law: Principles and Policies* 88 (3d ed. 2006). (4) Finally, the Court has permitted organizations to bring suit on behalf of their members as long as certain criteria are met. First, its members would have to have standing in their own right to bring suit. Second, the interests asserted have to be related to the organization's purpose. Third, neither the claim nor the relief sought requires the participation, as parties, of the organization's members. *See, e.g., Hunt v. Washington State Apple Advertising Commission,* 432 U.S. 333, 342–343 (1977) (holding that a member-elected advertising commission had standing to bring a constitutional challenge against a North Carolina regulation that discriminated against Washington State apple producers).

The Court also made clear in *Bond v. United States,* 131 S. Ct. 2355 (2011), that individuals seeking to challenge the constitutionality of a statute have standing to argue that the statute is beyond the power of Congress because it intrudes on the sovereignty of states. Such arguments do not belong to the states alone, the Court held. *Bond,* 131 U.S. at 2363-2364. The Court wrote that an "individual, in a proper case, can assert injury from governmental action taken in excess of the authority that federalism defines. Her rights in this regard do not belong to a State." *Id.* As Justice Ginsburg put it succinctly, "Bond, like any other defendant, has a personal right not to be convicted under a constitutionally invalid law." *Id.* at 2367 (Ginsburg, J., concurring).

To have standing to assert rights under a particular statute or regulation, a plaintiff must allege injury the statute was designed to protect against. For example, in *Air Courier Conference v. American Postal Workers Union,* 498 U.S. 517 (1991), the Court rejected attempts by the postal workers' union to invoke a statute granting the United States Postal Service a monopoly over mail delivery to prevent private companies from delivering mail overseas. The Court held that the protection of postal jobs was not within the zone of interests protected by that statute. The zone of interests test has been inconsistently applied over the years, and some have suggested that it applies only to "cases seeking judicial review of agency decisions under the Administrative Procedures Act." Chemerinsky, *supra,* at 102.

b. Ripeness. Ripeness seeks to ensure that the litigation occurs at the right time—that the injury alleged has occurred or is very likely to occur. Only when injury has not yet occurred is ripeness an issue. According to the Court, the basic rationale [for ripeness] is to prevent the courts, through avoidance of premature adjudication, from entangling themselves in abstract disagreements over administrative policies, and also to protect the agencies from judicial interference until an administrative decision has been formalized and its effects felt in a concrete way by the challenging parties. The problem is best seen in a twofold aspect, requiring us to [1] evaluate both the fitness of the issues for judicial decision and [2] the hardship to the parties of withholding court consideration.

Abbott Laboratories v. Gardner, 387 U.S. 136, 148–149 (1967).

The first of these two requirements enables the Court to determine whether the record, at present, is sufficient, or whether the case would benefit from additional facts being compiled. "The more a question is purely a legal issue the analysis of which does not depend on a particular factual context, the more likely it is that the Court will find ripeness." Chemerinsky, *supra,* at 111. As for the hardship on the parties, ripeness will generally be found (thus the court will hear the case) where (1) the plaintiff has suffered harm already; (2) where the harm is virtually certain to occur, even if no prosecution has actually commenced; or (3) plaintiff is exposed to specific, serious future harm. *See, e.g., United Public Workers v. Mitchell,* 330 U.S. 75 (1947); *see also Poe v. Ullman,* 367 U.S. 497 (1961).

c. Mootness. Just as the Court has traditionally refrained from issuing advisory opinions, it also declines to reach the merits of cases that no longer present live controversies — that are, in other words, moot. A good illustration of mootness is the Court's first encounter with racial preferences in higher education. The University of Washington School of Law was sued by Marco DeFunis, who alleged that despite superior grades and LSAT scores, he was rejected by the law school because of his race. He won in state trial court, which ordered him to be admitted; the state supreme court reversed, and the U.S. Supreme Court granted certiorari. By the time oral argument was held, however, DeFunis was close to graduating; the law school admitted that even if it won, it would allow DeFunis to graduate. The Court then declined to reach the merits, as DeFunis no longer had any real stake in the outcome. *DeFunis v. Odegaard,* 416 U.S. 312 (1974).

Of course the length of litigation means that, were the mootness doctrine rigorously applied, certain controversies would never be live by the time the Supreme Court heard the case. Thus, the Court has created an exception to the mootness doctrine for cases that are "capable of repetition yet evading review." For example, a pregnant woman's challenge to abortion regulations isn't moot even though the case wouldn't make it all the way to the Supreme Court before the end of the nine-month gestation period. To qualify for that exception, one must prove (1) that the controversy will not be litigated before it ceases to exist, and (2) that there is a reasonable chance this plaintiff will be subject to the same injury in the future. *See, e.g., Southern Pacific Terminal Co. v. Interstate Commerce Comm'n,* 219 U.S. 498 (1911); *see also Roe v. Wade,* 410 U.S. 113 (1973).

QUESTION 2. **An emolumental mess.**   Senator Solon is appointed to be Secretary of the Treasury. During the time Solon was in the Senate, she voted to increase the pay of several executive officials, including the Treasury Secretary. Peter, a constituent of Solon, sues, claiming the appointment violates the Emoluments Clause of Article I, § 6, clause 2, which reads that "[n]o Senator or Representative shall, during the Time for which he was elected, be appointed to any civil Office under the Authority of the United States, which shall have been created, or the Emoluments whereof shall have been increased during such time. . . . " Does Peter have standing to bring suit?

A. Yes, because Peter has suffered injury by the Secretary's failure to follow the Constitution.

B. Yes, because a portion of Peter's tax revenues that fund the Secretary's salary have been used to pay for an unconstitutional appointment.

C. No, because the injury is not redressable by a judicial decision.

D. No, because Peter has alleged a generalized grievance.

ANALYSIS.   It was probably easy to exclude **A** because you know that some "psychic injury" suffered by citizens who find out that their public officials aren't following the Constitution is not the kind of concrete, particularized injury-in-fact required by Article III. Similarly, the mere fact that some tiny portion of one's taxes go to pay for allegedly unconstitutional governmental actions also fails to satisfy the constitutional requirement unless *Flast v. Cohen* applies, which it does not because the controversy here does not involve congressional appropriations alleged to violate the Establishment Clause. So **B** is out, too. **C** isn't right either, because presumably a court *could* order that the appointment be rescinded or rule that actions taken by an ineligible official were null and void. That leaves **D**, which is the best answer. At most, Peter's complaint represents a complaint that he shares in common with millions of other citizens who might prefer that elected officials obey technical parts of the Constitution, like the Emoluments Clause. Be that as it may, courts will not allow that kind of generalized grievance to confer standing on someone who is not otherwise personally injured.

(handwritten margin note: Congress has given the money to the president)

QUESTION 3. **The tenacious taxpayer.**   Congress has appropriated money for the award of 25 Presidential Scholarships chosen by the President and an advisory board. Upon reading that one of the recipients intends to attend a sectarian college and study to be a missionary, Tom Taxpayer sues, claiming that the expenditure of federal funds violates the Establishment Clause. Does Taxpayer have standing to bring the suit?

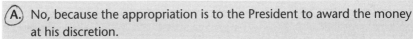

A. No, because the appropriation is to the President to award the money at his discretion.

B. No, because the claim represents a generalized grievance.

C. Yes, because the Establishment Clause is a specific limitation on Congress's taxing and spending power.

D. Yes, because taxpayers have standing to enforce lawmakers' compliance with specific constitutional limitations.

ANALYSIS. If you remembered that the Establishment Clause represented something of an exception to the rule against taxpayer standing, you might have been tempted to answer **C** because of *Flast v. Cohen*. But remember that the recent *Hein* case narrowly interpreted *Flast,* drawing a distinction between money spent by Congress itself and that which it delegated to the President to spend at his discretion. Therefore **A** is the correct answer. **B** is incorrect because the Establishment Clause functions as something of an exception to this general rule. **D**, though, is an incorrect statement of law; in general, taxpayers do *not* have standing to sue for alleged violations of the Constitution where the violation itself has resulted in no concrete injury to the plaintiff.

QUESTION 4. Standing in the shadow. Dan was convicted of violating a federal law requiring commercial farming operations to be "carbon neutral," that is, the farms do not add significantly to greenhouse gasses or to global warming. Under the federal legislation, state agricultural officials are charged with conducting inspections and issuing certificates. Dan failed to obtain a certificate. He alleges that the federal legislation commandeers state officials to implement a federal program and is thus unconstitutional. The State is not a party to the lawsuit. In response, the federal government seeks dismissal of the lawsuit saying that Dan lacks standing to assert his defense. Only the State, the federal government argues, may seek to vindicate those federalism interests. How should the court rule?

A. For Dan, because he has an interest in ensuring the government acts in a constitutional manner.

B. For Dan, because he may challenge the constitutionality of an act under which he is being prosecuted.

C. For the government, because Dan is seeking to make claims that belong to third parties not before the Court.

D. For the government, because Dan has suffered no injury.

ANALYSIS. On the one hand, Dan seems to satisfy all of the requirements of *Lujan* (injury-in-fact that's fairly traceable to the government, and likely to be remedied by a favorable decision); therefore, his interest in the case is *not* simply forcing the government to act constitutionally (which is not sufficient to get standing). Therefore neither **A** nor **D** is correct. While he *is* raising claims of third parties, doing so is not always a bar to standing, so **C** is not an accurate statement of the law either. That leaves **B**, which is what the Court recently held in *Bond v. U.S.*

QUESTION 5. Are you (in) kind?   Disturbed at reports that Americans are "bowling alone," as one author put it—declining to join various civic organizations like Rotary, the Kiwanis, etc., State decides to create financial incentives to keep those groups financially solvent. State allows individuals to donate up to $1000, which may be deducted from the income on which one pays state income tax. In addition, however, the state furnishes individuals with an additional credit of up to $500 against any state income taxes owed, for donations made over $1000. Donations to places of worship and religious orders are eligible. A group calling itself Freethinkers for Fiscal Responsibility made up of state taxpayers, challenges the credit, calling it an unconstitutional state-sponsored giveaway to churches. The State, meanwhile, alleges the taxpayers have no standing to challenge the program. A reviewing court should:

A. Side with the taxpayers because the scenario is covered by *Flast v. Cohen*.

B. Side with the taxpayers because they have an interest in ensuring that tax revenues are not spent on unconstitutional programs.

C. Side with the State, because taxpayers have no right to challenge the constitutionality of state spending programs.

D. Side with the State, because the aid does not involve legislative appropriations to religious entities.

ANALYSIS.   Let's eliminate some prospects at the outset. First, from your reading, you know that taxpayer standing is difficult to maintain. In fact, taxpayers do *not* have an undifferentiated interest in ensuring money is spent in a constitutional manner—or at least that interest is not sufficient to maintain a suit in federal court. So **B** is not right. However, it goes too far to say that taxpayers *never* have any ability to challenge spending decisions; that's inconsistent with *Flast*. **C**, therefore, is incorrect as well. As between the remaining choices, one has to remember that cases like *Hein* and *Winn* have chipped away at *Flast*, so that it stands for little more than its result. As a consequence, *Winn* refused to expand *Flast* to cover instances in which government is aiding religion through tax expenditures (tax credits and deductions) as opposed to direct appropriations. The best answer, therefore, is **D** and not **A**.

QUESTION 6. **Do you feel a draft?**   U.S. military commitments have taxed the armed forces to the point that Congress revives the draft. Now men 18 to 25 are chosen by lottery to serve for at least two years in the armed forces. Under the lottery system, lower numbers are called up first; higher numbers, if needed, will be called up in the future. Which of the following plaintiffs would likely be found to have standing if any files suit challenging the legality of the draft?

A. Parents of a 17-year-old male alleging that the draft is unconstitutional in the absence of a congressional declaration of war.
B. A 19-year-old female who argues that the draft violates the Thirteenth Amendment's ban on involuntary servitude.
C. An 18-year-old male who drew a low lottery number and has received instructions to report for a physical.
D. Any of the above.

ANALYSIS.   Because the draft affects only males of a certain age, the plaintiff in **B** couldn't suffer any harm. Similarly, although parents can sometimes assert the rights of their minor children, it's unlikely that they or their child are likely to be found to have suffered any imminent harm. It's unclear that, in a year, he will have been assigned a lottery number or, if he is, whether he will be subject to a call-up or not. Thus **A** is not correct either. If **A** and **B** are excluded, then **D** cannot be the correct answer. That leaves **C**, which is not only the only answer left, but presents someone whose injury could be described as concrete and particularized—has not only gone through the lottery, but has actually been ordered to report.

QUESTION 7. **A taxing opinion.**   The IRS issues a revenue ruling that granted favorable tax treatment to nonprofit hospitals that offered only emergency room care to indigent patients, as opposed to offering both free emergency and nonemergency care. Indigent plaintiffs and organizations that advocate for the poor challenge the ruling, claiming that it violates both the Internal Revenue Code and the Administrative Procedures Act, which governs the issuance of regulations by administrative agencies like the IRS. If the court dismisses the suit for lack of standing, it would likely do so because:

A. The plaintiffs have suffered no harm.
B. The injury is not imminent.
C. The lack of free, nonemergency care is not fairly traceable to the revenue ruling.
D. The plaintiffs are not in the zone of interest of the APA or the Code.

ANALYSIS.   The facts here are those of *Simon v. Eastern Kentucky Welfare Rights Organization*, 426 U.S. 26 (1976), in which the Court held that plaintiffs had no standing to challenge an IRS exemption for hospitals providing free emergency care only to indigents. There was no proof, the Court held, that the unavailability of nonemergency care for indigents was traceable to the IRS's revenue ruling. Therefore **C** is the correct answer. **A** and **B** are incorrect, because the continuing lack of access to indigent health care could be a concrete, particularized harm. **D** is incorrect because the APA, at least, is being invoked for the precise reason it was created: to ensure that agencies follow certain procedures in enforcing the laws they were tasked with administering.

QUESTION 8. Not-so-fresh air.   Emissions from coal power plants in State A are alleged to cause problems in adjoining State B. If left unchecked, the emissions could cause harm to crops and to persons with respiratory problems in State B. So far, the EPA, which has jurisdiction to regulate air quality, has declined to take enforcement action against the plants in State A. Which of the following parties would be most likely to have standing to challenge the EPA's nonenforcement?

A. State B, if State B can demonstrate that it stands to bear the costs of treating the respiratory ailments of citizens insured by the state, which are likely to develop in the future as a result of the air pollution.

B. A resident of State B who suffers from asthma, which can be triggered by air pollution, like the emissions from State A.

C. A resident of State B whose crops are at risk from acid rain produced by the emissions.

D. **B** or **C**.

ANALYSIS.   Even though the harm is neither certain nor imminent, and even though the EPA's enforcement action might raise causation and redressability problems, after *Massachusetts v. EPA*, State B would be in the best position to challenge the EPA. The other potential plaintiffs would have difficulty demonstrating the imminence of the harm, or of pleading facts making the harm fairly traceable to the EPA's nonenforcement of its own regulations. Because neither **B** nor **C** are good answers, neither is **D**. That leaves **A** as the best answer.

QUESTION 9. Rescue me!   David is being held at a military base without charges on suspicion of conspiring to commit acts of terrorism in the United States. David's father, Arthur, seeks to challenge his son's confinement in federal court, because David himself has not been permitted access to a lawyer. Would Arthur have standing to challenge his son's incarceration?

stay away from strong assertions

A. No, because Arthur has suffered no harm.
B. No, because Arthur may not assert the rights of third persons.
C. Yes, because David is unable to assert his own rights.
D. Yes, because parents may always assert the rights of children.

ANALYSIS. Ordinarily plaintiffs cannot raise claims of third parties, but there are exceptions. So **B** is an incorrect statement of law. One exception is where a special relationship exists between the plaintiff and the third party, as that which exists between a parent and a child. If you remember the discussion of the *Newdow* case, however, you will recall that there the Court *denied* standing to the father who was challenging the use of "under God" in the Pledge of Allegiance because he was a noncustodial parent. Therefore **D** is incorrect. Parents do not *always* have the right to assert their children's rights. **A** is not so much incorrect as beside the point; in some cases, as noted, the courts permit those who have suffered no personal harm to raise the claims of others. That leaves **C**, which is the right answer. Another exception to the third-party standing rule is where the third party is unable to vindicate her own rights. David's situation would seem to fit this exception perfectly.

4. Political questions

Although the Court has indicated that some constitutional questions are not susceptible to judicial resolution since *Marbury v. Madison,* most discussion of the modern political question doctrine begins with *Baker v. Carr,* 369 U.S. 186 (1962), and the six criteria that Justice Brennan extrapolated from the Court's prior cases. *Baker* arose in the context of an equal protection challenge to Tennessee's malapportioned legislature brought by urban voters who alleged that the malapportionment rendered their votes unequal to those rural voters who were overrepresented in the state legislature.

Not 15 years before, in *Colegrove v. Green,* 328 U.S. 549, 556 (1948), the Court refused to hear another reapportionment case, with Justice Felix Frankfurter arguing that the Court "ought not enter this political thicket." Here again, in *Baker,* the state argued that the dispute over apportionment was a nonjusticiable "political" question and that, although framed as an equal protection claim, the suit was in reality an attempt to get the Court to hear a claim under Article IV, § 4, which guarantees each state a "republican form of government." The Court held as far back as *Luther v. Borden,* 48 U.S. 1 (1849), that the Guarantee Clause was not judicially enforceable; that states must look to Congress or the President for enforcement. *See also Pacific States Tel. & Tel. Co. v. Oregon,* 223 U.S. 118 (1912) (refusing to hear challenge to direct lawmaking procedures on grounds initiative and referendum violated the Guarantee Clause). Further, the state argued that controversies regarding the structure of state political institutions were, by definition, "political questions" and not justiciable.

The *Baker* Court rejected this capacious definition of political question in favor of the following factors, synthesized from various cases involving different subjects:

> Prominent on the surface of any case held to involve a political question is found [1] a textually demonstrable constitutional commitment of the issue to a coordinate political department; or [2] a lack of judicially discoverable and manageable standards for resolving it; or [3] the impossibility of deciding without an initial policy determination of a kind clearly for nonjudicial discretion; or [4] the impossibility of a court's undertaking independent resolution without expressing lack of the respect due coordinate branches of government; or [5] an unusual need for unquestioning adherence to a political decision already made; or [6] the potentiality of embarrassment from multifarious pronouncements by various departments on one question.
>
> Unless one of these formulations is inextricable from the case at bar, there should be no dismissal for non-justiciability on the ground of a political question's presence.

369 U.S. at 216.

The Court held that it correctly refused to hear Guaranty Clause claims in cases like *Luther v. Borden* because the Clause "is not a repository of judicially manageable standards which a court could utilize independently in order to identify a State's lawful government," and not because the subject matter itself precluded any judicial intervention. *Id.* at 223. By contrast, "[j]udicial standards under the Equal Protection Clause are well developed and familiar, and it has been open to courts since the enactment of the Fourteenth Amendment to determine . . . that a discrimination reflects no policy, but simply arbitrary and capricious action." *Id.* at 226. It did not follow for the Court that because a claim could not be brought under the Guarantee Clause, it couldn't be brought under *any* constitutional provision.

Despite *Baker*'s pretensions to precision, few of the criteria are in any sense definite or self-defining. Some of the criteria seem never to have been seriously considered or applied by the Court. Is there any constitutional case involving judicial review of Congress's or the President's actions, for example, that *doesn't* carry the risk of "expressing lack of the respect due coordinate branches of government"? Other factors seem to be repetitive. If, for example, a Court cannot decide a case "without an initial policy determination of a kind clearly for nonjudicial discretion," isn't that a pretty good sign that there is "a textually demonstrable commitment of the issue to a coordinate political department"? Subsequent cases have answered some, but not all of these questions.

QUESTION 10. A political question question. Which of the following would be *least* likely to be held a political question by a reviewing Court?

A. A suit by members of Congress alleging that the President's commitment of military forces overseas without a congressional declaration of war was unconstitutional.

B. A suit by the President against members of the Senate whose refusal to hold confirmation hearings on judicial nominees has resulted in the inability of the President to fill vacancies in the federal judiciary.

C. A suit alleging that a federal hate crimes law exceeded the scope of Congress's powers under Article I, § 8 brought by a criminal defendant charged with violating the law.

D. A suit by a judge who was impeached and removed from office for alleged sexual harassment of lawyers and court staff, who claimed his impeachment and removal were unconstitutional because his offenses did not rise to the level of "high crimes and misdemeanors."

ANALYSIS.   This is intended to be a basic warm-up question. If you are stumped, read through the *Baker* factors again and perhaps glance at a copy of the Constitution. The first two factors are whether the Constitution seems to have committed the power to another branch, or whether the question presents difficulties in the creation of standards by the courts. In **A**, for example, the Constitution does give Congress the power to declare war, but it also makes the President the commander-in-chief of the military. The document says nothing about resolving conflicts when, for example, the President commits military forces without a formal declaration of war. In addition, the decision whether and when to commit military forces involves substantial issues of policy that are probably better left to the political branches. Similarly, in **B** the President and the Senate have shared responsibilities for nominating and confirming judicial nominees, but what happens when there is a stalemate between the branches? Can the judiciary *order* the Senate to hold hearings? Force a vote on nominees? It's likely that a court would simply let the branches work it out for themselves. In **D**, not only does the Constitution assign the *sole* power of impeachment and the *sole* power to try impeachments to the House and Senate, respectively, but the Constitution contains no criteria for defining "high crimes and misdemeanors." Therefore, **C** is the better answer, because questions about the scope of congressional power and the meaning of words like "commerce" and Article I form the warp and woof of constitutional law. If you didn't choose C because you thought that the controversy was "political"—that is, concerning the powers of the political branches—your confusion is understandable because the "political question" is something of a misnomer. Issues aren't nonjusticiable simply because they involve "political" disagreements or controversies involving one or more of the "political" branches. Much constitutional litigation involves intense political disagreements, or challenges by one branch to actions of another.

The very next political question case made clear that the Court makes these threshold decisions about whether and to what extent the *Baker* criteria are present. Thus the Court is not obliged to take Congress's word that the

Constitution had committed to it the power to pass on the qualification of its members, including the power to add to those minimal qualifications listed in Article I. This attitude is in keeping with the modern Court's jealous guarding of its prerogative to authoritatively interpret the Constitution and bind other actors with its interpretations.

In *Powell v. McCormack*, 395 U.S. 486 (1969), the Court rejected the Speaker of the House's claim that the political question doctrine barred the Court from hearing a challenge by the controversial congressman Adam Clayton Powell to the House's refusal to seat him at the beginning of the 90th Congress.[6] (Powell was reelected in 1968 and took his seat in 1969, but sued for back pay.)

The Speaker of the House claimed that because the Constitution gave Congress the power to "Judge . . . the Elections, Returns, and Qualifications of its own Members," U.S. Const. art. I, § 5, cl. 1, there was a "textually demonstrable constitutional commitment" to the House of the question of Powell's exclusion. 395 U.S. at 519. The Court was thus without power, the argument went, to review the House's decision. *Id.* Further, the House argued that judicial review that produced a contrary decision to the House would result in "embarrassment" to the House. *Id.* at 548–549.

The Court made clear, however, that whether and the extent to which a textually demonstrable commitment had been made *was* a question for the Court. It wrote that "whether there is a 'textually demonstrable constitutional commitment of the issue to a co-ordinate political department' of government and what is the scope of such commitment are questions we must resolve. . . ." *Id.* at 521. Ultimately, the Court concluded that although the House did have the power to judge the qualifications of its members, those qualifications, too, were set by the Constitution and could not be supplemented by the House. Article I, § 2, clause 2 sets age, residency, and citizenship qualifications; no additional qualifications to holding one's seat could be added, the Court held. *Id.* at 548. Congress could discipline its members, the Court noted, by seeking expulsion of a member.[7]

The Court, moreover, rejected the argument that the Court could not resolve the controversy without "embarrassment" to Congress. Chief Justice Warren wrote that the argument "that the case presents a political question because judicial resolution of petitioners' claim would produce a 'potentially embarrassing confrontation between coordinate branches' of the Federal Government" was untenable because "[o]ur system of government requires that federal courts on occasion interpret the Constitution in a manner at variance with the construction given the document by another branch. The alleged conflict that such an adjudication may cause cannot justify the courts' avoiding their constitutional responsibility." *Id.* at 549.

---

6. Powell was alleged to have diverted House funds for personal use and to have made false reports to the House.

7. *See* U.S. Const. art. I, § 5, cl. 2 (stating that "Each House may . . . punish its Members for disorderly Behavior, and, with the Concurrence of two thirds, expel a Member. . . . ").

After *Powell,* many wondered whether the political question doctrine was becoming one of those doctrines more honored in the breach. But in *Goldwater v. Carter,* 444 U.S. 996 (1979), a plurality of Justices found that the question whether rescission of a treaty required two-thirds approval by the Senate was a political question. And in *Nixon v. United States,* 506 U.S. 224 (1993), the Court concluded that most, if not all, questions regarding the impeachment and removal process were nonjusticiable.

Nixon involved the impeachment trial of a federal district court judge who had been convicted of accepting bribes. Nixon was tried before a committee of senators pursuant to a Senate rule permitting such procedures, as opposed to the entire Senate. The committee heard evidence during four days of hearings, it summarized all disputed facts for the whole Senate, and furnished a full transcript of the proceedings. Moreover, both the House managers and Judge Nixon submitted final briefs to the entire Senate, which then heard oral arguments by both sides, including a statement from Nixon himself. Senators had the opportunity to ask questions of both sides, as well. At the conclusion of the oral arguments, the requisite two-thirds majority voted to remove Nixon from office. 506 U.S. at 227–228.

Nixon argued that the whole Senate, not simply a part of it, had to preside over his trial. After reviewing the actual workings of the Rule XI proceeding under which Nixon was tried, Chief Justice Rehnquist defined "political question" largely in terms of two *Baker* factors:

> A controversy is nonjusticiable—i.e., involves a political question—where there is "a textually demonstrable constitutional commitment of the issue to a coordinate political department; or a lack of judicially discoverable and manageable standards for resolving it. . . ." But the courts must, in the first instance, interpret the text in question and determine whether and to what extent the issue is textually committed. . . . As the discussion that follows makes clear, the concept of a textual commitment to a coordinate political department is not completely separate from the concept of a lack of judicially discoverable and manageable standards for resolving it; the lack of judicially manageable standards may strengthen the conclusion that there is a textually demonstrable commitment to a coordinate branch.

Id. at 228–229.

The Court concluded that it had no standards for deciding how the Senate should "try" impeachments. The Constitution itself, the majority noted, seemed to prescribe a minimum number of procedural safeguards on impeachment trials (the Senators were under oath, conviction required a two-thirds supermajority, and, when the President was on trial, the Chief Justice presided). *Id.* at 229–230. "These limitations," Chief Justice Rehnquist wrote, "are quite precise, and their nature suggests that the Framers did not intend to impose additional limitations on the form of the Senate proceedings by the use of the word 'try.' . . ." *Id.* at 230.

As the Court indicated, its conclusion was reinforced by the use of the word "sole" in connection with both impeachment and trial in Article I, § 3, which suggested to the Court that the judiciary was to have no role in review-ing impeachment proceedings. *Id.* at 230–231. In addition to the problem of manageable standards and the textual commitment in the Constitution itself, the Court also presciently referred to "the lack of finality and the difficulty of fashioning relief counsel against justiciability. . . . This lack of finality would manifest itself most dramatically if the President were impeached." *Id.* at 236.

Following *Nixon,* it appears that the textually demonstrable commitment and lack of manageable standards prongs will be doing most of the work, with finality and remedy concerns playing supporting roles. For example, in *Vieth v. Jubelirer,* 541 U.S. 267 (2004), the Court came within one vote of over-turning *Davis v. Bandemer,* 478 U.S. 109 (1986), and holding that the Court could devise no judicially manageable standards for deciding when partisan gerrymanders—manipulation of districts so as to advantage one party over another—violated the Equal Protection Clause. To the extent the "pruden-tial" limits—risk of embarrassment from multivocal pronouncements on an issue and the inability to decide without expressing "disrespect" for another branch—will continue to play a role at all, it would likely be in the area of foreign affairs and foreign policy, where the Court has traditionally har-bored doubts about its institutional competence relative to that of the other branches.

However, as the Court reminded in *Zivotofsky v. Clinton,* 132 S. Ct. 1421 (2012), the Court is firmly in the interpretive driver's seat when it comes to applying the *Baker* factors. *Zivotofsky* concerned a conflict between executive branch policy not to take a position whether the City of Jerusalem was part of Israel or not and a congressional statute instructing State Department offi-cials to list "Jerusalem, Israel" on U.S. passports for American citizens born in that city. 132 S. Ct. at 1425. The court of appeals threw out the plaintiff's lawsuit on political question grounds. "It reasoned that the Constitution gives the Executive the exclusive power to recognize foreign sovereigns, and that the exercise of this power cannot be reviewed by the courts." *Id.* at 1426. The Supreme Court reversed the court of appeals and remanded for a hearing on the merits of the statute's constitutionality. Chief Justice Roberts wrote that "[t]he federal courts are not being asked to supplant a foreign policy decision of the political branches with the courts' own unmoored determination of what United States policy towards Jerusalem should be. Instead, Zivotofsky requests that the courts enforce a specific statutory right. To resolve his claim, the Judiciary must decide if Zivotofsky's interpretation of the statute is correct, and whether the statute is constitutional. This is a familiar judicial exercise." *Id.* at 1427. Quoting from the briefs of the parties, Roberts further concluded that the contending claims about the respective powers of the President and of Congress "sound in familiar principles of constitutional interpretation" and establish that discoverable and applicable standards *are* available to courts to resolve the case on the merits. *Id.* at 1430. Justice Breyer cited four prudential reasons—that the case involved foreign affairs, courts might have to make foreign policy decisions to decide the merits, the interest in judicial resolution of the case wasn't particularly strong, and the ability of the branches to work out the differences among themselves—in concluding that he would have affirmed the lower court. *Id.* at 1437-1441 (Breyer, J., dissenting).

QUESTION 11. On the house. Representative Ray has a reputation for being a gadfly. Regardless of who is in power, she always peppers colleagues and members of the executive branch with harsh questions about government actions and policies. Wildly popular in her district, many of her colleagues—and members of the executive branch—find her abrasive, rude, and uncollegial. In fact, she is so unpopular that following reelection, she was seated with the House once the new term began, but soon found herself expelled by her colleagues, pursuant to Article I, § 5, clause 2, which permits both houses of Congress to exclude members with a two-thirds vote. Furious, Ray sues, claiming that she was expelled simply for being too good at her job. She claims that her expulsion was unconstitutional and seeks reinstatement. The Speaker of the House, on the other hand, claims that expulsion is a political question and that the suit is nonjusticiable. For whom should the federal judge in the case rule?

A. The Speaker, because the Constitution commits the power to expel to each House of Congress.

B. The Speaker, because the Court could not decide the case without expressing disrespect for the House's judgment.

C. Ray, because the House may not expel her except for cause.

D. Ray, because the Court can interpret the Constitution to decide whether a claim is justiciable or not.

ANALYSIS. This scenario is a slight variation on the facts in *Powell v. McCormack*. The House's decision not to seat Representative Powell was a compromise. Members voted for his exclusion who would not have voted to expel him after Powell was seated. In Ray's case, she was seated, then expelled by the requisite two-thirds majority. After *Powell*, the Court will review claims of justiciability, especially claims that the Constitution commits some power or other to a particular branch, but that does not mean that it will pass on the ultimate merits. In *Nixon*, for example, the Court agreed with the Senate's lawyers that the Constitution *did* commit power to try impeachments to the Senate alone, and thus did not attempt to define the limits of what constituted a valid trial by the Senate. Therefore, **D** cannot be correct. Further, the Constitution is silent as to the reasons for expulsion; although Article I, § 5 says that members may be "punished" for "disorderly behavior," it says nothing about expulsion, except that it requires a two-thirds supermajority. Thus **C** is incorrect as well. Although **B** might be true, that argument against justiciability was rejected in *Powell*; as the Court noted, many times it is called on to invalidate actions undertaken by Congress or by the executive in ways that might be taken (certainly by those branches) as evincing disrespect, but that did not prevent the Court from exercising judicial review. That leaves **A** as the best answer: The Constitution places that power with each House, and there is a safeguard in the supermajority requirement. Further, the text itself furnishes no criteria that courts could use to fashion judicially manageable or applicable standards. That bolsters the conclusion that the Constitution commits that power to each House alone.

QUESTION 12. Wait just amendment!   Article V of the U.S. Constitution reads:

> The Congress, whenever two thirds of both houses shall deem it necessary, shall propose amendments to this Constitution, or, on the application of the legislatures of two thirds of the several states, shall call a convention for proposing amendments, which, in either case, shall be valid to all intents and purposes, as part of this Constitution, when ratified by the legislatures of three fourths of the several states, or by conventions in three fourths thereof, as the one or the other mode of ratification may be proposed by the Congress. . . .

In reaction to what was seen as irresponsible spending by the U.S. Congress, momentum built once again to pass a Balanced Budget Amendment (BBA) to the U.S. Constitution, which would require that federal outlays each year not exceed revenues. The BBA received the requisite two-thirds votes of both houses of Congress. Congress then submitted the BBA to the states for ratification by state legislatures, where the affirmative votes of 38 states were needed for the BBA to become part of the Constitution.

According to the U.S. Code, the Archivist of the United States decides when the threshold has been crossed. When the Archivist receives official notice at the National Archives and Records Administration "that any amendment proposed to the Constitution of the United States has been adopted, according to the provisions of the Constitution," the Archivist "shall . . . cause the amendment to be published, with his certificate, specifying the States by which the [amendment] may have been adopted, and that the [amendment] has become valid . . . as a part of the Constitution of the United States." 1 U.S.C. § 106b.

As the BBA approached the number of states needed for ratification, some states experienced second thoughts. Following state elections, Arizona and Nevada both voted to rescind their prior ratification of the BBA. Fears expressed by the BBA's opponents who now controlled the legislatures of both states—that the BBA's passage would empower courts to force spending cuts and even to raise taxes—proved persuasive. With Arizona and Nevada now both voting "no," the number of states voting to ratify fell from 37 to 35. The original proponents of the BBA in those states, however, as well as the congressional delegations from both states whose members favored the amendment, took the position that the rescissions were ineffective and that only one more state legislature needed to ratify the BBA for it to become effective.

A few weeks later, New Mexico voted to ratify the BBA, putting the number of states at either 38 or 36, depending on whether Arizona and Nevada's rescissions were valid. As the debate was raging, the Archivist of the United States published the BBA as the new Twenty-Eighth Amendment to the Constitution and certified that it had been validly adopted and was a valid part of the Constitution. His certificate listed Arizona and Nevada as having ratified the BBA; it made no mention of their alleged rescissions.

Furious, members of the legislatures in Arizona and Nevada who voted to rescind their states' early ratification filed suit in federal court seeking to enjoin the enforcement of the Amendment and an order requiring the Archivist to decertify the BBA.

What is the strongest argument *against* justiciability?

A. Article V mentions Congress, and not the courts in discussing the amendment process.

B. A judicial decision decertifying the Amendment would demonstrate disrespect toward Congress.

C. Article V contains no standards for determining when a state had effected a valid ratification of an amendment.

D. A and C

ANALYSIS. This is another question that gives me the opportunity to discuss a case that didn't seem to fit neatly in the earlier discussion. In *Coleman v. Miller*, 307 U.S. 433 (1939), a plurality of the Court argued that questions related to the amendment process were nonjusticiable. The facts in *Coleman* were similar to those in the question: Kansas rejected, then ratified, a constitutional amendment banning child labor. Legislators sued, claiming that the subsequent ratification was invalid. Chief Justice Hughes, writing for a plurality, thought that such questions were political questions and nonjusticiable. Even if you didn't know about *Coleman*, the choices presented you with some compelling arguments against justiciability. Let's start with the one you could reject. As we've seen, arguments that judicial involvement will evince "disrespect" toward another branch cut almost no ice with contemporary courts. Therefore, **B** would not be a strong argument. On the other hand, in *Nixon* and again in *Vieth*, members of the Court have stressed the primacy of textual commitments to other branches and the lack of manageable and applicable standards. That Article V mentions Congress—and Congress alone—might, like the reference to the "sole" power of the House and Senate to impeach and try impeachments, hint that the judiciary was not to have a role in assessing the validity of constitutional amendments. Thus, **A** is a strong argument. It is equally true, however, that Article V doesn't say anything about criteria to be used in establishing whether and to what extent a state has validly ratified an amendment sent to it by Congress for ratification. So **C** seems like a pretty good argument, too. For that reason, **D** is the best answer. In addition, because the amendment process—like the impeachment process—is at least a theoretical check on the Court itself, that might militate against judicial involvement in passing on the validity of amendments that could conceivably limit judicial power or reverse particular Supreme Court decisions. The Court deployed similar arguments in *Nixon* against judicial involvement in the impeachment process. It might also prove confusing to have multiple branches of the government issuing conflicting opinions on an amendment's validity.

QUESTION 13. Goldwater redux. When China fell to the Communists in the late 1940s, the Nationalist Government fled to the island of Formosa (renamed Taiwan) and claimed to be the rightful government of China. The United States entered into a defense treaty (ratified by the necessary 2/3 of the Senate) pledging to defend Taiwan against attack by mainland China. In order to normalize relations with mainland, the President of the United States renounced the treaty. Members of the Senate sued, claiming that the President acted unconstitutionally; another 2/3 vote of the Senate was required to renounce a ratified treaty, they argued. For its part, the Executive Branch noted that the President has the power to receive ambassadors, while the text of the Constitution is silent as to the rescission of treaties. The President further urges the court to declare the issue a nonjusticiable political question. What is the strongest argument *in favor of* the President's position?

A. The court has to decide whether the President's power is circumscribed by the Senate's power to ratify treaties.

B. The Constitution is silent on rescinding or abrogating treaties.

C. The court may not review a textually demonstrable commitment of power to the Executive Branch.

D. The controversy is at bottom a political disagreement among the branches.

ANALYSIS. I tried to make this a little more difficult. Remember the President is trying to get the court to dismiss the case as nonjusticiable. If all the court need do is use the familiar techniques of constitutional interpretation to decide who has the better argument, *Zivotofsky* says that's simply the court exercising the power "to say what the law is," as *Marbury* instructed. Therefore, **A** is not a strong argument for the President. Moreover, recall that the "political question doctrine" doesn't really have anything to do with whether or not the controversy is "political" or whether it involves a disagreement among the political branches. So **D** isn't a strong argument for the President either. **C** is an incorrect statement of law. As *Powell v. McCormack* and *Zivotofsky* make clear, a court is not obliged to defer to another branch's claim that the Constitution makes a textually demonstrable commitment of power to that branch. That leaves **B**, which is the best answer. Recall that *Nixon* stressed the connection between *Baker*'s lack of judicially applicable standards and the textually demonstrable commitment criteria. If the Constitution is silent about rescission of treaties, that leaves little for a court to go on for fashioning or applying standards for determining whether the abrogation was constitutional or not. The lack of standards, in turn, might suggest that the Constitution commits that determination to another branch or branches. On the other hand, though, *Zivotofsky* seems to suggest a narrower role for the political question doctrine than one might have inferred from cases like *Goldwater*. It's difficult to imagine a set of legal questions that would *not* generate some answer if a court used "familiar principles of constitutional interpretation," as the Chief Justice put it.

5. *Congressional power to alter federal courts' jurisdiction*

One intriguing possibility for limiting judicial review both in the Supreme Court and the lower federal courts arises from language in Article III of the Constitution. First, Congress is empowered to create lower federal courts other than the Supreme Court. Second, as to the Court itself, Congress possesses the ability to make "Exceptions" to and "Regulations" of its appellate jurisdiction. Combined, these powers have presented the intriguing—or frightening—possibility that Congress could respond to unpopular court opinions by simply passing so-called jurisdiction-stripping statutes. This section discusses the (sparse) case law on the congressional control of federal jurisdiction, and closes with some speculation why, for critics of the federal courts, the Supreme Court in particular, jurisdiction stripping has not lived up to its potential.

First, to clear some underbrush, the Court has held that the greater power of creating lower courts implies the lesser power to alter the jurisdiction of those courts. *See Sheldon v. Sill*, 49 U.S. 441 (1850). Moreover, despite the mandatory "shall" of Article II, § 2, the Court has held that Congress is not obliged to give original or appellate jurisdiction to federal courts over all matters listed therein. *Id.* We turn later to the question of whether this power, coupled with the power to make exceptions to the Supreme Court's appellate jurisdiction, means that Congress could exclude certain otherwise cognizable federal questions from any federal judicial review.

Most of what we know about the congressional power to limit the Supreme Court's appellate jurisdiction comes from the rather long-in-the-tooth *Ex Parte*

McCardle, 74 U.S. 506 (1869). Like *Marbury, McCardle* involves some political back story that might have influenced the course the Court took, although it's difficult to know for sure. McCardle was a Mississippi newspaper editor who fulminated in print against federal military occupation of his state. Fed up, the military governor of Mississippi, invoking provisions of the Reconstruction Acts, had McCardle imprisoned. McCardle petitioned for a writ of habeas corpus, alleging among other things that the Reconstruction Acts were unconstitutional. The Court eventually got the case, heard oral arguments, and was poised to rule on the constitutionality of those Acts when Congress amended the statute that served as the basis for McCardle's appeal.

The Court concluded that Congress's actions, undertaken pursuant to the power to make "exceptions" to its appellate jurisdiction, deprived it of the power to hear the case. "The provision of the act of 1867, affirming the appellate jurisdiction of this court in cases of habeas corpus is expressly repealed. It is hardly possible to imagine a plainer instance of positive exception," wrote Chief Justice Chase. 74 U.S. at 514. Disclaiming any ability to inquire into motive, the Court noted that "[w]ithout jurisdiction the court cannot proceed at all in any cause. Jurisdiction is power to declare the law, and when it ceases to exist, the only function remaining to the court is that of announcing the fact and dismissing the cause." *Id.*

Cryptically, though, the Court closed with the observation that the repealing act did not "except from jurisdiction any cases but appeals from Circuit Courts under the act of 1867. It does not affect the jurisdiction that was previously exercised [over habeas corpus]." *Id.* at 515. This procedure, known as habeas corpus aided by certiorari, was difficult and complicated, but apparently was still available. It is unclear, though, whether the sentence meant that some appellate review had to be available as a matter of constitutional law, or was just an observation that the 1868 Act did not repeal all appellate review of habeas corpus. What the Court meant makes a difference. If it meant to suggest that some appellate review was constitutionally required, then that means that true jurisdiction stripping—a bill disabling the Court's ability to hear, say, abortion cases—would not be possible.

It appeared the Court might get the chance to answer this question in *Felker v. Turpin,* 518 U.S. 651 (1996), a case involving congressional restrictions on state prisoners' ability to obtain habeas review of their state court convictions. Because, as in *McCardle,* habeas corpus aided by certiorari remained a theoretical possibility for securing review, the Court saw no need to address whether appellate jurisdiction could be *completely* stripped from the Court.

McCardle's ambiguity has spawned a cottage industry among scholars speculating about the scope and limits of Congress's power to restrict the Court's appellate jurisdiction. These debates are largely academic, as few serious attempts to eliminate, for example, the Court's jurisdiction over abortion cases have ever gotten very far in Congress. On one side are those who think that the Exceptions Clause pretty much means what it says, and is a potential check on an overweening Court.[8] On the other are those who essentially follow the late Harvard Professor Henry Hart, who wrote a famous article in which he argued that the power could not be used to undermine the "essential functions" of the Court, which others have argued include resolving conflicts over law and maintaining federal law as the supreme law of the land.[9]

Whatever the extent of those so-called internal limits on Congress's jurisdiction-stripping power, all agree that the Constitution imposes "external" limits as well—limits derived from other constitutional protections, like those in the Bill of Rights. It is clear that Congress could not, for example, bar claims by litigants of a particular race.

Nor can Congress instruct the courts to decide particular questions in a certain way. *United States v. Klein,* 80 U.S. 128 (1872), saw the Court strike down a congressional statute that purported to treat pardons granted to those suing in the Court of Claims to recover compensation for property seized by the government during the Civil War as conclusive evidence of disloyalty and instructed the Court to dismiss such claims. Had Congress simply denied to the Court the right to hear appeals of compensation cases from the Court of Claims that would have been within Congress's power under the Exceptions Clause. *Id.* at 145 ("If [the act] simply denied the right of appeal in a particular class of cases, there could be no doubt that it must be regarded as an exercise of the power of Congress to make 'such exceptions from the appellate jurisdiction' as should seem to it expedient"). But according to the Court, prescribing such a rule of decision "passed the limit which separates the legislative from the judicial power." 80 U.S. at 147. (The congressional statute also had the effect of disregarding presidential pardons, another reason the Court gave for invalidating the statute.) Note, however, that Congress can change the underlying law—even in the middle of a dispute—that alters the outcome of the matter. Congress just can't attempt to alter *specific results* of controversies governed by otherwise unchanged law. *Robertson v. Seattle Audubon Society,* 503 U.S. 429 (1992) (upholding congressional change in laws governing logging regulations, which altered results in two pending suits that could have come out differently under old rules).

Similarly, Congress cannot reinstate a cause of action once courts have entered a final judgment. *Plaut v. Spendthrift Farm, Inc.,* 514 U.S. 211 (1995). It may, however, change underlying substantive law in a way that results in pending cases being decided differently than they would have been prior to the change. Such changes would then apply only to cases in which final judgment had not yet been entered.

But jurisdiction-stripping measures aimed at the Court have probably foundered as much on practical difficulties as on constitutional doubts. The

---

8. *See, e.g.,* Herbert Wechsler, *The Courts and the Constitution,* 65 Colum. L. Rev. 1001 (1965).

9. Henry M. Hart, Jr., *The Power of Congress to Limit the Jurisdiction of Federal Courts: An Exercise in Dialectic,* 66 Harv. L. Rev. 1362 (1953); Leonard Ratner, *Congressional Power Over the Appellate Jurisdiction of the Supreme Court,* 109 U. Pa. L. Rev. 157 (1960).

measures are often spawned by unpopular or controversial Supreme Court decisions. Yet removing that subject matter from the Court's appellate jurisdiction does not result in the prior decision's reversal. That decision is still the law of the land and, technically, lower courts and state courts are bound by it. It's possible that removing the threat of review and reversal would embolden some judges to "underrule" the prior case by simply ignoring it, but it is doubtful that all — or even many — federal and state judges would be so willful. Assuming that most judges will continue to apply binding Supreme Court precedent in good faith, jurisdiction stripping seems like the proverbial closing of the barn door after the horse has run off.

Could Congress limit the jurisdiction of lower courts and the Supreme Court's appellate jurisdiction so as to deprive certain cases of any federal forum? Again, this is the subject of considerable academic debate. Some scholars (citing a portion of the Court's opinion in *Martin*) argue that for those subjects listed in Article III, some federal forum must exist, even if it is a specially created court with exclusive federal jurisdiction over certain matters mentioned in Article III. Others argue that the ability to control jurisdiction and assign certain subjects exclusively to state courts was part of a Framing-era compromise regarding federal courts.[10] Again it is unclear how effective this curb would be, given that offending Supreme Court opinions would still bind the state courts. In any event, few such radical curbs on federal judicial power have come close to passing in recent years.

QUESTION 14. Jurisdictional roulette. Which of the following would be most likely to be invalidated if challenged in federal court?

 A. Legislation that amended the Supreme Court's appellate jurisdiction rendering it unable to hear abortion cases; such cases would be heard by a new federal appeals court that would handle only abortion cases.

 B. A statute barring atheists from challenging the use of "under God" in the Pledge of Allegiance in federal court.

 C. A statute requiring abortion cases to be brought in state court, with a possible appeal to the U.S. Supreme Court after all state appeals had been exhausted.

 D. Legislation reversing a Supreme Court interpretation of a wage and hour statute holding that time traveling to and from work counted toward total hours worked during a week.

---

10. *Compare* Lawrence Sager, *The Supreme Court, 1980 Term—Foreword: Constitutional Limitations on Congress' Authority to Regulate the Jurisdiction of the Federal Courts*, 95 Harv. L. Rev. 17 (1981) *with* Martin Redish, *Constitutional Limitations on Congressional Power to Control Federal Jurisdiction: A Reaction to Professor Sager*, 77 Nw. U. L. Rev. 143 (1982).

ANALYSIS.   This is a nice review question to start us off slowly. Although the use of the Exceptions Clause to "zone" certain cases out of the Supreme Court is controversial, *McCardle* approved and the text of the Constitution seems to authorize it. Moreover, in the first answer, a federal appellate forum—the abortion court—would be available to resolve conflicts and enforce federal law. So **A** is not the best answer. The problem with **C** is that Congress clearly has the power to alter the jurisdiction of the lower courts, as part of their power to create inferior courts, like the abortion court in the first answer. Further, in **C** the Supreme Court still retains its role as the court of last resort. The facts in **D** are similar to those that resulted in the passage of the federal Portal-to-Portal Act, 29 U.S.C. § 251. Congress is entitled to change substantive law in ways that may have the effect of reversing a Supreme Court's interpretation of a statute and extinguishing a possible cause of action that has not been reduced to final judgment. That leaves **B**, the correct answer: Whatever the scope of Congress's Exceptions Clause power, it may not wield it in a way that offends other provisions of the Constitution. Barring appeals by atheist litigants *because of* their atheism would likely present severe First Amendment and Due Process Clause problems,[11] even if disabling courts from hearing challenges to the Pledge brought by *any* litigant would not.

QUESTION 15. Heads I win. Tails you lose. In an effort to expedite processing of those being held by the government as enemy combatants, the executive branch has authorized military review panels for detainee appeals of their designation as "enemy combatants." To prevent interminable appeals, Congress passes legislation preventing the Supreme Court from hearing appeals from the decisions of those review panels and instructing lower federal courts that any challenge to the decisions of those review panels is to be taken as conclusive proof that the plaintiff is, in fact, an enemy combatant. Such a law would, if challenged, likely be found:

A. Unconstitutional, because the Court may not have its appellate jurisdiction altered in cases involving civil liberties.

B. Unconstitutional, because the legislation prescribes a rule of decision for federal courts in particular cases.

C. Constitutional, because the law simply changes the underlying law the federal courts are to apply.

D. Constitutional, because Congress's greater power to create lower courts includes the lesser power to alter their jurisdiction.

---

11. Although the Fourteenth Amendment's Equal Protection Clause applies only to the states, the Supreme Court has found an "equal protection component" in the Fifth Amendment's Due Process Clause. *Bolling v. Sharpe,* 347 U.S. 497 (1954) (invalidating segregation in District of Columbia schools).

ANALYSIS.   The facts here are meant to recall those in *United States v. Klein*, where Congress attempted to prescribe a rule of decision in the Court of Claims regarding the legal effect of receipt of a presidential pardon. **A** is not a correct statement of the law; nothing categorically prohibits Congress from altering jurisdiction in cases involving civil liberties. **D** is correct, but the legislation here does more than simply strip jurisdiction from the Supreme Court and the lower federal courts. It purports to instruct the lower courts in how they are to treat cases in which appeals are taken from the status review boards' decisions. Therefore, **C** isn't correct as a factual matter. That leaves **B**, which is the correct answer. As in *Klein*, the effect of the legislation is not unlike a kind of legislative directed verdict — Congress is telling the lower courts how they are to decide the cases. Such prescriptions violate separation of powers principles and exceed the power to alter jurisdiction granted or implied by Article III.

6.   *The Eleventh Amendment*

The Eleventh Amendment was proposed and ratified as a response to the U.S. Supreme Court's decision in *Chisholm v. Georgia*, 2 U.S. 419 (1793), in which the Court interpreted Article III to permit a citizen of one state to sue another state in federal court without that state's consent. What followed was — at least on its face — a limitation of federal judicial power: "The Judicial power of the United States shall not be construed to extend to any suit in law or equity, commenced or prosecuted against one of the United States by Citizens of another State, or by Citizens or Subjects of any Foreign State." U.S. Const. amend. XI. What these words mean, exactly, has been the source of a contentious academic and judicial debate.

According to the Court in *Hans v. Louisiana*, 134 U.S. 1 (1890), the Amendment was intended to restore the doctrine of sovereign immunity following the *Chisholm* decision, but also stood for much more than a repudiation of *Chisholm*. *Hans* held that the Eleventh Amendment ensures that nonconsenting states cannot be sued in federal court. After *Hans*, the Court has tended to enforce the Amendment beyond the scope of its text, treating it instead as a proxy for the structural principle of sovereign immunity. For example, despite the literal language of the Amendment, the Court held the suit in *Hans* was barred, even though it was commenced by a citizen of Louisiana. Later cases applied the bar to suits in *state* courts, as well as to hearings before federal administrative agencies. *Federal Maritime Comm'n v. South Carolina State Ports Authority*, 535 U.S. 743 (2002); *Alden v. Maine*, 527 U.S. 706 (1999); *see also Edelman v. Jordan*, 415 U.S. 651 (1974) (barring suits by state's own citizens). In other cases, the Court has enforced the Eleventh Amendment as a restriction on both the courts' ability to hear suits against states and Congress's ability to enact statutes that would make states defendants to such suits. *See, e.g., Seminole Tribe v. Florida*, 517 U.S. 44 (1996) (holding that Congress could not abrogate state sovereign immunity using its Article I power to regulate Indian commerce). But in *Tennessee Student Assistance Corp. v. Hood*, 541

U.S. 440 (2004) and *Central Virginia Community College v. Katz,* 546 U.S. 354 (2006), the Court permitted a suit against state agencies to determine the dischargeability of a debt in bankruptcy. In both cases, the Court ruled that unlike many other Article I powers, the states did not retain sovereign immunity with regard to bankruptcy laws that Congress might pass.

The Eleventh Amendment is not an absolute limitation on jurisdiction. It can be waived by states, or it can be abrogated by Congress validly acting under the Fourteenth Amendment, *Fitzpatrick v. Bitzer,* 427 U.S. 445 (1976), but only if Congress makes a "clear statement" of its intent to do so. *Atascadero State Hospital v. Scanlon,* 473 U.S. 234 (1985).

The significance of the *Seminole Tribe* line of cases became clear when the Court decided *Boerne v. Flores,* 521 U.S. 507 (1997), in which the Court held that Congress could use the Fourteenth Amendment's § 5 enforcement power[12] only where the legislative remedy was "congruent and proportional" to the alleged violation and the severity of the harm suffered. As a practical matter this meant that the Court would closely scrutinize instances of congressional abrogation of sovereign immunity to ensure that the remedies were commensurate with the judicially recognized violations Congress sought to address.[13] The effect was a narrowing by the Court of Congress's enforcement ability, presumably arising from the Court's sensitivity — reflected in the Eleventh Amendment cases — to protecting states' sovereign immunity against undue involuntary abrogation.

Because of the Eleventh Amendment's potential — if widely applied — to frustrate efforts to bring state governments to heel, the Court has created a number of important exceptions to the general rule prohibiting suits against nonconsenting states. Waiver and congressional abrogation through the Fourteenth Amendment are two, but there are others. For example, the United States itself may bring suit against a state, and states may sue one another. Cities and other political subdivisions may also be sued.

Most important, state officers may be sued for prospective injunctive relief (and, in a few cases, for money). *Ex Parte Young,* 209 U.S. 123 (1908). The *Ex Parte Young* exception is premised on the notion that a state officer who acts unlawfully is not within the scope of his or her authority, because that authority does not run to violating federal law or the Constitution. Although a legal fiction — the officer is, after all, an officer of the state, and acting "under color of state law" even when acting outside the scope of his or her authority — *Ex Parte Young* "long has been recognized as a primary method of limiting the effect of the Eleventh Amendment and of ensuring state compliance with federal law." Chemerinsky, *supra,* at 203.

---

12.   Section 5 of the Fourteenth Amendment reads: "The Congress shall have power to enforce, by appropriate legislation, the provisions of this article."

13.   Congressional enforcement of civil liberties is covered in detail in Brannon Padgett Denning, The Glannon Guide to Constitutional Law: Individual Rights and Liberties, Ch. 10 (2012).

Eleventh Amendment immunity is a complex subject with lots of doctrinal twists and turns,[14] but remember these key points and you will likely know most of what you need to know about the Eleventh Amendment:

1. States may not be sued in state or federal court, or hauled before federal administrative agencies, for money damages by their own citizens or those of another state or citizens of other countries unless
   a. The State has waived sovereign immunity; or
   b. Congress has clearly abrogated state sovereign immunity using its remedial power under the Fourteenth Amendment. Such remedy must be both "congruent and proportional" to the alleged violation of constitutional rights.[15]
2. The United States can bring suit against states free from the Eleventh Amendment's restrictions.
3. Under *Ex Parte Young*, state officers may be sued in actions seeking prospective relief, like an injunction.
4. Political subdivisions of states do not possess sovereign immunity.
5. States do not retain sovereign immunity with regard to federal bankruptcy laws passed by Congress.

The Court's sovereign immunity decisions in the 1990s were closely divided 5–4 decisions. More recent cases, like *Katz* and *Hood*, were also closely divided, but in favor of federal jurisdiction. It remains to be seen whether they are harbingers of a retreat from the rigorous application of sovereign immunity of the late Rehnquist Court.

D.   The Closer

QUESTION 16. **Taking the Pledge.**   In response to the Ninth Circuit Court of Appeals' decision holding that the recitation of the Pledge of Allegiance in public schools with the phrase "one Nation under God" violated the Establishment Clause, members of Congress proposed the "Pledge Protection Act." Section 2 of the PPA reads, "[n]o court created by Act of Congress shall have any jurisdiction, and the Supreme Court shall have no appellate jurisdiction, to hear or decide any question

---

14. If you need more detail than is available here, Chemerinsky, *supra*, at § 2.10 provides an excellent overview.

15. The congruence and proportionality test is discussed in detail in Denning, *supra* note 13, at 284-295.

pertaining to the interpretation of, or the validity under the Constitution of, this section or the Pledge of Allegiance. . . ." The parents of school-children who had previously filed suit to have "under God" in the Pledge declared unconstitutional file suit alleging that the PPA is unconstitutional. Which of the following would be their strongest argument?

 A. The PPA deprives the Court of its essential function by preventing it from hearing the case.

 B. The PPA deprives the federal judiciary of the power to "say what the law is."

C. Article III requires that some federal forum exists to hear federal questions.

D. Congress may not use its jurisdiction-stripping power to alter outcomes in particular cases.

ANALYSIS.   This was a tricky one! (But, hey, these are supposed to be more difficult.) The question, however, is made somewhat easier if you read the operative part of the PPA carefully. Note that § 2 of the PPA not only purports to strip jurisdiction from lower federal courts and from the Supreme Court, but also seeks to deprive courts of the power to review this section—that is, § 2—for constitutionality. Recall that even the Court in *McCardle* assumed that it had the power to review Congress's amendment of the habeas corpus statute that deprived it of the power to hear McCardle's appeal. Trying to prevent courts from reviewing acts for constitutionality seems to go beyond mere jurisdiction stripping and to keep it from exercising what *Marbury* said was "emphatically the province and duty of the judicial department"—"to say what the law is." The answer, therefore, is **B**. **A** is not the best answer, because the Court has never held the "essential function" argument is a limit on the exercise of the Exceptions Clause. That limit has been suggested by scholars like Henry Hart. Likewise, though Joseph Story famously argued for the Court in *Martin* that Article III's grant of subject matter jurisdiction was mandatory, and thus some federal forum had to be available to hear such questions. Although that position has found favor with scholars, the Court did not adhere to it in subsequent cases. Finally, **D** may be true (see *Klein*), but the PPA doesn't seek to alter any outcomes. In fact, jurisdiction stripping itself can't guarantee any particular outcome. At best, it represents a reaction to prior decisions, and reflects a hope that other courts—state courts in this case—*will* come to different conclusions. Again, however, the decision prompting the jurisdiction stripping in the first place—at least if it was a Supreme Court decision—will still be binding on lower courts, and not all lower courts will abandon stare decisis, ignore binding precedent, or both to reach a different conclusion.

✺ Denning's Picks

1.	Veto-gate	**B**
2.	An emolumental mess	**D**
3.	The tenacious taxpayer	**A**
4.	Standing in the shadow	**B**
5.	Are you (in) kind?	**D**
6.	Do you feel a draft?	**C**
7.	A taxing opinion	**C**
8.	Not-so-fresh air	**A**
9.	Rescue me!	**C**
10.	A political question question	**C**
11.	On the house	**A**
12.	Wait just amendment!	**D**
13.	Goldwater redux	**B**
14.	Jurisdictional roulette	**B**
15.	Heads I win. Tails you lose.	**B**
16.	Taking the Pledge	**B**

3

Allocation of Power in a Federal System: Express, Implied, and Reserved Powers and Limits

CHAPTER OVERVIEW
A. Overview
B. *McCulloch v. Maryland* and the Doctrine of Implied Powers
C. Implied Restrictions on State Powers: *McCulloch* and *U.S. Term Limits*
D. The Closer
✦ Denning's Picks

A. Overview

The United States is a *federal* system. The Constitution creates a central government, allocates power to that government, and places limits on the exercise of those powers. But unlike unitary governments, as in France, for example, the United States is also made up of 50 states, each with its own legislative, executive, and judicial branches. Moreover, at least theoretically, these state governments (not to mention the thousands of substate governments with jurisdiction over counties and municipalities) have near-plenary legislative power, whereas Congress's legislative authority is circumscribed by the enumerated powers in Article I, § 8 and other sections of the Constitution, such as the enforcement clauses of various amendments.[1] Whereas Congress must point to an enumerated power to justify action, state and local governments exercise "the police power," which enables them to

---

1. *See, e.g.,* U.S. Const. amend. XIV, § 5 ("The Congress shall have power to enforce, by appropriate legislation, the provisions of this article.").

legislate for the health, safety, and welfare of their citizens, subject only to the limits of their state constitutions, and, of course, the U.S. Constitution.

In only a few instances does the Constitution grant Congress *exclusive* power to act, displacing state power even in the absence of affirmative congressional action. One example is found in Article I, § 8, which gives Congress the power to coin money. There is a complementary restriction on state power to do the same in Article I, § 10. More often, though, Congress and states have *concurrent power*—the power to tax, for example, is exercised both by Congress and the states. As discussed in Chapter 5, however, the Constitution requires state law to give way if state and federal laws are in conflict.

The fact that state and federal powers overlap in so many areas, and the fact that the federal government is one of limited authority, mean that questions frequently arise in constitutional law regarding the proper allocation of power and the location of boundaries between the state and federal governments. The scope of important congressional powers is taken up in Chapter 4; Chapter 5 covers important limits on the power of state governments. This chapter, however, addresses some very general questions regarding the allocation of power between the states and the federal government. It is, in other words, all about default rules: When the Constitution is silent, where does power get allocated between the federal and state governments?

First, we take up the question of whether Congress must find explicit sanction for each law it passes in Article I, § 8, or whether certain powers may be *implied* from the grant of other powers. That question was answered by Chief Justice Marshall in the first part of the famous 1819 case *McCulloch v. Maryland,* which ruled on the constitutionality of the Second Bank of the United States.

The second half of the chapter takes up a related question: In the absence of congressional legislation, are there any limits on the exercise of *state* power other than those mentioned specifically in the Constitution? As it happens, *McCulloch* addressed this question as well.

B.   *McCulloch v. Maryland* and the Doctrine of Implied Powers

In the 1790s, Alexander Hamilton, George Washington's Secretary of the Treasury, designed an audacious financial plan to improve the credit of the United States and position the country as a major trading power. Among his plans was the creation of a corporate Bank of the United States, modeled after the Bank of England. The stock of the bank would be offered to private investors, who would own it along with the U.S. government. Of course, Article I, § 8 mentions nothing about the power of Congress to create corporations, and a fierce debate about Congress's constitutional ability to create the bank ensued.

When the dust settled, the pro-Bank forces had won. President Washington was uncertain, however; he asked for three opinions from his cabinet. Attorney General Edmund Randolph and Secretary of State Thomas Jefferson were of the opinion that the bank was unconstitutional, and urged Washington to veto the bill. Alexander Hamilton, however, delivered a tour de force opinion justifying the creation of the bank and articulating a broad theory of implied powers. Washington was convinced, and signed the bill.

The First Bank of the United States, however, was chartered for a specific time. When its charter came up for renewal in the early nineteenth century, Congress allowed it to lapse. Following the War of 1812, when a wave of nationalism swept the country, a Second Bank of the United States was chartered; even early bank opponents like James Madison — who led the anti-bank forces in the House of Representatives during the debates over the First Bank — conceded its constitutionality. The Second Bank became unpopular in the wake of a financial panic; individual states, like Maryland, attempted to tax branches of the national bank out of existence. When McCulloch, the manager of the Baltimore branch of the Second Bank of the United States, refused to pay the state tax, the case of *McCulloch v. Maryland,* 17 U.S. 316 (1819) ensued.

There were two questions at issue: (1) the constitutionality of the Second Bank of the United States, and (2) assuming its constitutionality, whether Maryland could tax the bank. We take up the second question in the next section.

Marshall's opinion began by acknowledging the occurrence of the earlier debate over the First Bank of the United States, and stated that "[i]t would require no ordinary share of intrepidity to assert that a measure adopted under these circumstances was a bold and plain usurpation to which the constitution gave no countenance." 17 U.S. at 402. Nevertheless, Marshall took up the question of the bank's constitutionality anew.

He opened with a discussion of the nature of the Union. Contrary to a growing chorus of voices claiming that states were the original parties to the Constitution and that they retained significant aspects of sovereignty, Marshall argued that the nature of the Union was one in which "the People" gave consent to the creation of a new form of government through the special ratifying conventions. "From these conventions," he concluded, "the constitution derives its whole authority." 17 U.S. at 403. "The government of the Union," he added, is "emphatically and truly, a government of the people." *Id.* at 404–405.

He then observed that the government created was one of enumerated powers, and conceded that the power to create corporations was not found in the powers listed in Article I, § 8. But he then contrasted the wording of the Constitution with the Articles of Confederation. "[T]here is no phrase in the instrument," as was present in the Articles, "exclud[ing] incidental or implied powers and . . . requir[ing] that everything granted . . . be expressly and minutely described." *Id.* at 406.[2] Marshall noted that neither Article I, which delegated powers to Congress, nor the Tenth Amendment, which reserved to the states powers not delegated to the Congress nor forbidden to the states, included the word "expressly." *Id.* "[A] fair construction of the whole instrument," that is, the Constitution, was required to answer the question whether Congress could incorporate the bank.

Marshall then constructed a logical argument intended to show that enumeration of ends—such as those ends listed in Article I, § 8—implied a choice of means, including the creation of a corporation to further some enumerated power. "[A] government intrusted with such ample powers . . . must also be intrusted with ample means for their execution. The power being given, it is in the interest of the nation to facilitate its execution." 17 U.S. at 408. Unless express language in the Constitution compels it, Marshall wrote, we should not artificially limit Congress's choice of means—which are not enumerated—to achieve its enumerated ends. And creating a corporation is a *means,* not an *end* in and of itself; therefore, it was not surprising, he argued, that it is not listed among congressional ends in Article I, § 8. The "power of creating a corporation is never used for its own sake, but for the purpose of effecting something else." *Id.* at 411.

Marshall then let the other shoe drop: The Constitution did not leave the question of implied powers to logic. Among the powers listed in Article I, § 8, is the power to pass "all laws which shall be necessary and proper for carrying into execution the foregoing powers [in Article I, § 8], and all other powers vested by this constitution in the government of the United States, or in any department thereof." U.S. Const. art. I, § 8, cl. 18.

Chief Justice Marshall rejected Maryland's argument that "necessary" denoted that which was essential or indispensable to the execution of a power, opting instead for reading the term to mean "convenient" or "expedient." He bolstered his reading by reference to the qualification of necessary by the word "absolutely" in Article I, § 10. He also noted that the Necessary and Proper Clause was included not in restrictions on Congress's powers found in Article I, § 9, but in the section in which powers were granted. Further, Marshall argued that the Clause, by its terms, was intended to enlarge, not to circumscribe, the powers of Congress.

Marshall then stated something like a test for assessing whether Congress may exercise implied powers under the Necessary and Proper Clause:

1. The *end* must be legitimate (i.e., within Congress's power).
2. The *means* used to effectuate that end must be "appropriate," by which Marshall explained he meant:
   a. "plainly adapted" to the end,
   b. not prohibited to Congress by the Constitution, and
   c. consistent with the letter and spirit of the Constitution.

---

2.   Article II of the Articles reads, "Each state retains its sovereignty, freedom, and independence, and every power, jurisdiction, and right, which is not by this Confederation expressly delegated to the United States, in Congress assembled."

17 U.S. at 421. He concluded that a corporation and a bank "is a convenient, a useful, and essential instrument in the prosecution of [Congress's] fiscal operations. . . . " *Id.* at 422.

The upshot of Marshall's opinion, and its rejection of Maryland's more restrictive interpretation of the Necessary and Proper Clause, was that the Court would grant Congress considerable leeway in supplementing its enumerated powers with implied powers intended to carry into execution either Congress's powers or those powers lodged elsewhere in the federal government. Critics feared that this would mean that enumeration in Article I would prove to be of little use in restraining Congress. Marshall acknowledged this, and closed with a warning of sorts. Should Congress, he wrote,

> in the execution of its powers, adopt measures which are prohibited by the constitution; or should congress, under the pretext of executing its powers, pass laws for the accomplishment of objects not intrusted to the government; it would become the painful duty of this tribunal, should a case requiring such a decision come before it, to say that such an act was not the law of the land.

Id. at 423. The Court, however, has never articulated a standard for determining when a particular exercise of congressional power is "pretextual" and, thus, invalid.

Marshall's deferential position is still the position of the Court. In current parlance, the Court reads *McCulloch* as holding that all powers "rationally related" to executing or carrying out Congress's enumerated powers are constitutional. It has so held most recently in the case of *Sabri v. United States*, 541 U.S. 600 (2004). *Sabri* involved a constitutional challenge to a federal statute prohibiting bribery of state and local officials of entities receiving $10,000 or more of federal funds. A real estate developer convicted of violating the statute sued to reverse his conviction, claiming that such a law exceeded congressional power. Rejecting Sabri's argument, the Court wrote that

> Congress has authority under the Spending Clause to appropriate federal moneys to promote the general welfare, Art. I, § 8, cl. 1, and it has corresponding authority under the Necessary and Proper Clause, Art. I, § 8, cl. 18, to see to it that taxpayer dollars appropriated under that power are in fact spent for the general welfare, and not frittered away in graft or on projects undermined when funds are siphoned off or corrupt public officers are derelict about demanding value for dollars. See generally *McCulloch v. Maryland*, [17 U.S. 316 (1819)] (establishing review for means–ends rationality under the Necessary and Proper Clause).

541 U.S. at 605.

Arguably, though, the "rational basis" test is not necessarily the equivalent of Marshall's test in *McCulloch*. Under the rational basis test, the Court generally presumes constitutionality, and thus would permit an exercise of implied power as long as there is evidence that a rational Congress could have concluded that X was helpful or expedient or useful in exercising power Y. The

Court will even presume evidence of utility to have been present or available to Congress, despite absence of that evidence in the record. By contrast, as Justice Thomas pointed out in his concurring opinion in *Sabri,* Chief Justice Marshall's test requires that the end be "appropriate" and "plainly adapted" to the end, and notes that power must not be "pretextual." Justice Thomas argued that such language was more restrictive than the Court's rational basis test. 541 U.S. at 612–613 (Thomas, J., concurring).

The Court seemed to continue its deferential review of congressional claims of necessity in *United States v. Comstock*, 130 S. Ct. 1949 (2010), in which the Court upheld the civil commitment of prisoners deemed "sexually dangerous" after completion of their prison sentences. Respondents alleged that the law authorizing civil commitment exceeded Congress's power under Article I, section 8. Seven justices concluded that the law was authorized by the Necessary and Proper Clause. *Comstock*, 130 S. Ct. at 1956. Justice Breyer, writing for the majority, gave five reasons for upholding the civil commitment act.

First, he noted that "the Necessary and Proper Clause grants Congress broad authority to enact federal legislation" and that the Court had concluded that "whether the Necessary and Proper Clause grants Congress the legislative authority to enact a particular statute" depended on whether the statute was "rationally related to the implementation of a constitutionally enumerated power." *Id.* at 1956. Second, Justice Breyer characterized the statute as "a modest addition to a set of federal prison-related mental-health statutes that have existed for many decades," even though most of the earlier statutes ended commitment when the term of imprisonment ended. *Id.* at 1958-1959. Third, the statute, argued the Court, was reasonable because the federal government had a responsibility as custodian to "extend[] its longstanding civil-commitment system to cover mentally ill and sexually dangerous persons . . . in order to protect nearby (and other) communities from the danger federal prisoners may pose." *Id.* at 1961. Fourth, the act respects state interests by authorizing the state where the prisoner was tried or domiciled and inviting the state to take custody of the individual. *Id.* at 1962. Finally, the Court held that the "links between [the statute] and an enumerated power are not too attenuated." *Id.* at 1963. Specifically, the Court declined to hold that "when legislating pursuant to the Necessary and Proper Clause, Congress' authority can be no more than one step removed from a specifically enumerated power." *Id.* "[F]rom the implied power to *punish*," the Court explained, "we have *further* inferred both the power to imprison . . . and the federal civil-commitment power." *Id.*

The origins of many of Justice Breyer's five factors in *Comstock* are unclear. The dissent complained that the "Government identifies no specific enumerated power or powers as a constitutional predicate for [the statute], and none are readily discernable." *Id.* at 1973 (Thomas, J., dissenting). Justice Thomas also criticized the majority for applying its "newly minted test [which] cannot be reconciled with the Clause's plain text or with two centuries of our precedents interpreting it." *Id.* at 1975 (Thomas, J., dissenting). Indeed, if Congress is permitted to use the Clause as a bootstrap, passing legislation that is "necessary" to execute other statutes passed in turn as "necessary" to some congressional power, it is difficult to see what sort of judicially enforceable limit exists. At some point, the exercise seems to approach the "pretext" limit Marshall himself suggested in *McCulloch*.

The narrower reading of the Clause expressed by Justice Thomas in his *Sabri* concurrence and in the *Comstock* dissent garnered support in the hotly contested litigation over the Affordable Care Act (ACA). Among the ACA's controversial provisions was a requirement that individuals either purchase health insurance that satisfied minimum requirements or pay a penalty. *National Federation of Independent Business v. Sebelius*, 132 S. Ct. 2566 (2012) (hereinafter "*NFIB*"). Among the arguments deployed in support of the so-called "individual mandate" was that it was authorized under the Necessary and Proper Clause. While the Court ultimately upheld the mandate as a permissible exercise of Congress's taxing power,[3] five Justices rejected the argument that the mandate was "necessary" to any enumerated power.

Writing for himself, Chief Justice Roberts rejected the Government's argument that the Clause authorized the individual mandate because it was "an 'integral part of a comprehensive scheme of economic regulation,'" namely the provisions that prohibited insurers from denying coverage to individuals with preexisting conditions or for charging them more for insurance based on their health. *NFIB*, 132 S. Ct. at 2591. In prior cases, Roberts explained, the laws upheld "involved exercises of authority derivative of, and in service to, a granted power." *Id.* at 2592. "The individual mandate, by contrast, vests Congress with the extraordinary ability to create the necessary predicate to the exercise of an enumerated power." *Id.* However "necessary" the individual mandate was, it was not—in the opinion of the Chief Justice—"proper." The joint dissent agreed that "the Necessary and Proper Clause is exceeded not only when the congressional action directly violates the sovereignty of the States but also when it violates the background principle of enumerated (and hence limited) federal power." *Id.* at 2646 (Scalia, Kennedy, Thomas & Alito, JJ., dissenting). For her part, Justice Ginsburg characterized the Chief's Justice's reading of the Necessary and Proper Clause as "long on rhetoric" but "short on substance" and "[l]acking [in] case law support . . . . " *Id.* at 2626, 2627 (Ginsburg, J., concurring in part and dissenting in part).

There is considerable tension between the conflicting interpretations of the Necessary and Proper Clause in *Comstock* and *NFIB*. The task of reconciling the decisions is made all the more difficult by two things: (1) the fact that Chief Justice Roberts and Justices Kennedy and Alito joined the *Comstock* majority and (2) uncertainty over the status of the five Justices' opinions in *NFIB*. Because Chief Justice Roberts ultimately upheld the individual mandate

---

3. *See infra* Chapter 4.C. for a discussion of *NFIB*.

under the taxing power, his ruminations on the constitutionality of the mandate could be characterized as non-binding *dicta*. In any event, the authors of the joint dissent did not join his lone opinion. The most we can conclude is that there were five votes in *NFIB* for a more narrow reading of the Necessary and Proper Clause than the *Comstock* Court's reading. Reconciliation or synthesis of the two conflicting visions contained in both cases must await future decisions.

QUESTION 1. Going postal.   Assume that a congressional statute authorizes the federal government to exercise eminent domain to acquire property for new post offices. That is, the statute enables the government to force private land owners to sell their land to the federal government if it cannot acquire it through negotiated agreement. The government wants land owned by Farmer Filburn, and begins eminent domain proceedings against the parcel on which the government wishes to place the postal facility. Filburn claims that the statute is unconstitutional. He points out that nothing in Article I gives to Congress the power of eminent domain. Will Farmer Filburn likely prevail on his claim?

A. No, because eminent domain would be helpful to the government in exercising its constitutional power to "establish Post Offices," given in Article I, § 8.

B. No, because eminent domain is indispensable to the power to establish post offices.

C. Yes, because Congress may exercise only enumerated powers given in Article I, § 8.

D. Yes, because eminent domain is not a power expressly given to Congress by Article I.

ANALYSIS.   You ought to have found this question straightforward after reading about *McCulloch*. First, you know that Congress is not restricted to those powers explicitly enumerated in Article I. As Chief Justice Marshall pointed out in the opinion, the word "expressly" is omitted both from the delegation of legislative power in Article I and in the Tenth Amendment, which also speaks of powers "delegated" to Congress. The framers' omission of that word, he argued, was intentional, and left open the possibility of implied powers. Therefore, you can eliminate **C** and **D** right off the bat, as they are erroneous statements of law.

That leaves a choice between **A** and **B**. Again, however, there is an erroneous statement of law in **B**: Congress need *not* demonstrate that a particular implied power is indispensable or essential to the exercise of an enumerated power to take advantage of the Necessary and Proper Clause. *McCulloch* held that the power need only be helpful or useful. Therefore, **A** is the best answer.

QUESTION 2. Stormy Weathers. Title 18 of the U.S. Code, § 2115, reads:

> Whoever forcibly breaks into or attempts to break into any post office, or any building used in whole or in part as a post office, with intent to commit in such post office, or building or part thereof, so used, any larceny or other depredation, shall be fined under this title or imprisoned not more than five years, or both.

Robin Weathers was arrested and convicted for violating § 2115 after he was caught inside the Monteagle, Tennessee post office with fistfuls of mail and assorted packages. He has challenged the constitutionality of this statute, arguing that while Article I, § 8 gives to Congress the power to "establish Post Offices and post Roads," nothing in Article I gives Congress the power to pass criminal laws. How should a court rule on his appeal?

A. Affirm the conviction, because Congress was acting pursuant to its police powers.
B. Reverse the conviction, because Congress has no Article I power to create criminal offenses, other than its power to "define and punish Piracies and Felonies committed on the high Seas, and Offences against the Law of Nations."
C. Reverse the conviction, because state law could adequately deal with mail thefts.
D. Affirm the conviction because punishing theft of the mail is "necessary and proper" way to carry out the "establish[ment] of Post Offices."

ANALYSIS.   This was another warmup, to see how carefully you read what went before. **A** cannot be the correct answer, because Congress — unlike state governments — does not possess plenary legislative power. It must trace its authority to act to powers enumerated in Article I, § 8. But because *McCulloch* tells us that Congress is not limited to *express* Article I powers, you know that **B** is incorrect, as the power to create crimes does not necessarily have to be given affirmatively to exist. Moreover, whether state law could deal adequately with mail thefts is beside the point — the issue is whether Congress, should it choose to do so, could criminalize theft of the mails independent of the states. Therefore **C**, too, is incorrect. That leaves **D**, which is correct because Congress could think that criminalizing mail theft is "necessary and proper," which is to say expedient and useful, to the establishment of post offices in the first place.

QUESTION 3. Reach out and threaten someone.   Thomas Quill calls the White House switchboard and threatens to kill the President of the United States. After an investigation by the Secret Service, Quill is charged with and convicted of violating 18 U.S.C. § 871(a), which prohibits "knowingly and willfully . . . mak[ing] [a] threat against the President. . . ." Facing a fine and up to five years' imprisonment, Quill appeals his conviction, claiming that Congress lacks the authority to criminalize threats against the President. Having read the Court's disposition of Robin Weathers's case, Quill points out that there is no power in Article I, § 8 to which criminalizing threats to the life of the President could be considered "necessary and proper." How should a reviewing court rule?

A. Affirm Quill's conviction because criminalizing threats against the President is necessary and proper to Congress's power to provide for the general welfare found in Article I, § 8, clause 1.

B. Affirm Quill's conviction because criminalizing threats against the President is necessary and proper to allow the President to, as Article II, § 3 states, "take Care that the Laws be faithfully executed. . . ."

C. Reverse Quill's conviction because criminalizing threats to the President could not conceivably be necessary and proper to any of Congress's Article I, § 8 powers.

D. Reverse Quill's conviction because the passage of criminal laws is reserved to the states by the Tenth Amendment to the Constitution.

ANALYSIS. This was a little bit trickier. The key to answering the question is to remember the precise phrasing of the Necessary and Proper Clause. Not only may Congress pass laws necessary and proper to execution of its own powers, but it may also pass laws necessary and proper to "other powers vested by this constitution in the government of the United States, or in any department thereof." U.S. Const. art. I, § 8, cl. 18. Thus, **C** is wrong, because one need look to other potential sources of power in the Constitution to decide whether a particular exercise of the Necessary and Proper Clause power is constitutional. Careful reading would have led you to exclude **D** as well, as Congress need not have explicit power to pass a particular law.

Between the remaining answers, **A** is incorrect because there is *no* general power to legislate "for the general welfare" in Article I. Such a power would render the rest of § 8 superfluous! Congress does have the power to "lay and collect Taxes, Duties, Imposts, and Excises, to pay the Debts and provide for the common Defence and general Welfare of the United States," U.S. Const. art. I, § 8, cl. 1, but that is not the same as having a general legislative power to so provide.

That leaves **B**, which is the best answer. Congress might think it helpful or useful to criminalize threats against the life of the President so as to ensure that she is able to carry out her executive duties. The Necessary and Proper Clause gives Congress implied powers to furnish means to other officials to discharge the ends of their offices, just as it furnishes Congress itself with the power to choose means to achieve its legislative ends.

QUESTION 4. **The case of the contentious carjacker.** Under federal law, one who, with intent to produce death or serious bodily harm, "takes a motor vehicle that has been transported, shipped, or received in interstate or foreign commerce from the person or presence of another by force and violence or by intimidation" is guilty of the federal crime of carjacking and subject to a lengthy prison sentence. 18 U.S.C. § 2119. Ferris Felon is convicted of a carjacking that occurred entirely within the boundaries of a single state and challenges the constitutionality of § 2119, claiming that it exceeds Congress's power under Article I, § 8. Felon notes that nothing in Article I gives Congress the power to pass criminal laws or regulate automobiles; and that carjacking is, at best, indirectly related to the power of Congress to regulate "commerce among the several states." Is Felon's argument likely to succeed in reversing his conviction and invalidating § 2119?

A. Yes, because § 2119 is not necessary and proper to any enumerated power.
B. Yes, because the statute is a pretextual regulation of interstate crime.
C. No, if Congress could have rationally concluded that criminalizing carjacking would aid in the regulation of interstate commerce.
D. No, because any connection to any enumerated power will suffice to authorize congressional action.

ANALYSIS. Finding the right answer to this question has become a little more difficult in light of the conflicting visions of the Necessary and Proper Clause featured in cases like *Comstock* and *National Federation of Independent Business*. But careful reading can help you reason to the best answer. As we'll see in the next chapter, Congress has the ability to regulate not only interstate commerce qua interstate commerce, but also the ability to regulate "instrumentalities" of interstate commerce, like cars. The Necessary and Proper Clause clearly authorizes this: Congress could think that it might more effectively regulate "commerce among the several states" if it could regulate instrumentalities of commerce by, say, prescribing safety standards for automobiles, trains, ships, and the like. The question then is whether Congress may pass laws that are necessary to *another* law that was necessary to an enumerated power? Criminalizing carjacking under this theory would be okay, despite the lack of mention in Article I about either autos or criminal laws, because such a law is a "necessary and proper" regulation of a particular instrumentality of commerce that Congress may regulate because regulation of those are "necessary and proper" to the regulation of interstate commerce. *Comstock* clearly holds that necessary and proper laws need not be restricted to one remove from the enumerated power. So **A** is not the best answer. Nor is **B**. Chief Justice Marshall mentioned that "pretextual" regulations would be invalidated, but neither he, nor subsequent Courts, have been able to articulate where that line resides. At the same time, as both *Comstock* and *NFIB* make clear, there *is* an outer limit to what the Necessary and Proper Clause would permit. That means **D** is not the best answer either. That leaves **C**, which commanded five votes in *Comstock* (along with two concurring opinions), and is—the statements of five justices in *NFIB* notwithstanding—probably the most accurate statement regarding laws like § 2119.

C.   Implied Restrictions on State Powers: *McCulloch* and U.S. Term Limits

The second half of *McCulloch* posed a different question: In the absence of a specific textual prohibition on state power and in the absence of an otherwise valid exercise of congressional power with which a state law conflicts,[4] are there implicit or *structural* (as opposed to *textual*) limits on state power? Specifically, even assuming that the creation of the Second Bank of the United States was constitutional, did the Constitution further limit Maryland's ability to tax a local branch of that bank?

A logical answer might be "no." After all, the argument against such limits might run, the Tenth Amendment furnishes the appropriate default rule. It reads, "The powers not delegated to the United States by the Constitution, nor prohibited to it by the States, are reserved to the States respectively, or to the people." The attorney for Maryland surely could be forgiven for thinking that Maryland had a pretty strong case. After all, Article I, § 10's Import-Export and Tonnage Clauses contain the only explicit textual restrictions on state taxing power. Further, nothing in Article I gives Congress *exclusive* power over taxes. Therefore, it would seem that Maryland would be free to impose a tax on a bank—even a federal bank—within its jurisdiction, as long as nothing in its state constitution prohibited it from doing so.

Chief Justice Marshall, however, articulated a compelling structural argument that the nature of the Union created by the Constitution limited this particular exercise of Maryland's taxing power. If Maryland could tax the bank out of existence, other states could tax other branches, or other instrumentalities of the federal government. That would mean, de facto if not de jure, that the federal government was subordinate to the states.

He began with the following premise: The power to create the national bank of which the Court just approved included the power to preserve such creations. Those creations, moreover, are supreme vis-à-vis the states. From this he constructed the following syllogism:

---

4.   In that case, the federal law would trump the state law by virtue of the Supremacy Clause of Article VI. See Chapter 5 for a discussion of preemption.

1st. That a power to create implies a power to preserve. 2d. That a power to destroy, if wielded by a different hand, is hostile to and incompatible with these powers to create and to preserve. 3d. That where this repugnancy exists, that authority which is supreme must control, not yield to that over which it is supreme.

17 U.S. at 426. Because the state's taxing power could be exercised to destroy the federal bank, Marshall reasoned, there must be implied limits to the state's power to tax federal instrumentalities. Otherwise, states would be able to tax them out of existence.

Marshall rejected Maryland's argument that the political safeguards would prevent abuse of the taxing power, observing that the people of the United States, whose representatives created the bank, are not sufficiently represented in Maryland to provide security against oppressive taxation. "In the legislature of the Union alone are all represented," Marshall wrote. "The legislature of the Union alone, therefore, can be trusted by the people with the power of controlling measures which concern all, in the confidence that it will not be abused." *Id.* at 431. If Maryland could tax its branch, other states could, and the federal government could easily suffer the proverbial death by a thousand cuts.

McCulloch still states the default rule for state taxation and regulation of federal instrumentalities: State and local governments are prohibited from directly taxing or regulating federal instrumentalities in the absence of express congressional authorization to do so. *See, e.g., United States v. State Tax Comm'n,* 421 U.S. 599, 610 (1975) (holding sales of liquor on military bases immune from state taxation); *Sperry v. Florida,* 373 U.S. 379, 385 (1963) (state prohibited from applying unauthorized practice of law statute to federal patent agents authorized by U.S. Patent Office).

QUESTION 5. Battling bases.   The State of Ames is home to a large number of federal military installations. Responding to local governments' complaints about the strain that playing host to soldiers and their families puts on local resources, the state authorizes a special property tax on military bases located in the state. The revenue will be distributed, on a per-capita basis, to localities where the bases are located. Would such a property tax be constitutional?

A. No, under the rule established in *McCulloch v. Maryland.*
B. No, unless Congress authorized such a tax.
C. Yes, if the state can demonstrate a serious need.
D. A and B.

ANALYSIS.   *McCulloch* held that, absent congressional permission, federal instrumentalities are not subject to state or local taxation. There is no hardship exception. Therefore **C** is incorrect. Because both **A** and **B** are correct, the best answer is **D**.

> **QUESTION 6. Driver 8, take a break.**   Fred is an employee of the
> U.S. Postal Service and is required, as part of his job, to deliver the mail
> by truck all over the State of Maryland. As part of his duties, Fred was
> checked out by other federal employees and approved for driving his
> delivery truck. Fred did not, however, obtain a special Maryland license to
> operate the size of truck he drives. On his rounds one day, Fred is stopped
> by a state police officer, ticketed, and fined for not having the required
> Maryland license. He appeals his conviction. What result?
>
> **A.** Fred's appeal is rejected; there is no right to drive in contravention of
> state law.
> **B.** Fred's appeal is rejected, because the Postal Service is not a federal
> instrumentality.
> **C.** Fred's conviction is reversed, unless Congress had specifically required
> Postal Service drivers to comply with appropriate state laws.
> **D.** Fred's conviction is reversed because federal employees can never be
> regulated by state law.

ANALYSIS.   The facts in this question are loosely based on those of *Johnson
v. Maryland,* 254 U.S. 51 (1920), in which the Court held that a driver for
the U.S. Postal Service could not be fined for failing to possess a state driver's
license, where the driver had been vetted for that task by the federal government. Under the principles of intergovernmental immunity derived from
McCulloch, **A** is incorrect, as is **B**, because the Postal Service is a federal instrumentality like the Second Bank of the United States. **D**, however, is also incorrect, because Congress could require compliance with state law. That leaves **C**
as the best answer.

Nearly 180 years later, the Court again returned to the question of implied
limits on state power in *U.S. Term Limits, Inc. v. Thornton,* 514 U.S. 779 (1995).
There the issue was the constitutionality of an Arkansas constitutional amendment limiting members of the state's congressional delegation to three terms in
the House of Representatives and two terms in the U.S. Senate. Although *Powell
v. McCormick* (discussed in Chapter 2) held that *Congress* could not add additional qualifications to federal officeholding, the Court was forced to concede
that *Powell* said nothing about the ability of states to do so. Nevertheless, relying in part on *McCulloch,* Justice Stevens held that states were constitutionally
barred from imposing additional qualifications on their federal legislators.

Arkansas had argued that because the power to add qualifications was
neither delegated to Congress nor denied by the Constitution to states, the
power was "reserved" to the states via the Tenth Amendment. The Court
responded that "the power to add qualifications is not part of the original
powers of sovereignty that the Tenth Amendment reserved to the States. . . .

[T]hat Amendment could only 'reserve' that which existed before." 514 U.S. at 802. And because Congress didn't exist before the Constitution created it, Stevens reasoned, no power to impose qualifications on representatives to that body could be said to have been reserved to states.

Further, "the Framers envisioned a uniform national system, rejecting the notion that the Nation was a collection of States, and instead creating a direct link between the National Government and the people of the United States." *Id.* at 803. In so doing, the Framers ensured that "representatives owe primary allegiance not to the people of a State, but to the people of the Nation." *Id.* Because the term limits disrupted that link, according to the Court, they could not stand. Allowing "individual States to formulate diverse qualifications for their representatives would result in a patchwork of state qualifications, undermining the uniformity and the national character that the Framers envisioned and sought to ensure." *Id.* at 822. It would also "sever the direct link that the Framers found so critical between the National Government and the people of the United States." *Id.*

QUESTION 7. The scarlet "D." In response to the *U.S. Term Limits* decision, assume that the Arkansas constitution was instead amended to require that the legend "Disregarded Voters' Instructions on Term Limits" appear next to the names of incumbents who served more than three terms in the House of Representatives or more than two terms in the U.S. Senate. For nonincumbent candidates who refuse to sign a pledge adhering to those limits, the constitution provides that "Declined to Pledge to Support Term Limits" appear by their names. Such an amendment would, if challenged, likely be held to be:

A. Unconstitutional, under *U.S. Term Limits.*
B. Constitutional, because it did not bar access to the ballot as did the amendment in the *Term Limits* case.
C. Constitutional, because states have reserved powers to instruct their representatives.
D. Unconstitutional, because states may not regulate federal elections.

ANALYSIS. The facts in this question are based on those in *Crook v. Gralike,* 531 U.S. 510 (2001), in which the U.S. Supreme Court unanimously struck down a Missouri constitutional amendment that did what the hypothetical amendment in the question did: require candidates who decline to support or abide by term limits to appear on the ballot with a legend indicating their failure to support those limits. The Court concluded that, in substance, the legends attempted to do indirectly what *Term Limits* held the states could not do directly: punish members who disregard term limits established by the state and its voters. Thus **B** is incorrect, because the Court declined to elevate form over substance.

D is an incorrect statement of the law. The Constitution obligates states to hold elections, but leaves voter qualifications as well as the conduct and management of elections up to the states, subject to later-added requirements in the Fifteenth, Nineteenth, and Twenty-Sixth Amendments dealing with race, sex, and age of voters, respectively. In *Gralike*, the Court rejected the notion that the right to "instruct" one's federal representatives meant that the state could require ballots to contain such language as was required by the amendment. Thus **C** is incorrect.

That leaves **A**. The Court concluded that *Term Limits* foreclosed Missouri's attempts to regulate their federal congressional delegation in this manner.

D.　The Closer

> **QUESTION 8. No vacancy.** Article II gives the President the power to nominate "Ambassadors, other public Ministers and Consuls, Judges of the supreme Court, and all other Officers of the United States" subject to Senate confirmation. Further, when the Senate is in recess, the President has the power "to fill up all Vacancies that may happen during the Recess of the Senate, by granting Commissions which shall expire at the End of their next Session." The President asks for, and Congress gives him, the power to make "acting" appointments for situations in which a vacancy occurs when the Senate is in session and either a nomination has not been made or the nomination is pending in the Senate. This Act provides that such acting appointment be made for no more than 120 days, after which time a nominee must be submitted to the Senate. Reappointments of acting officials for another 120 days may be made only if the Senate has not confirmed the pending nominee.
>
> After passage of this Act, the President appoints an acting head of the Environmental Protection Agency, who promulgates certain air quality regulations for coal-fired power plants. Olden Smokey, the CEO of Anthracite Power Co., challenges the regulations, which would cost Anthracite Power millions of dollars in compliance costs. Smokey alleges that Congress had no power under Article I, § 8 to authorize "acting" appointments, therefore the EPA's head's actions are null and void. A reviewing court should:
>
> A. Rule for Smokey, because Congress has no power to supplement the Constitution's methods of appointment in Article II.
> B. Rule for Smokey, because Article II quite clearly requires Senate confirmation for all appointments.

3. Allocation of Power in a Federal System: Express, Implied, and Reserved Powers and Limits   **61**

> **C.** Rule against Smokey because the Act is a rational means of assisting the President and the Senate in the nomination and confirmation of federal officials.
>
> **D.** Rule for Smokey, because the appointment of acting officials is not indispensible to the confirmation process.

ANALYSIS. This is a trickier form of a Necessary and Proper Clause question. If you thought that the Necessary and Proper Clause applied *only* to congressional powers in Article I, § 8, you aren't alone. Many folks forget that the Clause applies not only to "make all Laws which shall be necessary and proper for carrying into Execution the foregoing Powers [in Article I, § 8]," but also to "all other Powers vested by this Constitution in the Government of the United States, or in any Department or Officer thereof." The President and Senate are given the powers to nominate and confirm officers of the United States in Article II. Congress can pass laws necessary and proper to the execution of both responsibilities, even though no mention is made of them in Article I. Therefore **A** is incorrect.

B is an incorrect statement of law; the President is not required to get Senate confirmation for so-called recess appointments made when the Senate is not in session. (As we'll see in Chapter 6, moreover, Senate confirmation need not be required in the case of "inferior" executive branch officials either.)

D misstates the test for the Necessary and Proper Clause—the measure need only be expedient, or rationally related to some power, not indispensible. That leaves **C**, which is the best answer. Giving the President the power to make acting appointments when the Senate is in session can both ensure that important jobs are filled and that the Senate has ample time to perform due diligence on any nominee that is before it.

Denning's Picks

1.	Going postal	**A**
2.	Stormy Weathers	**D**
3.	Reach out and threaten someone	**B**
4.	The case of the contentious carjacker	**C**
5.	Battling bases	**D**
6.	Driver 8, take a break	**C**
7.	The scarlet "D"	**A**
8.	No vacancy	**C**

4

The Powers of Congress and Their Limits

CHAPTER OVERVIEW

A. Overview
B. The Commerce Power
C. The Taxing and Spending Power
D. Federalism-Based Limits on Federal Legislative Power
E. Constitutional Limits on the Treatymaking Power
F. The Closer
◈ Denning's Picks

A. Overview

We turn in this chapter from Congress's implied power, to the scope of—and limits on—those powers enumerated in Article I, § 8. The chapter begins with the scope of Congress's power over interstate commerce, then moves on to the Court's treatment of Congress's power to lay and collect taxes and spend the revenue derived therefrom. Taken together, these three powers, when supplemented by the Necessary and Proper Clause, serve as the engine of the modern administrative state. As we will see, however, the Court has attempted to lay down some limits lately. Chapter 4 ends with a discussion of the explicit and implied *limits* on the exercise of congressional power. The latter are analogous to those implied limits on state power acknowledged in *McCulloch v. Maryland* and discussed in Chapter 3. We discuss another important set of implied limits on state power in Chapter 5.

B.   The Commerce Power

1.   Introduction

Article I, § 8, cl. 3 of the Constitution confers on Congress the power to "regulate commerce with foreign nations, and among the several states, and with the Indian tribes." Nearly everyone of the Framing era agreed that control over interstate and foreign commerce ought to be centralized in the national government. The lack of centralized power was seen as a major defect of the Articles of Confederation. What we now know as the Commerce Clause was adopted without debate at the Philadelphia Convention. However, the unanimity left a number of questions unanswered: (1) What effects did the centralization of power in Congress have on the *states'* ability to regulate interstate commerce? (2) What was "commerce among the several states"? (3) What did it mean to "regulate" that commerce? (4) What powers were "necessary and proper" to Congress's regulatory power?

The lack of guidance from the delegates in Philadelphia meant that, ultimately, the Court would supply the answers. In doing so, the Court oscillated between a rigid, formal approach to congressional power that depended on the regulated activity being correctly placed in its proper category, and a functional approach to that power that took account of the dynamic and rapidly changing nature of the national economy. Often the Court's reversion to formalism was reactive, driven by a sense that unless limits were placed on Congress, the expanded, creative uses of its power would soon eclipse state legislatures. The Court's search for limits was also driven by the assumption that states possessed areas of regulatory control from which the federal government was excluded. The Court had largely abandoned formalism by the early 1940s, but it again attempted to limit Congress's power beginning in the mid-1990s, although just how deep the Court's commitment to those limits has recently been called into question.

2.   Pre-New Deal Commerce Clause cases

Surprisingly, the Court did not have occasion to interpret the Commerce Clause until 1824, 35 years after the ratification of the Constitution. In *Gibbons v. Ogden,* 22 U.S. 1 (1824), the Marshall Court was asked to pass on the constitutionality of New York's steamboat monopoly between that state and New Jersey. A rival company claimed the right to ply the same route by virtue of its federal coasting license. The existence of the coasting license enabled Marshall to sidestep the difficult question of whether the Commerce Clause prevented the states from regulating interstate commerce *at all.* For the coasting license to preempt a conflicting state regulation,[1] however, he still had to establish that this was a regulation of commerce "among the several states."

---

1.   Article VI of the Constitution proclaims that federal laws "made in pursuance of" the Constitution are "the supreme law of the land," notwithstanding contrary state laws or state constitutional provisions. Federal law is thus said to "preempt" conflicting state laws. Preemption is discussed more in Chapter 5.

Rejecting the argument that the license was "navigation," not "commerce," Marshall wrote that while commerce included "traffic . . . it is something more—it is intercourse. It describes the commercial intercourse between nations, and parts of nations, and all its branches. . . . " 22 U.S. at 189. Marshall conceded that the "completely internal" commerce of a state was beyond the reach of the commerce power, but added that the power did encompass "that commerce which concerns more States than one." 22 U.S. at 194. Within those boundaries, he concluded, Congress's power over interstate commerce "is complete in itself, may be exercised to its utmost extent, and acknowledges no limitations, other than are prescribed in the constitution. . . . [T]he sovereignty of Congress, though limited to specified objects, is plenary as to those objects." 22 U.S. at 196–197.

Following *Gibbons,* and until the late nineteenth century, the Court's Commerce Clause case law largely concerned the limits the Clause implicitly placed on state regulation of commerce.[2] However, in cases like *The Daniel Ball,* 77 U.S. 557 (1871), the Court upheld the ability of Congress to regulate ships carrying goods in interstate commerce, even if they were operating in waterways located entirely within one state. Thus, with the Necessary and Proper Clause, Congress could regulate not only commerce per se, but also those instrumentalities of commerce, like ships that carried commerce.

As the federal government began experimenting with regulatory bodies to superintend the rapid industrialization taking place throughout the country, Congress began to rely more on the commerce power as authority for doing so. The reaction to this expansion of governmental power was mixed, if not downright schizophrenic. Parallel lines of precedent emerged from the Supreme Court, one quite accommodating of congressional power; the other, more restrictive.

For example, in cases like *Champion v. Ames,* 188 U.S. 321 (1903), the Court upheld a national prohibition on the sending of lottery tickets through the mails. That Congress's motive in doing so was to eliminate lotteries was held to have no effect on Congress's ability to regulate the mailing of the tickets. Other cases similarly upheld the closing of interstate commerce to products deemed harmful or injurious—even injurious to morals. *See, e.g., Hoke v. United States,* 227 U.S. 308 (1913) (upholding the Mann Act, prohibiting the transport of women across state lines for "immoral purposes"); *Hipolite Egg Co. v. United States,* 220 U.S. 45 (1911) (upholding the Pure Food and Drug Act); and *Caminetti v. United States,* 242 U.S. 470 (1917) (upholding Mann Act as applied to noncommercial tryst taking place across state lines).

Similarly, the Court also upheld the regulation of intrastate activities deemed to be so intertwined with interstate commerce as to require regulation by Congress. The leading case here is *Houston, East & West Texas Railway Co. v. United States,* 234 U.S. 342 (1914), the so-called Shreveport Rate Case, in which the Court upheld the Interstate Commerce Commission's regulation of

---

2. The so-called dormant Commerce Clause doctrine is discussed in detail in Chapter 5.

intrastate railroad rates deemed to discriminate against interstate commerce. Then-Justice Charles Evans Hughes wrote, "Whenever the interstate and intrastate transactions of carriers are so related that the government of the one involves the control of the other, it is Congress, and not the state, that is entitled to prescribe the final and dominate rule." 234 U.S. at 351–352. Likewise the Court upheld the regulation of intrastate activities where such were included in the continuous movement of interstate commerce from one part of the country to the other. *See, e.g., Swift & Co. v. United States,* 196 U.S. 375 (1905) (upholding Sherman Act's anti-price-fixing provisions as applied to meat dealers who buy cattle engaged in a journey from pasture to slaughterhouse); *see also Stafford v. Wallace,* 258 U.S. 495 (1922) (upholding regulation of packers and stockyards as essential to regulation of interstate commerce in cattle).

At the same time, the Court invalidated exercises of congressional power on facts similar to those in earlier cases where the Court had upheld federal action. For example, in *Hammer v. Dagenhart,* 247 U.S. 251 (1918), the Court invalidated the Child Labor Act of 1916, which prohibited the movement in interstate commerce of goods produced by child labor. The Court distinguished the result in *Hammer* from that in *Champion v. Ames, Hoke, Hippolite Egg Co.,* and *Caminetti* on the somewhat spurious ground that, in those cases, the thing excluded from interstate commerce was, in and of itself, harmful (although one cannot imagine how lottery tickets or women could be described as inherently harmful). As the dissenters charged, however, it is difficult not to conclude that the majority's true objection was to the motives of Congress—to regulate working conditions of children in states, which the majority deemed to be beyond the reach of the federal government. That the logical extension of the Court's earlier cases seemed to countenance this very result caused the majority to blink and forced it to make the tendentious distinctions that it did.

The Court also made rather formalistic distinctions between "commerce" and activities it deemed not to be a part of commerce. In *United States v. E.C. Knight,* 156 U.S. 1 (1895), the Court invalidated the application of the Sherman Antitrust Act to an alleged monopoly in the sugar refining industry. According to the Court, the refining of sugar was "manufacture" not "commerce"; and "Commerce succeeds to manufacture, and is not a part of it." 156 U.S. at 12. This distinction between commerce on the one hand, and antecedent activities like manufacture, agriculture, production, and the like on the other, emerged in the 1930s to scuttle a number of federal initiatives intended to bring the country out of the Great Depression. A related doctrine inquired whether federal regulations "directly" regulated interstate commerce or were impermissible "indirect" regulations. *See, e.g., Carter v. Carter Coal Co.,* 298 U.S. 238 (1936).

3. *The New Deal and the "Constitutional Revolution of 1937"*

For four years, after the New Deal's economic experimentation and unprecedented federal intervention in the national economy, the Court regularly invalidated federal legislation because it regulated activities that were not "commerce," because it intervened in areas the Constitution reserved exclusively to the states, or both. In *A.L.A. Schechter Poultry Corp. v. United States,* 295 U.S. 495 (1935), the Court invalidated portions of the National Industrial Recovery Act, which authorized the promulgation of fair codes of competition in various industries. The regulation of chickens—and of wages and hours in the poultry industry—in New York City was deemed an insufficiently "direct" regulation of commerce. 295 U.S. at 546 (noting that "where the effect of intrastate transactions upon interstate commerce is merely indirect, such transactions remain within the domain of state power"). Note again the tension between that holding and contrary earlier cases like *Swift & Co.* and *Stafford v. Wallace.*

The same year, the Court invalidated the Railroad Retirement Act of 1934 on the same ground: The welfare of railroad workers was "remote" from commerce. *Railroad Retirement Board v. Alton,* 295 U.S. 330 (1935). The following year, *Carter v. Carter Coal Co.* saw the Court strike down the Bituminous Coal Conservation Act, which, among other things, empowered coal boards to set prices, wages, and hours in the industry. Again the Court held that the regulated activities were only indirectly related to commerce. The Court also resurrected the production–commerce distinction, writing that "[t]he employment of men, the fixing of their wages, hours of labor and working conditions, the bargaining in respect of these things . . . each and all constitute intercourse for the purposes of production, not of trade." 298 U.S. at 303. A close reading of the majority opinion, though, revealed a renewed concern that were the Act upheld, no judicially enforceable limit to the commerce power could ever be maintained, and that Congress could displace the state legislatures completely.

Infuriated by the Court's intransigence, and emboldened by his landslide 1936 victory, President Franklin Roosevelt proposed his infamous court-packing plan. The plan would have permitted Roosevelt to nominate an additional Supreme Court Justice for each Justice over age 70 who did not retire. Although the plan was ultimately defeated, the Court began to retreat from its restrictive positions.

Whether because of doctrinal changes already underway, personnel changes, President Roosevelt's failed court-packing plan, or some combination of these factors—historians disagree—the Court became much more solicitous of expansive exercises of the commerce power beginning in 1937. Thereafter, for nearly 60 years, the Court rejected every other Commerce Clause challenge brought against federal legislation. It abandoned its earlier formalism for a near-total deference to Congress.

Among the numerous cases involving the scope of Congress's commerce power that the Court decided during this period, three stand out: *NLRB v. Jones & Laughlin Steel Corp.,* 301 U.S. 1 (1937); *United States v. Darby,* 312 U.S. 100 (1941); and *Wickard v. Filburn,* 317 U.S. 111 (1942). Taken together, these decisions countenanced a dramatic expansion of congressional power to regulate the economy that the Court did not question until 1995.

The first of these cases, *Jones & Laughlin Steel Corp.,* involved a challenge to the National Labor Relations Act, which, among other things, outlawed "unfair labor practices" that affected interstate commerce, like discharging workers for union activities. Relying on cases like *Carter Coal,* the corporation asserted that Congress was regulating production, not commerce, which was reserved to the states. By contrast, the government emphasized that Jones & Laughlin was a vertically integrated company with nationwide operations. It relied on *Swift & Co.* and *Stafford v. Wallace* for the proposition that Congress could regulate activities that, though local in and of themselves, were part of the "stream of commerce."

In the end, the Court declined to embrace either position, instead stressing that Congress had the "plenary" power to protect interstate commerce from obstructions and interruptions, whatever the source. 301 U.S. at 37. Further, the Court held, "[a]lthough activities may be intrastate in character when separately considered, if they have such a close and substantial relation to interstate commerce that their control is essential or appropriate to protect that commerce from burdens and obstructions, Congress cannot be denied the power to exercise that control." *Id.* at 37.

In *Darby,* the Court upheld provisions of the Fair Labor Standards Act (FLSA), which established minimum wages and maximum hours for workers producing goods for interstate commerce, and barred goods produced in violation of those provisions from the interstate market. In doing so, the Court explicitly overruled *Hammer v. Dagenhart,* whose distinction between goods that were inherently harmful and those that were not "was novel when made and unsupported by any provision of the Constitution." 312 U.S. at 116. Further, the Court held that Congress's motive in prohibiting the shipment of goods in interstate commerce — to support the wage and hour provisions — was irrelevant to questions regarding the scope of its power. *Id.*

The Court also upheld the direct regulation of wages and hours on alternative theories. First, the Court held that Congress "having by the [NLRA] adopted the policy of excluding from interstate commerce all goods produced for the commerce which do not conform to the specified labor standards, it may choose the means reasonably adapted to the attainment of the permitted end, even though they involve control of intrastate activities." 312 U.S. at 121. The Court also thought that the wage and hour provisions were aimed at combating substandard labor conditions whose products competed unfairly with those produced in conformity with the wage and hour provisions of the FLSA. Therefore, those provisions, the Court held, are "so related to [interstate] commerce and so affects it as to be within the reach of the commerce power." *Id.* at 122, 123.

Finally, the Court held in *Wickard* that when Congress regulated a class of activities, no instance of such activity was beyond its reach, no matter how "local" it seemed, if it was rational for Congress to have concluded that, when aggregated, such activities had a substantial effect on interstate commerce. At issue was a wheat quota, imposed on farmers by the Agricultural Adjustment Act as part of a plan to arrest the decline in commodities prices caused by overproduction. Filburn exceeded his quota, was fined, and protested his fine on the ground that he produced the wheat for his own use, and that, in any event, he alone could not affect interstate commerce in any appreciable way.

In findings that accompanied the Act, though, Congress found that the "effect on consumption of homegrown wheat on interstate commerce is due to the fact that it constitutes the most variable factor in the disappearance of the wheat crop." 317 U.S. at 127. In other words, the price wouldn't go up any if farmers could act as Filburn had done, because the wheat grown and consumed at home competed with that on the market. Had Filburn stuck to his quota, he could have either reduced the amount of wheat he sold, reserving some for home use, or he would have had to purchase what he needed for his farm at market prices. The Court concluded that

> [h]ome-grown wheat . . . competes with wheat in commerce. The stimulation of commerce is a use of the regulatory function quite as definitely as prohibitions or restrictions thereon. The record leaves us in no doubt that Congress may properly have considered that wheat consumed on the farm where grown if wholly outside the scheme of regulation would have a substantial effect in defeating and obstructing its purpose to stimulate trade therein at increased prices.

Id. at 128–129.

4. *Post-New Deal cases*

Until 1995, it was generally assumed that limits on the commerce power were for the Congress, not the Court, to locate and enforce. The only significant cases following the New Deal involved the 1964 Civil Rights Act's reliance on the Commerce Clause to make illegal private discrimination in places of public accommodation. In a pair of cases, *Heart of Atlanta Motel v. United States,* 379 U.S. 241 (1964), and *Katzenbach v. McClung,* 379 U.S. 294 (1964), the Court—relying on New Deal precedents like *Darby* and *Wickard*—upheld this use of the commerce power to further civil rights.

Title II prohibited racial discrimination in places of public accommodation that affected interstate commerce. Included in the statute was a section presuming that effect if certain conditions obtained, including serving interstate customers, advertising in interstate commerce, or purchasing in interstate commerce a substantial portion of food sold at a restaurant. Of the two cases, *Heart of Atlanta Motel* was the easier. The motel at issue was located close to an interstate highway, advertised extensively in interstate commerce, and served numerous interstate travelers. 379 U.S. at 243. The Court noted that discrimination in places of accommodation like motels was deemed by Congress to constitute an obstruction to interstate commerce, which Congress was permitted to remove. *Id.* at 252–253. "Congress," it added, "was not restricted by the fact that the particular obstruction to interstate commerce with which it was dealing was also deemed a moral and social wrong." *Id.* at 257. Even if discrimination by a single motel did not affect interstate commerce, Congress was permitted to conclude that, in the aggregate, all similarly situated motels *would* have such an effect, and exercise power even over "local" motels.

Unlike the Heart of Atlanta Motel, Ollie's Barbeque restaurant served a purely local market. It was not located near a highway, and did not advertise at all, much less in interstate commerce. 279 U.S. at 296–297. It did, however, purchase nearly half of the food it sold in interstate commerce. Under the terms of Title II, the out-of-state purchases triggered the presumption that the restaurant "affected interstate commerce." Ollie's argued that it was strictly local, and could not possibly affect interstate commerce, even if it did purchase some food from interstate commerce. Again, the Court was unmoved. It alluded to the obstacles to interstate commerce posed by racial discrimination, and invoked *Wickard*-style aggregation in upholding the application of Title II to Ollie's. *Id.* at 303–304.

Wickard's role as a trump in Commerce Clause cases was again illustrated by *Perez v. United States,* 402 U.S. 146 (1971) and *Hodel v. Virginia Surface Mining and Reclamation Association,* 452 U.S. 264 (1981). In *Perez,* the Court upheld the application of a federal statute criminalizing loan sharking to an individual not otherwise a part of organized crime and whose operations were confined to New York City. Congress, the Court concluded, had a rational basis for thinking that even local, intrastate loan sharking could, if aggregated, affect interstate commerce. In *Hodel,* the Court upheld a federal strip mining act, despite the fact that land use regulation had traditionally been left to state and local governments.

After cases like *Perez* and *Hodel* affirmed the lengthy reach of the commerce power, conventional wisdom had it that no judicially enforceable limits on the Commerce Clause remained. Even discussion of theoretical limits was largely confined to law professors' hypotheticals and exam questions—if they were mentioned at all. That state of affairs changed, however, in 1995.

5.   Lopez, Morrison, *and* Raich: *Back to the future?*

Alfonso Lopez was a Texas twelfth-grader who took a gun to school to sell to a classmate, thus running afoul of the federal Gun Free School Zones Act (GFSZA), which prohibited possessing a firearm within 1,000 feet of a building that the defendant knows or reasonably should know is a school. To the surprise of many, the Supreme Court in *United States v. Lopez,* 514 U.S. 549 (1995), affirmed the Fifth Circuit's reversal of Lopez's conviction, and struck down the GFSZA as beyond the power of Congress to regulate interstate commerce.

In a judicial tour de force, Chief Justice Rehnquist synthesized the Court's prior jurisprudence, extrapolating from the cases three broad areas Congress may regulate under the Commerce Clause. First, Congress could regulate *channels* of interstate commerce, like roadways, waterways, and railroads. Second, Congress could also regulate *instrumentalities* of interstate commerce, including persons and things in interstate commerce. Finally, Congress may regulate those local, intrastate activities that *substantially affect* interstate commerce. *Lopez,* 514 U.S. at 558–559.

Noting that since the GFSZA regulated mere possession of a firearm, with no other connection to interstate commerce, Chief Justice Rehnquist wrote that to be valid, the GFSZA must be analyzed under the third category. To assist the Court's inquiry, the Court mentioned several factors that aided in a determination that particular activity substantially affected interstate commerce. First, the Court asked whether the activity was commercial or economic or not. Second, it asked whether the statute contained explicit language tying the regulated activity to interstate commerce (sometimes called the "jurisdictional element" or "jurisdictional nexus"). Third, findings provided by Congress could make explicit a connection to interstate commerce not apparent on the face of a statute. Fourth, the Court asked whether the regulated activity was part of a national regulatory scheme whose efficacy would be impaired by an inability to regulate—the example it gave was the AAA's attempt to raise commodities prices through quotas at issue in *Wickard v. Filburn.* Finally, the Court asked whether the connection between the regulated activity and interstate commerce was so attenuated as to require the Court to "pile inference upon inference" to connect the two. *Id.* at 561–564, 567. (Two scholars have called this element of *Lopez* the "non-infinity principle": If sustaining the congressional act requires one to adopt a limitless interpretation of the Clause, then the act must fall, lest Congress end up with a de facto police power.) An additional element, later incorporated by the majority, was offered in a concurring opinion by Justices Kennedy and O'Connor: whether the regulated activity was in an area of traditional state concern. *Id.* at 580 (Kennedy, J., concurring).

Applying these factors, the Court concluded that the GFSZA could not be said to substantially affect interstate commerce without conceding that *anything* could. The regulation of mere possession was in no sense economic or commercial activity. The statute contained neither an explicit statement tying the regulated activity to interstate commerce[3] nor findings that made the case for possession's effect on interstate commerce. It was in no sense vital to the maintenance of a national regulatory scheme and, as Justice Kennedy pointed out, it involved a subject—regulation of crime—generally left to the states. Were the Court to uphold the GFSZA on the theory offered by the government—that guns around schools create an unsafe atmosphere that affects student learning, resulting in an undereducated workforce and the loss of international competitiveness —then nothing would be beyond the power of

---

3. The statute was amended to require proof that the gun itself had, at some point, moved in or affected interstate commerce. See 18 U.S.C. § 922(q)(2)(A).

Congress. Such a holding, the Court concluded, would be inconsistent with the Framers' enumeration of congressional powers in Article I, § 8. *Id.* at 567.

Although *Lopez* did not overrule a single New Deal–era precedent, the dissent and commentators noted that neither did the Court defer to congressional judgment about effects on interstate commerce as it had in prior cases. Moreover, it was not clear which of the several factors the Court described, if present, would have saved the statute.

QUESTION 1. Make a run for the border. A federal statute states that "anyone who crosses state lines for the purpose of selling a controlled substance" shall be subject to five years imprisonment, large fines, or both. Freddie crosses from New Jersey into New York to sell a small amount of marijuana to an undercover police officer. He is arrested and convicted of violating the federal statute. He appeals his conviction claiming that Congress lacked authority to pass the statute under its commerce power. Freddie's conviction should be:

A. Reversed, because the statute failed to require that the sale have a substantial effect on interstate commerce.

B. Reversed, because crime cannot be "commercial" or "economic" activity.

C. Upheld, because sales, even of contraband, constitute economic activity under *Lopez.*

D. Upheld, because Congress can close the channels of interstate commerce to particular uses.

ANALYSIS. This question is intended to remind you that the action is not always in locating substantial effects on interstate commerce. The power of Congress to close the channels of interstate commerce to harmful or injurious uses dates back over a century. Thus, **A** is irrelevant; the statute doesn't *have* to mention substantial effects because it criminalizes crossing state lines to sell drugs. Further, neither **B** or **C** matters, although, as it happens, illicit activity can still be economic activity for Commerce Clause purposes. That leaves **D**, which is the correct answer. Congress may regulate the channels of interstate commerce, closing them off to particular uses, or harmful activities.

QUESTION 2. Don't make a federal case out of it. A federal statute makes it a crime to "take[] a motor vehicle that has been transported, shipped, or received in interstate or foreign commerce from the person or presence of another by force and violence or by intimidation," with "the intent to cause death or serious bodily harm." Jack is convicted of violating this statute, but, having heard about *Lopez,* appeals his conviction

> on the grounds that it exceeds Congress's constitutional authority. Jack's conviction should be:
>
> A. Overturned, unless the government can prove that carjacking has a substantial effect on interstate commerce.
> B. Overturned, because violent crimes such as carjacking are areas of traditional state activity.
> C. Upheld, because cars are instrumentalities of interstate commerce.
> D. Upheld, because crimes like carjacking represent a kind of forced wealth transfer that is economic, albeit illegal, activity.

ANALYSIS. In analyzing Commerce Clause questions, it's important not to assume that you have to jump into an extended discussion of the *Lopez* and *Morrison* factors that determine whether intrastate activity substantially effects interstate commerce and thus is subject to congressional regulation. Recall that the Court recognized two other broad areas of regulatory authority over (1) channels of interstate commerce and (2) instrumentalities of interstate commerce, including persons and things in interstate commerce. Thus **A** is incorrect. If the regulated activity could be framed as a regulation of channels or instrumentalities, then no inquiry into the activity's substantial effects is necessary. For the same reason **B** is incorrect. Whether Congress is regulating in an area usually regulated by states is relevant only if the regulated activity can be sustained, if at all, only by proof that it substantially affects interstate commerce.

D is incorrect, because even assuming that crime is a type of economic activity, that is precisely the kind of inference-upon-inference argument that the Court rejected in both *Lopez* and *Morrison*. It proves too much: Nearly everything is economic under that reading, and susceptible to congressional regulation. That means that Congress has precisely the sort of all-encompassing police power that *Lopez* and *Morrison* took pains to deny that the Constitution granted.

That leaves **C** as the best answer. Punishing carjacking either seeks to protect cars in interstate commerce (note the jurisdictional nexus) or their drivers, both of which could be characterized as instrumentalities of interstate commerce.

QUESTION 3. GFSZA redux. Following *Lopez*, Congress reenacted the GFSZA, which now reads that "[i]t shall be unlawful for any individual knowingly to possess a firearm that has moved in or otherwise affects interstate or foreign commerce, at a place the individual knows or has reasonable cause to believe, is a school zone." Jeremy is charged with violating the statute by bringing a gun to school to sell to another student. At trial, the U.S. Attorney presents evidence that the gun Jeremy possessed was manufactured out of state and crossed state lines before being purchased by Jeremy's father, from whom Jeremy had stolen it. Jeremy is convicted. He appeals his conviction, arguing that under *Lopez*, Congress lacks authority to criminalize mere possession. Would a reviewing court likely reverse his conviction?

A. No, because Congress may regulate things that move in interstate commerce.

B. No, because his possession substantially affects interstate commerce.

C. Yes, because possession is not economic activity.

D. Yes, because permitting Congress to regulate things simply because they travel in interstate commerce would mean no practical limit on its commerce power.

ANALYSIS.   The key to this question is the language in the revised statute, "a firearm that has moved in or otherwise affects interstate or foreign commerce." Recall that one of the Court's complaints about the GFSZA in *Lopez* was that it contained no "jurisdictional nexus" between the regulated activity and interstate commerce. The revised GFSZA corrected that, and provides a much easier case for upholding the statute, given what was proven at trial. What was proven, incidentally, was *not* that Jeremy's possession of the gun substantially affected interstate commerce, nor was such proof necessary under the statute. Therefore **B** is incorrect.

C is not correct either; the statute, unlike the unamended GFSZA, does not criminalize mere possession. It criminalizes possession of a weapon that has traveled in interstate commerce. Again, *Lopez* held that Congress could regulate "instrumentalities" of interstate commerce, including persons and things that moved in interstate commerce.

Although it is true that interpretation leaves Congress a great deal of power — perhaps too much — **D** incorrectly states the law. **A** is the best answer, and the one that lower courts have given in similar situations.

———————————

Five years later, the Court returned to the issue in *United States v. Morrison*, 529 U.S. 598 (2000), in which it again struck down a federal statute on Commerce Clause grounds. A part of the omnibus Violence Against Women Act (VAWA) provided a federal civil remedy for victims of violence motivated by gender. The majority opinion reaffirmed *Lopez*'s framework, stressing that a characterization of regulated activity as "economic" or "noneconomic" was "central" to the *Lopez* decision. 529 U.S. at 610. VAWA's civil-suit provision regulating "[g]ender-motivated crimes of violence," it noted, did not regulate "in any sense of the phrase, economic activity." *Id*. at 613. The Court expressed considerable skepticism that noneconomic activity could ever be aggregated à la *Wickard*. Further, the Court stressed the importance of a jurisdictional statement, which the civil-suit provision lacked, tying regulated activity to interstate commerce. Although VAWA was accompanied with numerous findings purporting to document the effects of gender-motivated violence on the economy, the Court found that these findings merely recited the kind of "inference upon inference" type of reasoning it rejected in *Lopez*. According to the Court, the "findings [were] substantially weakened by the fact that they rely so heavily on a method of reasoning that we have already rejected as unworkable if we are to maintain the Constitution's enumeration of powers." *Id.* at 615.

QUESTION 4. Machine Gun Kelly.   18 U.S.C. § 922(o) makes it unlawful to "transfer or possess" a machine gun "in or affecting interstate commerce." Kelly, an accomplished gunsmith, was charged with possession of a machine gun that he had made himself. He was convicted, and appealed on the ground that his intrastate possession of the machine gun could not substantially affect interstate commerce. Which of the following would be most helpful to Kelly's attempt to overturn his conviction?

[handwritten margin notes: 1) channels 2) 3) substantially affect]

A. Mere possession of the machine gun was not "economic" or "commercial" activity.

B. The statute contained no jurisdictional nexus.

C. The findings accompanying the statute mentioned the need to combat interstate and international arms sales by regulating possession.

D. The connection between individual possession and the interstate machine gun market was too attenuated to support regulation.

ANALYSIS.   If you read the language of the statute carefully, you could exclude **B** immediately. The language "in or affecting interstate commerce" is precisely what the Court meant when it referred to a jurisdictional nexus in *Lopez* and *Morrison*. Further, **C** would not be very helpful, because the presence of findings describing why the regulation of local, intrastate possession was necessary or in what way it was related to interstate commerce would *support* the constitutionality of the statute.

As between the remaining answers, **D** would not be as helpful, because it is not necessarily true that a "demand-side" approach to machine gun regulation requires the Court to "pile inference upon inference" as it would have had to do to uphold the GFSZA in *Lopez*. That leaves **A**, which is the best answer, because the *Morrison* opinion called the inquiry into the economic nature of the regulated activity "central" to *Lopez*. Further, *Lopez* itself declined to hold that simple possession was, in any sense of the word, "economic" activity; and *Morrison* strongly hinted that *Wickard* aggregation was unavailable for non-economic activity.

QUESTION 5. Arbitrate this!   The Federal Arbitration Act ("FAA") requires enforcement of a "written provision in . . . a contract evidencing a transaction involving commerce to settle by arbitration a controversy thereafter arising out of such contract . . . shall be valid, irrevocable, and enforceable." 9 U.S.C. § 2. Prior case law has interpreted "involving commerce" to mean "affecting commerce." Jerry lives in a state with laws that disfavor arbitration clauses, and defaults on a loan to a state bank whose loan officer Jerry claims defrauded him. When the bank secures an order requiring arbitration, Jerry cries foul. Congress, he argues, has exceeded its commerce power in ordering intrastate disputes arbitrated, contrary to the declared public policy of the state. Which of the following argument(s) is/are helpful to the bank seeking enforcement?

A. The FAA has a jurisdictional nexus.
B. The FAA regulates economic activity.
C. In the aggregate, all contracts containing arbitration clauses substantially affect interstate commerce.
D. Any of the above.

ANALYSIS.   The answer is **D**. Each of the statements would be helpful to the bank seeking to defend the FAA under *Lopez* and *Morrison*.

Despite the limited clarification provided by the Court in *Morrison*, questions still remained as to how far the Court intended to go to limit congressional power under the Commerce Clause. Critics of the Court's attempts noted the similarities between the *Lopez/Morrison* inquiry into an activity's economic or noneconomic nature and earlier Courts' insistence that activities like production and agriculture were not part of the commerce Congress was entitled to regulate.

In 2005, the Court gave at least a partial answer in *Gonzales v. Raich*, 545 U.S. 1 (2005), in which the Court upheld the application of the federal Controlled Substances Act to individuals who acquired marijuana locally for medicinal purposes, as permitted under California's compassionate use law. The defendant had argued that because she had been given the locally produced marijuana, the activity wasn't, in any sense of the word, "economic"; and that even if aggregated, all compassionate use of marijuana pursuant to state law would have a negligible effect on interstate commerce.

Writing for a majority of the Court, Justice Stevens instead saw the case as on all fours with *Wickard*. Because Congress could eliminate the entire interstate market in marijuana through the Controlled Substances Act, it could eliminate all use, possession, and growth of the same, no matter how "local" or "noncommercial" it might be. Reverting to the deference the Court had shown Congress pre-*Lopez*, Stevens wrote that "[w]e need not determine whether respondents' activities, taken in the aggregate, substantially affect interstate commerce in fact, but only whether a 'rational basis' exists for so concluding." 545 U.S. at 22. The decision was made possible by the fact that two members of the *Lopez/Morrison* majority—Justices Scalia and Kennedy—concurred with the *Lopez/Morrison* dissenters—Justices Stevens, Souter, Ginsburg, and Breyer—to produce the *Raich* decision.

The majority recognized, though, that *Lopez* and *Morrison* remained good law. For example, Justice Stevens stressed that growing marijuana—although perhaps noncommercial—was nevertheless economic. The activities regulated by the Controlled Substances Act, he wrote, "are quintessentially economic. 'Economics' refers to 'the production, distribution, and consumption of commodities.'. . . The CSA is a statute that regulates the production, distribution, and consumption of commodities for which there is an established, and lucrative, interstate market." *Id.* at 25–26. So defined, *Lopez* and *Morrison* made that economic activity eligible for the *Wickard*-style aggregation on which the *Raich* Court relied.

Moreover, the Court stressed that unlike either the GFSZA or the civil-suit provision of the VAWA, the Controlled Substances Act "was a lengthy and detailed statute creating a comprehensive framework for regulating the production, distribution, and possession of five classes of 'controlled substances.'" *Id.* at 24. *Lopez* itself had suggested that if intrastate activity was part of a "national regulatory scheme" whose efficacy would be undermined if that activity could not be reached, the Court might defer to Congress. 514 U.S. at 560–561.

> **QUESTION 6. A grave matter.** Certain states (notably New York) permit rental car agencies to be sued for negligence committed by a person to whom the agency rented a car. Recently, Congress enacted the so-called Graves Amendment as part of a larger transportation bill. The Graves Amendment reads, in relevant part:
>
> > **a) In general.**—An owner of a motor vehicle that rents or leases the vehicle to a person (or an affiliate of the owner) shall not be liable under the law of any State or political subdivision thereof, by reason of being the owner of the vehicle (or an affiliate of the owner), for harm to persons or property that results or arises out of the use, operation, or possession of the vehicle during the period of the rental or lease, if—
> > **(1)** the owner (or an affiliate of the owner) is engaged in the trade or business of renting or leasing motor vehicles; and
> > **(2)** there is no negligence or criminal wrongdoing on the part of the owner (or an affiliate of the owner).
>
> 49 U.S.C. § 30106. The practical effect of the Graves Amendment is to preempt causes of action for negligent entrustment against or imposing

vicarious liability on car rental agencies. Several suits have been filed alleging that the Graves Amendment exceeds Congress's commerce power. Which of the following descriptions of the amendment would be helpful in crafting arguments *in favor of* the statute's constitutionality?

A. The effect of the amendment is to regulate cars rented in a national rental market.
B. The effect of the amendment is to alter tort liability rules arising from intrastate rental transactions.
C. The effect of the amendment is to regulate the economic activity between rental agencies and their customers.
D. A or C.

ANALYSIS. This question is intended to demonstrate how the framing of an issue can make a difference when analyzing a law under the Commerce Clause. *Lopez* and *Morrison* held that Congress can regulate instrumentalities and channels of interstate commerce, in addition to local activities that substantially affect interstate commerce. The Graves Amendment arguably regulates rental cars, which are instrumentalities of interstate commerce. Framed in that manner, it would easily pass muster. Therefore, **A** would be a strong argument in favor.

On the other hand, it isn't cars per se that are regulated, but rather the Amendment alters liability rules that arise from the rental transaction itself. If anything is a "traditional state activity," it is the establishment of tort rules that govern local transactions—note there is nothing in the Amendment limiting it to interstate transactions. Therefore, framing the issue as in **B** would *not* be helpful; in fact, that's the way one might want to frame the issue if one was arguing against the Amendment's constitutionality.

And yet the statute does regulate an economic transaction—note that the Amendment restricts itself to those "engaged in the trade or business of renting or leasing motor vehicles"—and *Morrison* tells us those are the activities for which *Wickard*-style aggregation is possible. Therefore framing the issue as **C** does would be helpful as well. Because either **A** or **C** would be useful in defending the Amendment, the correct answer is **D**.

QUESTION 7. **Machine Gun Kelly part deux.** Suppose that the defendant from Question 4, earlier, was prosecuted in the wake of the *Raich* decision. He argues that the machine gun possession statute cannot constitutionally be applied to him, because his possession of a homemade machine gun could not substantially affect interstate commerce. A reviewing court would likely do what?

> **A.** Overturn his conviction, because his possession was not economic activity.
>
> **B.** Overturn his conviction, because even if aggregated, the class of homemade machine guns could not substantially affect interstate commerce.
>
> **C.** Uphold his conviction, because if Congress can regulate a class of activities, it may regulate each member of that class, no matter how local.
>
> **D.** Uphold his conviction, because the *Lopez/Morrison* framework is no longer good law.

ANALYSIS.   Kelly is basically making the same argument as the respondents in *Raich* made; it would likely be rejected for similar reasons. In this example, Congress is seeking to eliminate the interstate market for machine guns, hence it criminalizes "transfer or possession in or affecting interstate commerce." Kelly's homemade machine gun, like the homegrown marijuana made available in California, competed with other machine guns in the market the government wished to eliminate. As in *Raich*, his fashioning of the machine gun is likely to be considered economic activity, as it involves the production of some good. Thus, **A** would not be correct.

Further, the *Raich* Court declined to permit the respondents to create a subclass of "medicinal marijuana users" and argue that, even if aggregated, medicinal marijuana users would not substantially affect interstate commerce. Pot was pot, the Court responded; it was fungible. Therefore, **B** isn't a good argument either.

On the other hand, **D** is not true: The majority did not overrule or even question the future viability of *Lopez* and *Morrison*. It merely held they needed to be read with the Court's other, earlier Commerce Clause cases.

C, then, is the best answer; it is a succinct statement of *Raich*'s holding. If Congress can eliminate an interstate market in something, then the fact that an individual is a small-time participant in that market is no defense.

---

6.   National Federation of Independent Business v. Sebelius: *The Umpire Strikes Back*?[4]

In March 2010, President Barack Obama signed the Patient Protection and Affordable Care Act (PPACA), which enacted sweeping reforms to the nation's

---

4. The reference is to Chief Justice Roberts's confirmation hearing analogy between judging and umpiring. Confirmation Hearing on the Nomination of John G. Roberts, Jr. to Be Chief Justice of the United States: Hearing Before the S. Comm. on the Judiciary, 109th Cong. 56 (2005) (statement of Judge John G. Roberts, Jr.); *see also id.* at 55 ("Judges are like umpires. Umpires don't make the rules, they apply them.").

health care system. Among the PPACA's provisions was a requirement that individuals purchase health insurance by 2014 or pay a penalty. The individual mandate was tied to a separate provision that prohibited insurers from refusing to cover persons based on pre-existing conditions. The mandate, it was hoped, would address the "moral hazard" problem insurers feared: that people would not purchase insurance until they were sick, thereby depriving insurers of sufficient numbers of healthy people in their risk pools to cover expected payouts with premiums from persons who were not filing claims. *National Federation of Independent Business v. Sebelius*, 132 S. Ct. 2566, 2580 (2012).

The Obama Administration defended the individual mandate on alternative grounds: (1) that, in the aggregate, the uninsured substantially affect interstate commerce and thus Congress had authority under the Commerce Clause to require the purchase of insurance or (2) that the penalty is simply a tax on individuals' decisions not to purchase health insurance. *National Federation of Independent Business*, 132 S. Ct. at 2584. Opponents, in turn, claimed that penalizing economic *inactivity*—the failure to purchase a product—is unprecedented and that if it is upheld, it meant the end of any judicially enforceable limit on Congress's power to regulate interstate commerce. Challengers argued that upholding the mandate would mean government had the power to force people to buy myriad products or services regardless of their preferences. In *National Federation of Independent Business*, the Supreme Court, in a 4-1-4 decision, upheld the individual mandate, but on the ground that it was a constitutionally permissible exercise of the taxing power, not under the Commerce Clause. (More on the taxing power in the next section.)

Writing for himself, Chief Justice John Roberts agreed with four dissenting Justices (Scalia, Kennedy, Thomas, and Alito) that the regulation of "inactivity" was beyond Congress's commerce power. Roberts noted that "Congress has never attempted to rely on [the commerce] power to compel individuals not engaged in commerce to purchase an unwanted product." *Id.* at 2586 (opinion of Roberts, C.J.) (footnote omitted). Further, Roberts argued that the language of the Commerce Clause (i.e., granting the power "to regulate" commerce) "presupposes the existence of commercial activity to be regulated" lest subsequent enumerations in Article I be rendered superfluous. *Id.* (opinion of Roberts, C.J.). The Court's precedents, too, he continued, "expansive [as they] have been . . . uniformly describe the power as reaching 'activity.'" *Id.* at 2587 (opinion of Roberts, C.J.). Were Congress allowed "to justify federal regulation by pointing to the effect of inaction on commerce," he wrote, "countless decisions an individual could *potentially* make" would be brought "within the scope of federal regulation, and—under the Government's theory—empower Congress to make those decisions for him." *Id.* (opinion of Roberts, C.J.).

The authors of the unusual joint dissent agreed. "To go beyond" the Court's cases, the most expansive of which "involved commercial *activity* . . . and to say that the failure to grow wheat or the refusal to make loans affects commerce, so that growing and lending can be federally compelled, is to extend federal power to virtually everything." *Id.* at 2648 (Scalia, Kennedy, Thomas & Alito, JJ., dissenting). Such an interpretation threatens the constitutional order, according to the dissenters, "because it gives such an expansive meaning to the Commerce Clause that *all* private conduct (including failure to act) becomes subject to federal control, effectively destroying the Constitution's division of governmental powers. *Id.* at 2649 (Scalia, Kennedy, Thomas & Alito, JJ., dissenting).

Dissenting from the Chief Justice's opinion on the Commerce Clause, Justice Ginsburg alleged that the "limitation of the commerce power to the regulation of those actively engaged in commerce finds no home in the text of the Constitution or our decisions." *Id.* at 2621 (Ginsburg, J., concurring in part and dissenting in part). She predicted courts would have difficulty "in distinguishing statutes that regulate 'activity' from those that regulate 'inactivity.'" *Id.* at 2622 (Ginsburg, J., concurring in part and dissenting in part). She faulted the Chief Justice and the other dissenting Justices for not deferring to Congress's judgment that the mandate was a necessary regulation of interstate commerce. *Id.* at 2619 (Ginsburg, J., concurring in part and dissenting in part).

It is unclear what — if any — weight the opinions on the scope of the commerce power carries, especially as the joint dissent did not join that portion of Chief Justice Roberts's opinion. For his part, the Chief Justice claimed that the Commerce Clause analysis was necessary because "the statute reads more naturally as a command to buy insurance than as a tax" and that it was "only because the Commerce Clause does not authorize such a command that it is necessary to reach the taxing power question." *Id.* at 2600 (opinion of Roberts, C.J.). Whatever the precise precedential weight of the Commerce Clause arguments in *NFIB*, it seems that post-*Raich* reports of the death judicially enforced limits on congressional power may have been exaggerated.

C.   The Taxing and Spending Power

1.   *Introduction*

Next to the Commerce Clause, the power of Congress to tax, and then to spend that revenue, sometimes offering money to state and local governments conditionally, represents another important power of the federal government. The development of the Court's taxing and spending jurisprudence parallels that of the Commerce Clause. Initially, the Court resisted the ability of Congress to use its taxing and spending power to regulate indirectly what the Court's limits on the commerce power prevented Congress from regulating directly. During the New Deal, the Court relaxed these limits, deferring to Congress and leaving to the political process the articulation and enforcement of limits on both. Unlike with the Commerce Clause, however, the Court has shown no interest in even hinting at judicially enforceable limits to both powers even after *Lopez* was decided. The result was to deprive *Lopez* and *Morrison* of much of whatever sting those cases possessed, because even with restrictions on the commerce power, Congress remains free to regulate indirectly using either its taxing or spending powers.

2. *Taxing*

Early taxing cases permitted a measure of indirect regulation, because heavily taxing an activity discourages it. The Court approved congressional taxation of things like state bank notes, *Veazie Bank v. Fenno,* 75 U.S. 533 (1869); oleo-margarine, *McCray v. United States,* 195 U.S. 27 (1904); and narcotics, *United States v. Doremus,* 249 U.S. 86 (1919). When Congress attempted to tax firms employing child labor after the Court struck down its attempt to exclude their products from interstate commerce, however, the Court was keen to locate restrictions on Congress's taxing power, lest it create a way for Congress to invade the exclusive domain of states the Court assumed existed. As the Court did in *Hammer v. Dagenhart,* the Court relied on a tendentious distinction between true taxes and impermissible "penalities" to mark the line between valid and invalid exercises of the taxing power. If the Commerce Clause forbade the regulation of "production" or "agriculture," then the Court concluded it would be impermissible to permit Congress to regulate these things indirectly by use of its taxing power.

In *Bailey v. Drexel Furniture Co.,* 259 U.S. 20 (1922), the Court held that Congress's imposition of a 10 percent excise tax on the net profits of employers using child labor was an unconstitutional penalty. One measure of whether a tax was valid or invalid was the amount of revenue it raised. And although the Court claimed that an incidental motive did not affect the validity of the tax, "there comes a time in the extensions of the penalizing features of the so-called tax when it loses its character as such and becomes a mere penalty, with the characteristics of regulation and punishment." 259 U.S. at 38. However, the Court's real concern was expressed earlier in the opinion: To allow Congress to do indirectly what it could not do directly "would be to break down all constitutional limitation of the powers of Congress and completely wipe out the sovereignty of the States." *Id.*

As the Court began to retreat from the rigid interpretation of the Commerce Clause, and began to relax its assumption that states possessed exclusive regulatory powers that the federal government could not invade, the Court became less concerned with controlling indirect means of regulation through the tax and spend powers. After 1937, the Court also became less concerned with possible motives of Congress in exercising its powers in a particular way, even if it hesitated to repudiate explicitly the penalty–tax distinction articulated in *Drexel Furniture Co. See Sonzinsky v. United States,* 300 U.S. 506 (1937) (upholding $200 annual tax on firearms dealers because it was "productive of some revenue"); *United States v. Sanchez,* 340 U.S. 42 (1950) (upholding tax on marijuana); *United States v. Kahriger,* 345 U.S. 22 (1953) (upholding tax on bookies).

In upholding a tax on professional gamblers, *Kahriger* stressed the cases prior to *Bailey* in which the Court rejected arguments that mixed motives on Congress's part were enough to condemn a particular tax, and arguments that a tax was invalid if it was not primarily intended to raise revenue. Only two Justices thought that the "bookie tax" had gone too far and invaded the states' proper domain under the guise of the taxing power.

The tax-penalty distinction made something of a comeback in *National Federation of Independent Business v. Sebelius,* 132 S. Ct. 2566(2012). Although Chief Justice Roberts's opinion held that the mandated payment for not obtaining health insurance was not a permissible exercise of Congress's commerce power,[5] he voted to uphold it as a valid exercise of the taxing power. The holding was somewhat jarring because the Obama Administration had made a tactical decision during the congressional debate over the Affordable Care Act to term the payment a "penalty" and not a tax. When litigation commenced, however, the Administration began to invoke the taxing power as an alternative source of congressional power. As the Chief Justice put it, "the Government asks us to read the mandate not as ordering individuals to buy insurance, but rather as imposing a tax on those who do not buy that product." 132 S. Ct. at 2593.

While what Congress decided to call the payment made a difference for some things,[6] Chief Justice Roberts held that the Court was not bound by the labels chosen by Congress when passing on the scope of congressional power. *National Federation of Independent Business,* 132 S. Ct. 2594. He noted that the Court had previously looked behind labels in cases like *Drexel.* In that case, he wrote, the Court focused on "three practical characteristics" that "convinced us the 'tax' was actually a penalty." 132 S. Ct. at 2595. "First, the tax imposed an exceedingly heavy burden — 10 percent of a company's net income — on those who employed children . . . . Second, it imposed that exaction only on those who knowingly employed underage laborers. . . . Third, this 'tax' was enforced in part by the Department of Labor . . . ." *Id.*

In contrast, the "shared responsibility payment" could be considered a tax because the amount was not especially heavy. "[F]or most Americans," Roberts observed, "the amount due will be far less than the price of insurance and, by statute, it can never be more." *Id.* at 2595-2596 (footnote omitted).

---

5. *See supra* Chapter 4.B.6.

6. Federal law generally prohibits challenging a tax prior to having paid it. 26 U.S.C. § 7421(a). However, the Court concluded that Congress's use of the term "penalty" to describe the mandated payment signaled its intent that the payment was not a tax for purposes of the Anti-Injunction Act. 132 S. Ct. at 2583 ("The Anti-Injunction Act and the Affordable Care Act . . . are creatures of Congress's own creation. How they related to each other is up to Congress, and the best evidence of Congress's intent is the statutory text."); *id.* at 2584 ("The Affordable Care Act does not require that the penalty for failing to comply with the individual mandate be treated as a tax for purposes of the Anti Injunction Act. [The Act] therefore does not apply to this suit . . . .").

Unlike the child labor penalty, the payment in lieu of obtaining insurance contained no scienter requirement. Finally, Roberts noted that "the payment is solely collected by the IRS through the normal means of taxation—except that the Service is *not* allowed to use those means most suggestive of a punitive sanction, such as criminal prosecution." *Id.* at 2596. Justices Ginsburg, Breyer, Sotomayor, and Kagan, joined the Chief Justice's opinion upholding the mandate as a tax. *Id.* at 2629 (Ginsburg, J., concurring in part and dissenting in part). The joint dissenters, however, alleged that upholding the mandate as a tax was "not to interpret the statute but to rewrite it." *Id.* at 2654 (Scalia, Kennedy, Thomas & Alito, JJ., dissenting). They would have taken Congress at its word that the payment was a penalty and not a tax.

3. *Spending*

There are two questions here. First, are there restrictions on the power of Congress to spend revenue it collects from taxes it imposes? Second, may Congress *condition* receipt of federal money by states on states doing or refraining from doing certain things Congress might not be able to *directly* compel them to do? As to the first question, it is clear that the power "to pay the Debts and provide for the common Defense and general Welfare of the United States" is an independent power. Congress need not spend only in connection with its other enumerated powers in Article I, § 8. Defining the "general Welfare," moreover, is something the courts will leave to congressional discretion.

The answer to the second question requires a little more explanation. As with its restrictions on the taxing power prior to 1937, the Court drew questionable distinctions between valid conditional spending and invalid "coercion." In 1936, for example, the Court struck down a portion of the Agricultural Adjustment Act that paid subsidies to farmers for not producing; the subsidy was funded by taxes on processors of commodities. *United States v. Butler,* 297 U.S. 1 (1936). While acknowledging that the power to spend the revenue raised by taxes was not limited to spending on the subjects of other enumerated provisions, the *Butler* Court found that the spending "invade[d] the reserved rights of the states. It is a statutory plan to regulate and control agricultural production, a matter beyond the powers delegated to the federal government." 297 U.S. at 68. The Court rejected the argument that the plan was voluntary, finding it "coercive" because declining to participate meant a loss of benefits. *Id.* at 70–71.

As with the Court's question-begging distinction between taxes and penalties, the distinction between "coercive" and "voluntary" conditions began to erode almost immediately, as the Court began to worry less about protecting certain state prerogatives from federal interference. *See Steward Machine Co. v. Davis,* 301 U.S. 548 (1937). In *Helvering v. Davis,* 301 U.S. 619 (1937), in which the Court upheld aspects of the Social Security Act, Justice Cardozo argued for judicial deference to Congress when it came to the question of what constituted the "general welfare."

The modern spending test was articulated in *South Dakota v. Dole*, 483 U.S. 203 (1987), in which the Court upheld a conditional spending requirement that states raise their drinking ages to 21 or forfeit 5 percent of federal highway funds. Chief Justice Rehnquist wrote that as long as Congress (1) spends for the "general welfare" (as determined by Congress); (2) makes explicit and unambiguous the conditions that attend receipt of the money; (3) relates the conditions to the federal interest in a particular program; (4) does not otherwise violate the Constitution in making the conditions; and, perhaps (5) isn't "coercive," then the Court will not strike down the program. 483 U.S. at 207–208. The Court was satisfied that the fit between the condition (raise the drinking age) and the purpose of the funds (ensuring highway safety) was sufficient to satisfy the test. *Id.* at 208–209.

Justice O'Connor dissented in *Dole,* arguing that a distinction should be made between conditions and regulations. The former would state how the money was to be spent, to ensure fidelity to congressional intent in making the money available in the first place. Regulations, for O'Connor, included anything that went beyond saying how the appropriated money should be spent. Because telling states to raise their drinking age did not tell them how to spend the highway funds Congress had appropriated to them, it was a regulation, and thus could only be accomplished if Congress otherwise had the power in Article I, § 8 to regulate directly. She thought that Congress did not, thus it could not achieve the same end through its spending power. *Id.* at 216–217 (O'Connor, J., dissenting).

Despite calls to do so, particularly in light of the new restrictions placed on Congress's commerce power in *Lopez* and *Morrison,* O'Connor's position has not been adopted by the rest of the Court. *See, e.g, Sabri v. United States,* 541 U.S. 600 (2004) (upholding conviction for statute prohibiting bribery involving federal funds, despite lack of nexus between the bribery and the federal funds themselves). However, in *National Federation of Independent Business v. Sebelius,* 132 S. Ct. 2566 (2012), the Court invoked *Dole*'s "no-coercion" rule to hold that States could not be compelled to participate in a dramatic expansion of Medicaid, the federal-state program providing insurance for low-income families. As part of the Affordable Care Act's effort to reduce the number of persons in the U.S. without health insurance, the Act greatly expanded the coverage of Medicaid. "The Medicaid provisions of the Affordable Care Act . . . require[d] States to expand their Medicaid programs by 2014 to cover *all* individuals under the age of 65 with incomes below 133 percent of the federal poverty line." *Id.* at 2601. States were also obligated to cover those persons with a benefits package established by federal law. If states declined to participate, they would lose not only the money Congress had set aside for the new program, but all *existing* Medicaid funding as well. *Id.* at 2603. That condition, according to the Chief Justice, meant that "the financial 'inducement' Congress [chose] is much more than 'relatively mild encouragement'—it is a gun to the head." *Id.* at 2604. It meant that states really had no choice to accept or reject the federal offer, as *Dole* requires. The Medicaid expansion, moreover, "accomplishe[d] a shift in kind, not merely degree," one that "enlist[ed] the States in a new health care program." *Id.* at 2605, 2606. Chief Justice Roberts didn't invalidate the expansion, however; he (along with Justices Breyer and Kagan) held that states must be allowed to decline to participate in the expanded program without hazarding their existing Medicaid funding. *Id.* at 2608. The joint dissent agreed that the expansion and conditions were coercive, *id.* at 2662 (Scalia, Kennedy, Thomas & Alito, JJ., dissenting), but argued the proper remedy was to invalidate the program. *Id.* at 2667 (Scalia, Kennedy, Thomas & Alito, JJ., dissenting) ("We should not accept the Government's invitation to attempt to solve a constitutional problem by rewriting the Medicaid Expansion so as to allow States that reject it to retain their pre-existing Medicaid funds.").

It was somewhat surprising that seven members of the Court found the conditions attached to the Medicaid expansion to be "coercive." The Court had not, heretofore, seemed interested in limiting Congress's power to condition spending in any meaningful way. *See, e.g., Sabri v. United States*, 541 U.S. 600 (2004) (declining to limit Congress's authority to criminalize bribery associated with the receipt of federal funds, despite the lack of a nexus between the bribery and the federal funds themselves). It remains to be seen whether the Medicaid expansion was so dramatic and the conditions so onerous as to make it a one-of-a-kind law, or whether this signals a renewed effort to find judicially enforceable federalism limits and impose them on Congress. Even the joint dissent made clear that "[w]hether federal spending legislation crosses the line from enticement to coercion is often difficult to determine, and courts should not conclude that legislation is unconstitutional on this ground unless the coercive nature of an offer is unmistakably clear." *Id.* at 2662 (Scalia, Kennedy, Thomas & Alito, JJ., dissenting). Suffice it to say that what is "unmistakably clear" to the joint dissenters is unlikely to be so for, say, Justices Breyer or Kagan.

QUESTION 8. The GFSZA rides again!   Assume that, following *Lopez*, Congress repassed the GFSZA, this time unambiguously requiring states receiving federal funds for various educational programs to pass a state version of the GFSZA; that is, prohibiting possession of a gun within 1,000 feet of a building the possessor knows or reasonably should know is a school. Failure to do so would result in a loss of 5 percent of those funds. Would such a provision pass constitutional muster?

A. No, because Congress may not do indirectly through the spending power what it cannot do directly through, e.g., the Commerce Clause.

B. Yes, because the purpose of the condition, ensuring school safety, is sufficiently related to the purpose of the funds, assisting states to provide adequate education.

C. No, because given the dependence of state and local schools on federal funds, any such condition would be, by definition, coercive and not voluntary.

D. Yes, because Congress may determine what constitutes the general welfare for spending.

ANALYSIS.   *Dole* sets forth the modern test for the spending power, but it has at least been clear since 1937 that Congress can use its spending power to regulate indirectly. Therefore **A** is incorrect because it does not correctly state the law.

Likewise, the Court abandoned its distinction between truly voluntary spending and spending programs that were coercive. Thus, **C** is also an incorrect statement of law. As between the remaining answers, it is true that the Court will defer to congressional judgments about what constitutes spending for "the general welfare," but that is not a sufficient condition for upholding the spending, so **D** would not be as good as the remaining answer, **B**. *Dole* made clear that there needed to be some (not very tight) connection between the condition and the federal interest in the program itself. It is likely that requirement could be satisfied by the connection between school safety and educational funding.

QUESTION 9. **On the Dole.**   Assume for purposes of this question that instead of the 5 percent at stake in *Dole,* states refusing to raise their drinking age would face the loss of 100 percent of all federal highway funds. Would that fact have any bearing on the constitutionality of the requirement?

A. Yes, because at that point, the condition becomes coercive and the Court will strike it down on that basis.

B. Yes, because the *Dole* Court held that only 5 percent may be withheld from states.

C. No, because the Court has repudiated the voluntary–coercive distinction present in its earlier case law.

D. No, as long as the condition is unambiguous.

ANALYSIS.   Given the last question, you might have been drawn to **C**, but although the Court has moved away from *Butler*'s claim that conditional spending was often "coercive" if one faced the loss of benefits for noncompliance with the condition, *Dole* did concede that *at some point* a coercive condition might be held to be invalid, without suggesting where that point might be. Seven Justices in *National Federation of Independent Business*, moreover, were willing to put some teeth into what had been a theoretical limit. The Court did not hold that 5 percent was any sort of maximum amount that Congress could withhold, so **B** is incorrect. **D** is incorrect for the reason stated earlier: The Court has held that coercion, at least that which is "unmistakeably clear," is fatal to a congressional condition.

That leaves **A**, which is the best answer. If *any* condition were to be invalidated as coercive, it would likely be one that required states to forfeit *all* money from the federal government.

QUESTION 10. **The fat tax.** Troubled over statistics correlating high rates of child and adult obesity with chronic health problems among the nation's uninsured and underinsured, Congress imposes a 10 percent excise tax on the net profits of companies who knowingly market "unhealthy" foods, as defined by statute, to children. Producers allege that the tax is really a penalty. This "obesity impact fee" is collected by the Department of Health and Human Services and used to fund obesity prevention programs. Their challenge is likely to:

A. Succeed, if they can prove that the tax is intended to discourage production of the snacks rather than raise revenue.
B. Succeed, because the tax violates the reserved powers of the state.
C. Succeed, unless Congress otherwise has the power to prohibit the sale of unhealthy snacks.
D. Succeed, because it is not a valid tax.

ANALYSIS. While it looked as if *Bailey v. Drexel Furniture Co.*'s distinction between valid taxes and invalid penalties had been superseded, *National Federation of Independent Business* revived that distinction, contrasting the penalty invalidated in *Bailey* with the valid tax imposed on an individual's refusal to obtain health insurance by the Affordable Care Act. Chief Justice Roberts pointed to three things that distinguished the latter from the former: (1) the onerous nature of the tax; (2) the presence of a scienter requirement; and (3) whether the IRS collects the revenue from the "tax." Here, the "fat tax" looks more like the child labor tax in *Bailey* than the payment for not having insurance in *National Federation of Independent Business*. **D**, therefore, is the best answer. **A** is not correct because all taxes discourage the activity taxed to some degree. **B** is incorrect because the taxation of products isn't an area *exclusively* set aside for states. **C** is incorrect because the power to tax is an independent power and does not need to be tied to another enumerated power.

D.   Federalism-Based Limits on Federal Legislative Power

1.   Introduction

Recall that in Chapter 3 we discussed implicit limits the Court has inferred from the Constitution and applied to state powers. As it happens, there are some similar implicit limits the Court has placed on the powers of Congress as well; specifically, on Congress's commerce power. These are controversial topics that have been criticized vehemently by members of the Court who find no constitutional sanction for such limits. These critics argue that the Court is repeating the error of older New Deal-era Courts that sought to limit congressional power to preserve areas of state authority presumed to be exclusive, and not amenable to federal regulation. Advocates of such limits point out that the Constitution presupposes a union composed of semisovereign states that delegate some powers to a national government and retain other aspects of their sovereignty. Because the Constitution was framed with the states in mind, they reason, surely there are limits to what Congress might compel states to do.

For a brief period from the mid-1970s until the mid-1980s, the Court signaled its intent to place substantive limits on the exercise of congressional power vis-à-vis the states out of respect for our federal system. The Court abandoned this effort, however, only to revive certain procedural restrictions in the 1990s. Thus, although there are no longer limits as to the *ends* Congress may require the states to pursue, there are limits as to the *means* Congress may adopt in pursuit of those ends. This section first discusses the Court's brief experiment with substantive limits, inaugurated by *National League of Cities v. Usery,* 426 U.S. 833 (1976); then discusses the procedural "anti-commandeering principle" announced in *New York v. United States,* 505 U.S. 144 (1992).

2.   Substantive limits: The rise and fall of National League of Cities v. Usery

Initially, the Fair Labor Standards Act (FLSA) exempted state and local governments from its wage and hour requirements, in part owing to concerns about federalism and the federal government's power to dictate such standards to states. The Court upheld a partial extension of the FLSA in *Maryland v. Wirtz,* 392 U.S. 183 (1968), as a valid exercise of Congress's commerce power. When the FLSA was again extended to cover more state and local employees, another constitutional challenge was mounted. In a surprise decision, the Court overruled *Wirtz,* and invalidated the extension of the FLSA to state and local employees.

The challenge in *National League of Cities* concerned not the scope of Congress's power over commerce (i.e., whether Congress was properly regulating conduct that "affected" or "substantially affected" interstate commerce), but whether congressional power could be exercised at all over certain areas of state activity (what *National League of Cities* called "traditional governmental functions"). There were deemed to be certain narrow areas of state activity immune from congressional regulation. Specifically, in *National League of Cities,* the objection was that by prescribing wages and hours for municipal employees, cities would be forced to either cut services elsewhere or raise taxes to cover the increased costs. Principles of federalism, the Court reasoned, dictated that local voters, not Congress, should choose the appropriate mix of services and compensation for their employees. As restated by a subsequent case, the rule of *National League of Cities* was that Congress could not (1) regulate states as states; (2) regarding matters that were attributes of state sovereignty; (3) where compliance with federal requirements would impair states' abilities to structure "integral operations" in areas of "traditional governmental functions" unless (4) an overriding federal interest justifies state submission. *Hodel v. Virginia Surface Mining & Reclamation Ass'n,* 452 U.S. 264, 287–288 & n. 29 (1981).

The Court, however, struggled to define "traditional governmental functions." Following *National League of Cities,* in fact, the Court did not strike down a single other exercise of congressional power over the states. By 1985, one (reluctant) member of the *National League of Cities* majority, Justice Harry Blackmun, changed his mind and wrote for a new majority that rejected *National League of Cities* and the entire concept of substantive federalism restrictions on congressional power. *Garcia v. San Antonio Metropolitan Transit Authority,* 469 U.S. 528 (1985).

The *Garcia* Court concluded that the search for standards to distinguish traditional from nontraditional governmental functions was a futile one. Certainly there was nothing in the Constitution from which such criteria could be derived. Thus, the Court concluded, "the fundamental limitation that the constitutional scheme imposes on the Commerce Clause to protect 'States as States' is one of process rather than one of result." 469 U.S. at 554. The "sovereign interests" of states, the Court held, were "more properly protected by procedural safeguards inherent in the structure of the federal system than by judicially created limitations on federal power." *Id.* at 552.

3. The anti-commandeering principle

Federalism limits on federal power were not quite done, however, despite *Garcia*'s apparent signal that the Court was withdrawing from the field. The difference was that particular ends were no longer foreclosed to Congress; the focus, rather, was on limiting the means Congress might use to achieve its ends. For example, in 1991, the Court announced that it would not interpret congressional mandates to alter the balance of power between federal and state governments absent a "clear statement" that Congress intended such an alteration to occur. *Gregory v. Ashcroft,* 501 U.S. 452 (1991) (declining to apply the

Age Discrimination in Employment Act to mandatory retirement provision for state judges in state constitution). Then, in *New York v. United States,* 505 U.S. 144 (1992), the Court announced a new procedural limit on the power of Congress—the so-called anti-commandeering principle.

At issue in *New York* was a congressional program intended to remedy the problem of low-level radioactive waste disposal in the country. Among the provisions was one that required states to enter into compacts with adjacent states to dispose of the waste or to take title to all such waste produced in the state. The Court invalidated this provision because it found that it "commandeered" the state legislatures by requiring them to pass particular laws or suffer the consequences. The Court distinguished *Garcia,* noting that while the statute at issue there was generally applicable, the legislation in *New York* applied to states as states alone. 505 U.S. at 160. By contrast, "[t]he Constitution has never been understood to confer upon Congress the ability to require the States to govern according to Congress' instructions." *Id* at 162.

Congress can pass its own statutes and, through preemption, require states to comply. Congress can also attach conditions to the receipt of federal funds to encourage states to bend to congressional will. *Id.* at 167–168. Because Congress could not command state legislatures to pass a particular bill and similarly could not command the legislature to take title to all of the low-level radioactive waste in the state, it could not require legislatures to make a "choice" between those two either. 505 U.S. at 176 ("Because an instruction to state governments to take title to waste, standing alone, would be beyond the authority of the Congress and because a direct order to regulate, standing alone, would also be beyond the authority of Congress, it follows that Congress lacks the power to offer the States a choice between the two.").

The Court traced the anti-commandeering principle to background principles of federalism "so basic that, like the air around us . . . are easily overlooked." *Id.* at 187. The Court noted that were Congress able to use state legislatures in this manner, accountability for unpopular policies would be obscured. Congress could take credit for having "solved" a particular problem, whereas States acting at the behest of the federal government to implement particular policies would bear the brunt of constituent complaints. *Id.* at 168–169.

A few years later, the Court extended the anti-commandeering principle to state and local executive officers. *Printz v. United States,* 521 U.S. 898 (1997). Federal gun control legislation known as the "Brady Bill" required that background checks be run on prospective purchasers of handguns. The legislation required that a computerized database be created enabling such checks to be run instantaneously at the point of sale. Until that database was established, however, the Brady Bill required that those background checks be performed within five days by the Chief Law Enforcement Officer (CLEO) where the sale took place.

The Court struck down those provisions, holding that history, structure, and precedent demonstrated that such commandeering of executive officials was unconstitutional. First, the Court noted that even during wartime Congress seemed to have operated on the assumption it could only request—not command—state executive officials to offer assistance in implementing federal programs. *Id.* at 907–917. Second, in addition to the points made about commandeering's obfuscation of authority, the Court pointed out that it subverted separation of powers, too. If Congress could merely commandeer the executive apparatus of states, it need not work with the President, whose cooperation is normally needed to see laws executed. *Id.* at 922–923. Finally, the Court noted it had "held in *New York* that Congress cannot compel the States to enact or enforce a federal regulatory program" and that "Congress cannot circumvent that prohibition by conscripting the State's officers directly." *Id.* at 935. Justice O'Connor concurred on the assumption that requiring states to merely report certain statistics that they otherwise keep would not run afoul of the anti-commandeering principle. *Id.* at 936 (O'Connor, J., concurring).

Critics noted that taken to its logical conclusion, the anti-commandeering principle posed problems for the Court's preemption doctrine (discussed in the next chapter). Why, they wondered, was requiring states to obey federal law not a form of commandeering? But the Court was unwilling to go this far; it distinguished commandeering from preemption in *Reno v. Condon*, 528 U.S. 141 (2000).

At issue in *Condon* was the constitutionality of the Drivers' Privacy Protection Act (DPPA), which forbade any person (defined to include States) from selling data collected from driver's licenses. The State of South Carolina, which made money selling such data to various marketing firms, sued, claiming that the law violated the anti-commandeering principle. The Court first found that the DPPA easily fell within the scope of the commerce power, because Congress was regulating things (data) in interstate commerce. 528 U.S. at 148. The Court then unanimously rejected South Carolina's arguments that the DPPA violated the Tenth Amendment because it "thrusts upon the States all of the day-to-day responsibility for administering its complex provisions," and thereby makes "state officials the unwilling implementors of federal policy," by requiring the State's employees to learn and apply the Act's substantive restrictions, which consume the employees' time and thus the State's resources. 528 U.S. at 150. Quoting from an earlier case, *South Carolina v. Baker,* which upheld a congressional prohibition on state issuance of unregistered bonds, the Court responded:

> Such "commandeering" is, however, an inevitable consequence of regulating a state activity. Any federal regulation demands compliance. That a State wishing to engage in certain activity must take administrative and sometimes legislative action to comply with federal standards regulating that activity is a commonplace that presents no constitutional defect.

It continued:

> Like the statute at issue in *Baker,* the DPPA does not require the States in their sovereign capacity to regulate their own citizens. The DPPA regulates the States as the owners of data bases. It does not require the South Carolina

Legislature to enact any laws or regulations, and it does not require state officials to assist in the enforcement of federal statutes regulating private individuals. We accordingly conclude that the DPPA is consistent with the constitutional principles enunciated in *New York* and *Printz.*

528 U.S. at 150–151 (quoting *South Carolina v. Baker,* 485 U.S. 505, 514–515 (1988)).

Because these principles are designed to protect the interests of *states,* may *individuals* invoke them to challenge the constitutionality of congressional legislation? Lower courts had split on whether individuals had standing to allege that federal laws impermissibly encroached on states' interests.[7] But the Court in *Bond v. United States,* 131 S. Ct. 2355, 2363-2364 (2011), held that an "individual, in a proper case, can assert injury from governmental action taken in excess of the authority that federalism defines. Her rights in this regard do not belong to a State."

QUESTION 11. Hurricane help. In the wake of Hurricane Katrina, Congress decided to develop comprehensive emergency management plans that incorporated "best practices" according to disaster management specialists. Congress wants to get all states to enact these plans, so that it can be sure that in the initial hours following a disaster, states will be able to meet the needs of their citizens until federal help arrives. Which of the following means may Congress *not* use?

A. Pass a comprehensive plan and require state officials to implement the federally mandated provisions.

B. Pass a comprehensive federal plan that bypasses states and puts federal officials in charge, preempting nonconforming state plans.

C. Provide financial incentives to states to develop a plan that meets minimum federal standards.

D. Pass a comprehensive plan and offer state officials the choice between creating and implementing a state plan that complies with federal minimum standards or submitting to that federally designed plan.

ANALYSIS. Although Congress may not force states to pass federal legislation under *New York v. United States,* it may regulate directly, and preempt conflicting state law. Therefore **B** is perfectly legal. Similarly, Congress may use its spending power to encourage states to do things that it might not be able to require them to do directly. This point was stressed in both *New York* and *Printz.* Therefore **C** is fine as well. **D** is also permissible. The choice offered there is between submitting to a comprehensive federal plan that will preempt

---

7. Standing is discussed in Chapter 2.C.3.a.

contrary state law and the state designing and implementing its own plan, which conforms to some minimum standard, as the federal government often does with its environmental statutes. That choice is *unlike* the choice in *New York v. United States,* where the state was offered the "choice" between two alternatives (take title to the waste or pass a specific piece of legislation that Congress dictated), neither of which Congress had the power to compel. That leaves **A**, in which the federal government wants to commandeer state officials to implement a federal program. *Printz* held that this is not permitted.

E.   Constitutional Limits on the Treatymaking Power

1.   Introduction

Article II, § 2 of the Constitution gives the President the power "to make Treaties, provided two thirds of the Senators present concur." Congress as a whole, by virtue of the Necessary and Proper Clause, has power "to make all laws which shall be necessary and proper for carrying into Execution" treaties the United States enters into. U.S. Const. art. I, § 8, cl. 18. Further, the Supremacy Clause says that "all treaties made, or which shall be made, under the authority of the United States, shall be the supreme law of the land." U.S. Const. art. VI, § 2. Unlike the provision of Article VI requiring that "laws of the United States" be "made in pursuance" of the Constitution to be supreme, treaties need be made only "under the authority of the United States" to be supreme. Though this provision was likely worded to preserve treaties that pre-dated the Constitution, questions remain about the scope of the treaty-making power and of any enabling legislation passed to implement treaties as a matter of domestic law. Specifically, the Court has been asked to address whether (1) Congress might, by dint of authority from a treaty, pass legislation that would otherwise violate federalism limitations on Congress, and (2) whether treaties might be negotiated and ratified that violate provisions of the Constitution. This section takes each in turn.

2.   Structural limits and the treatymaking power

In *Missouri v. Holland,* 252 U.S. 416 (1920), the Court rejected a challenge to a federal law concerning migratory birds that implemented a treaty between the United States and Great Britain on the same subject. Among other things, the law regulated aspects of bird hunting within the states. Missouri objected that the law infringed on its reserved rights, argued that treaties are not valid if they violate the Constitution, and that Congress's powers did not increase when it legislated pursuant to a treaty. 252 U.S. at 432 (noting the argument that "what an act of Congress could not do unaided, in derogation of the powers reserved to the States, a treaty cannot do").

Although not disputing that there were limits to the treatymaking power, Justice Holmes, for the Court, thought it equally "obvious that there may be matters of the sharpest exigency for the national well being that an act of Congress could not deal with but that a treaty followed by an act could." *Id.* at 433. Then Justice Holmes observed that the treaty did not "contravene any prohibitory words to be found in the Constitution." *Id.* Therefore, the question was whether it was "forbidden by some invisible radiation from the general terms of the Tenth Amendment," adding that "in deciding what that amendment has reserved," the Court "must consider what this country has become." *Id.* at 434.

Although states may regulate the killing and sale of birds by its citizens, "it does not follow that its authority is exclusive of paramount powers." *Id.* Holmes noted that birds migrate and that, contrary to the State's claim, no one really "owns" them. He concluded:

> Here a national interest of very nearly the first magnitude is involved. It can be protected only by national action in concert with that of another power. The subject matter is only transitorily within the State and has no permanent habitat therein. But for the treaty and the statute there soon might be no birds for any powers to deal with. We see nothing in the Constitution that compels the Government to sit by while a food supply is cut off and the protectors of our forests and our crops are destroyed. It is not sufficient to rely upon the States. The reliance is vain, and were it otherwise, the question is whether the United States is forbidden to act. We are of opinion that the treaty and statute must be upheld.

Id. at 435.

3. *Treaties and individual rights*

The somewhat opaque reasoning of *Missouri v. Holland* made some fearful that the treatymaking power would be used either to obliterate federalism or curb civil liberties. Such fears culminated in an attempt, spearheaded by Ohio Senator John Bricker, to formally amend the Constitution to make clear that treaties could not violate its provisions. While the Eisenhower administration worked to defeat the amendment in Congress, a plurality of the Supreme Court allayed the worst fears of the Bricker Amendment's supporters in *Reid v. Covert,* 354 U.S. 1 (1957).

The wives of two servicemen were convicted of murdering their husbands following trials by military courts martial, as permitted by executive agreements with Great Britain and Japan. The defendants argued that the court martial proceedings violated their Fifth and Sixth Amendment rights to a jury trial preceded by indictment by a grand jury. The government argued that the legislation providing for courts martial for civilian dependents of military personnel overseas was "necessary and proper to carry out the United States' obligations under the international agreements made with those countries." 354 U.S. at 16.

Justice Black's response, writing for a plurality of the Court, was categorical: "[N]o agreement with a foreign nation can confer power on the Congress, or on any other branch of Government, which is free from the restraints of the Constitution." *Id.* There is nothing in the Supremacy Clause, he added, "which intimates that treaties and laws enacted pursuant to them do not have to comply with the provisions of the Constitution." *Id.* The only reason the Clause omitted the "in pursuance of" language with regard to treaties "was so that agreements made by the United States under the Articles of Confederation . . . would remain in effect." *Id.* at 16–17. Justice Black distinguished *Missouri v. Holland,* stressing that "the treaty involved was not inconsistent with any specific provision of the Constitution" and adding that at most it meant that where the United States can make valid treaties, the Tenth Amendment is no barrier. *Id.* at 18.

QUESTION 12. A command[eering] performance. The President of the United States has made the United States party to a multilateral treaty committing the country to reducing emissions of pollutants that are thought to contribute to global warming. The Senate consents to the treaty by the requisite two-thirds majority and it goes into effect. The House and the Senate together then pass implementing legislation required by the treaty. Among the provisions in the implementing legislation is a requirement that state officials aid in the implementation and enforcement of regulations promulgated by the federal Environmental Protection Agency. Prince, one of the state officials who will be required to assist in the enforcement of these new regulations, sues, claiming that the legislation constitutes unconstitutional commandeering of state executive officials. A reviewing court should find the statute:

A. Constitutional under the rule in *Missouri v. Holland.*
B. Unconstitutional, because it forces state executive officials to implement a federal program.
C. Constitutional, because the legislation is necessary and proper to implementing the treaty.
D. Unconstitutional, because treaties may not violate individual rights.

ANALYSIS. The facts here resemble those in *Printz v. United States,* discussed earlier. The question asks whether it would make a difference if the commandeering was countenanced by a treaty, as opposed to ordinary legislation. **D** is incorrect because it is irrelevant—there are no individual rights at issue here.

Answer **B** is also wrong, because it assumes the matter in question: whether legislation passed pursuant to a treaty is limited by federalism concerns to the same degree that "ordinary" legislation would be. Similarly, **C** might be true, but it doesn't answer the question whether other parts of the Constitution limit the power.

The best answer is **A**. *Missouri v. Holland* seems to hold that when enacting legislation pursuant to a treaty, certain of the Constitution's structural provisions do not limit Congress the same way as they do when Congress is legislating unaided. Although *Missouri v. Holland* controls, the issue is nevertheless a difficult one. The Court could very well revisit this issue, in light of cases like *Printz* and *New York v. United States;* but, for now, *Missouri v. Holland* remains good law.

QUESTION 13. Gun control goes global. On June 26, 2008, the U.S. Supreme Court held that the Second Amendment guarantees an individual right to keep and bear arms, and invalidated a D.C. ordinance that made it difficult to keep a gun in your home or business for self-defense. Imagine that the United States becomes a party to an international treaty aimed at curbing the proliferation of small arms, including handguns. The treaty obligates signatories to take steps to combat gun sales and gun violence domestically, as part of a global strategy to reduce gun deaths. Pursuant to that treaty, which is duly approved by the Senate, Congress passes legislation outlawing the possession of handguns by private citizens. What is the strongest argument against the constitutionality of such a statute?

A. The subject matter is not suitable for a treaty.
B. The Court's decision in *Reid v. Covert.*
C. *Heller's* holding that the Second Amendment guarantees an individual right to private gun ownership for self-defense.
D. B and C.

ANALYSIS.   If you read the preceding paragraphs closely, this was an easy question—even if you had never heard of *Heller*. Answer **A** is incorrect, because nothing in the Constitution or the Court's case law has suggested that certain subjects are not appropriate ones for treatymaking.

B is more promising, because if *Reid* stands for the proposition that legislation passed pursuant to a treaty cannot itself violate explicit provisions of the Constitution, then a law banning guns would be suspect in light of the Second Amendment. Until *Heller,* however, there had been a debate whether the Amendment guaranteed an individual right of private gun ownership or not. Therefore, **C** would also be a strong argument for the law's unconstitutionality, as it settled the debate. Because both **B** and **C** are strong arguments against the law, the correct answer is **D**.

F.   The Closer

> **QUESTION 14. The Port Protection Act.** After a survey indicated that the nation's ports were vulnerable to terrorist attack, Congress passed the 2009 Port Protection Act. The Act has three main components. Title I requires all ports to comply with security measures to be promulgated by the Department of Homeland Security; specifically, the Act requires rigorous new inspection of shipping containers that come into the ports by the thousands each year. Title II allocates money to state and local governments to assist them in bringing the ports up to the new, stringent federal standards. Title III requires state and local officials to aid federal officials in inspecting the ports for compliance with the new standards.
>
> Mark Price is the Director of the Port Authority for the City of Immobile in the State of Floribama. Trying to cope with a reduction in funding, lack of personnel, and the aftermath of a powerful recent hurricane, Price regards these new requirements as an intolerable imposition. He challenges the Port Protection Act, claiming that it is unconstitutional. Of the three titles, which, if any, would be vulnerable to constitutional challenge?
>
> **A.** Title I, because there is no requirement in the statute itself that the regulated ports "substantially affect" interstate commerce.
> **B.** Title II, because the spending in Title II benefits only a select group of state and local governments and, therefore, does not advance the "general welfare."
> **C.** Title III, because it impermissibly commandeers state executive officials.
> **D.** None; all titles of the Port Protection Act would pass constitutional muster.

ANALYSIS.   Hey, no one said these Closers were supposed to be easy! It is true that there is no mention in the facts that the legislation applies only to ports "substantially affecting" interstate commerce, but don't forget that the substantially affects factors, like the jurisdictional requirement, do not, apparently, apply to regulations of "channels" or "instrumentalities" of interstate commerce. Ports are part of the channels of interstate (and foreign) commerce; the shipping containers themselves are instrumentalities of that commerce. Therefore, **A** would not be the correct answer.

Nor would **B**, which argues that because Congress has designated money for a select group of cities and states (i.e., those with ports), that spending is not "general." Although the Court did apply that limitation in the past, the current law, articulated in *Dole* among other places, is that defining the "general welfare" is a decision for Congress to make. Title III, however, requires state and local officials to assist federal officials in the implementation of the new regime. This is classic commandeering, which *Printz* held was unconstitutional.

If you thought that the combination of the spending in Title II and the conscription in Title III was covered by *Dole,* remember that case required that the tie between the condition and the spending be clear and unambiguous. In the Port Protection Act, it is unclear that the two are even connected, much less that the receipt of the money offered in Title II is unambiguously contingent on the participation of the state and local port officials. Therefore **C** is the correct answer, and **D** is incorrect.

 # Denning's Picks

1.	Make a run for the border	**D**
2.	Don't make a federal case out of it	**C**
3.	GFSZA redux	**A**
4.	Machine Gun Kelly	**A**
5.	Arbitrate this!	**D**
6.	A grave matter	**D**
7.	Machine Gun Kelly part deux	**C**
8.	The GFSZA rides again!	**B**
9.	On the Dole	**A**
10.	The fat tax	**D**
11.	Hurricane help	**A**
12.	A command[eering] performance	**A**
13.	Gun control goes global	**D**
14.	The Port Protection Act	**C**

5

Limits on State Power to Regulate Interstate Commerce

A. Overview

This chapter discusses some of the express and implied restrictions the Constitution and the Court impose on the ability of states to regulate commerce traveling across borders. The chapter begins with the most important of these, the dormant Commerce Clause doctrine (DCCD), an implied restriction on states that prohibits them from exercising their taxing or regulatory powers to discriminate against or otherwise burden interstate commerce. Next up is perhaps the most important explicit restriction on state power in this area, the Privileges and Immunities Clause of Article IV, § 2, which requires states to treat citizens of other states as they do their own citizens, at least where certain "fundamental rights" are involved. The chapter ends with a discussion of the various preemption doctrines. Unlike the DCCD, which applies when Congress has not acted affirmatively, preemption follows from the operation of the Supremacy Clause of Article VI and displaces conflicting or inconsistent state law whenever federal and state legislation address the same or similar subjects.

B. The Dormant Commerce Clause Doctrine

1. Introduction

The DCCD is a term used to describe the set of judicially enforceable restraints on state power[1] to regulate interstate commerce that the Court has inferred from the Constitution's grant of power to Congress over commerce. Early Court decisions rejected the argument that the mere grant of power to Congress over interstate commerce displaced all state power and was thus exclusive. *Gibbons v. Ogden,* 22 U.S. 1 (1824).

Subsequent Courts struggled with drawing the line between permissible and impermissible state and local regulations of interstate commerce. Early Marshall Court opinions seemed to hold that although states could exercise their "police powers" to protect the health, safety, and welfare of their citizens, despite some incidental effect on interstate commerce, any state regulation of interstate commerce qua commerce was impermissible. *Willson v. Black Bird Creek Marsh Co.,* 27 U.S. 245 (1829).

The Taney Court was much more amenable to state power generally, and it retreated somewhat from the Marshall Court's strong nationalism, but its members could not agree on a single rationale for its DCCD cases, leading to much confusion as to where to lay down the constitutional markers. Finally, in the 1851 case of *Cooley v. Board of Wardens,* 53 U.S. 299 (1851), Justice Benjamin Curtis concluded that the line was to be drawn according to the nature of the subject regulated. "Local" subjects could tolerate a variety of rules, whereas those subjects that were in their nature "national" required a rule prescribed by Congress, if they were to be regulated at all. States did not have the power, he concluded, to regulate national subjects.

But *Cooley* articulated no criteria for distinguishing between national and local subjects; courts spent the remainder of the nineteenth and much of the early twentieth century developing formulae to implement Curtis's grand compromise. One such test asked whether the state tax or regulation "directly" regulated commerce, or whether its effects were felt only "indirectly." Dissatisfaction with the malleability of this test led the Court to begin to frankly balance the burdens on interstate commerce against the local benefits conferred by the regulation, a balancing that is still part of our modern DCCD. *See, e.g., South Carolina State Hwy. Dept. v. Barnwell Bros., Inc.,* 303 U.S. 177 (1938); *So. Pacific Co. v. Arizona,* 325 U.S. 761 (1945).

About the same time the Court was employing the direct–indirect test to evaluate state and local laws, another line of cases appeared in which the

---

1. Throughout the discussion of the DCCD, I use the phrase "state" power or "state" law. It should be noted, however, that the DCCD applies to local laws as well. Thus for "state," read "state and local laws." *See, e.g., Dean Milk v. Madison,* 340 U.S. 349 (1951).

Court struck down laws that subjected out-of-state commerce to different (usually unfavorable) regulations or taxes than in-state commerce. *See, e.g., Welton v. Missouri,* 81 U.S. 275 (1876). This antidiscrimination principle, too, is an enduring and robust part of the modern DCCD. The reason given for the focus on discrimination was largely historical: The Court assumed that the Framers intended to prevent the discrimination that existed during the Confederation Era and centralized commercial regulatory power in Congress in part to prevent a recurrence of the conditions assumed to have prevailed prior to the Constitution's ratification.

Today, the Court uses a two-tier standard of review in DCCD cases. Strict or heightened scrutiny is triggered upon a showing that a state law or local ordinance discriminates against interstate commerce (1) on its face, (2) in its effects, or (3) was passed with a discriminatory purpose. Discriminatory or protectionist legislation is presumed invalid, subjected to strict scrutiny, and nearly always invalidated. In such cases, the state bears the burden of proving (1) a legitimate (i.e., nondiscriminatory or nonprotectionist) end and (2) the lack of any less discriminatory alternatives to effectuate that end.

In contrast to strict scrutiny, a balancing test is employed when the law is facially neutral and the purpose and effects are equally untainted by protectionism or discrimination. Here the challenger must prove that the burden on interstate commerce clearly exceeds the local benefits claimed for the law. I describe each tier in more detail below, especially the discriminatory effects and discriminatory purpose prongs of the DCCD.

2. *Facially discriminatory laws*

Facially discriminatory laws are those that explicitly subject out-of-state commerce to less favorable treatment than in-state or local commerce because of its geographic origins. The Supreme Court treats facially discriminatory laws as "virtually per se illegitimate," and permits them only where the state or local government can demonstrate (1) that their end is legitimate, that is, not motivated by economic protectionism, and (2) that there are no less discriminatory means to effectuate that legitimate end.

Philadelphia v. New Jersey, 437 U.S. 617 (1978), featured the paradigmatic example of a facially discriminatory law: New Jersey law banned the import of out-of-state solid waste. The Court held that the actual purpose of New Jersey's law excluding out-of-state waste (i.e., its "end") was irrelevant, because the means used by New Jersey (erecting a barrier excluding out-of-state products) was equally impermissible. In other words, assuming that, as it claimed, New Jersey was merely trying to conserve its landfill space (as opposed to enriching in-state economic actors at the expense of out-of-state actors), it could not do so by, in the Court's words, "isolating the State from the national economy" and attempting to "saddle those outside the State with the entire burden of slowing the flow of refuse into New Jersey's remaining landfill sites." Thus, although New Jersey's law might not be "protectionist" in the sense of protecting an industry from out-of-state competition, it was inconsistent with the vision of the Framers, who wished to demolish the barriers states had erected against one another's commerce and thus to avoid the political friction often spawned by those barriers.

QUESTION 1. Clean hands. Alabama is home to an environmentally friendly manufacturer of paper products. To encourage environmentally responsible packaging and to promote the consumption of alternatives to environmentally harmful materials, Alabama prohibits the importation of all out-of-state paper products. Assume that Alabama's stated purpose, to preserve the environment, is sincere. Alabama's regulation is likely

A. Unconstitutional, because Alabama does not have a legitimate interest in environmental protection.
B. Unconstitutional, because Alabama could limit the use of all paper products in the state.
C. Constitutional, because the law was not passed to enrich in-state paper producers.
D. Constitutional, because there is no federal law with which Alabama's law conflicts.

ANALYSIS. These are a close approximation of the facts in *Philadelphia v. New Jersey.* Recall that the DCCD applies when Congress has not acted; it is an implicit restriction on state power that does not depend on the existence of affirmative congressional action. Therefore **D** is incorrect.

A and **C** are likewise incorrect, because recall that the DCCD can be violated by ends as well as means. Even if Alabama has a legitimate interest in protecting the environment (which it does), and that motive, not some illegitimate interest in economic protectionism, was behind the law's passage, it still treats out-of-state paper products differently than those produced in-state based on the origins of those products. The law is facially discriminatory and, because, as **B** suggests, Alabama has nondiscriminatory alternatives available to it, the law is likely to be invalidated by a court. Thus, **B** is the correct answer.

QUESTION 2. Something fishy. State biologists in Maine have learned that parasites have been diminishing fish stocks in other states. To preserve its native fish population, which has so far avoided contamination, the legislature passes a law banning the importation of baitfish into the state from other states. Biologists testify that the ban is the only way to ensure that the parasites won't infect native fish stocks, because there is no efficient way to test incoming baitfish for the parasite. Out-of-state baitfish suppliers sue, claiming the Maine law violates the DCCD. A reviewing court should

> **A.** Invalidate the law, because it is facially discriminatory.
> **B.** Invalidate the law, because it is motivated by simple economic protectionism.
> **C.** Uphold the law as a valid exercise of Maine's police power.
> **D.** Uphold the law, because there is no other effective means for the state to protect its wildlife.

ANALYSIS. There are no facts given suggesting that Maine's legislative purpose is in question here. Therefore **B** is incorrect. Moreover, **C** is true, insofar as Maine is exercising its police power here, but that is irrelevant for DCCD purposes. A pure heart does not insulate government regulations from review under the DCCD. As in Question 1, the ends chosen to effectuate that end might be invalid. Based on Question 1, you might have jumped at **A**, but facts are given that make **D** the correct answer.

Remember that although facially discriminatory laws are presumptively invalid, they may survive scrutiny if there is a legitimate interest and no less discriminatory means available to the state to effect that interest. According to the facts, Maine wanted to protect its fish from these harmful parasites, clearly a legitimate state interest; moreover, the facts indicate that there is no efficient way to test for the presence of parasites in any incoming fish, so the state claims that it must bar their importation completely. If that is true, then such a law would likely overcome the presumptive unconstitutionality of facially discriminatory measures.

3. *Facially neutral laws*

Facially discriminatory laws are relatively rare, and are rarely upheld when passed. More common are facially neutral laws alleged to discriminate covertly against interstate commerce, either by the law's actual operation ("effects") or because it was intended to apply only to out-of-state commerce ("purpose"). As we shall see, the presence of either a discriminatory effect or discriminatory purpose is sufficient to trigger the application of strict scrutiny. We begin, though, with the polar opposite of strict or heightened scrutiny—the so-called *Pike* balancing test.

a. Facially neutral laws that are neutral on their face, as well as in purpose and effect. As noted earlier, the Court, dissatisfied with the direct–indirect test, began to "balance" the costs to interstate commerce against the local benefits derived from the law. A lineal descendant of *Cooley*'s national–local distinction, the presumption behind balancing is that if the costs to interstate commerce outweighed the local benefits, then a national rule was needed—and that such a rule had to come from Congress, if at all. The Court has offered a few other reasons in its cases: that laws may function as a drag on interstate commerce, or that states should not be able to subject interstate commercial actors to conflicting and contradictory laws.

In *Southern Pacific Co. v. Arizona*, 325 U.S. 761 (1945), for example, the Court concluded that Arizona's train-length law burdened interstate commerce more than it benefited the workers the law was supposed to benefit, and struck the limit down. On the other hand, in *South Carolina State Hwy. Dept. v. Barnwell Bros.*, 303 U.S. 177 (1938), the Court concluded that the state's interest in maintaining safe roads justified its restriction of the width and weight of commercial trucks operating on South Carolina roadways and outweighed any costs to out-of-state trucking companies.

Today, this balancing is commonly referred to as *Pike* balancing, after *Pike v. Bruce Church, Inc.*, 397 U.S. 137 (1970), the case in which the modern balancing test was famously articulated. According to *Pike* balancing, nondiscriminatory statutes are presumed valid, and will be invalidated only if the burdens on interstate commerce "clearly exceed" what *Pike* calls the "putative local benefits."

Balancing has had its critics. In the past, Justices Hugo Black and William Douglas argued that balancing benefits and burdens of nondiscriminatory laws was a legislative function in which the Court had no business engaging. More recently, Justice Scalia has been a vociferous critic, complaining that asking courts to balance benefits and burdens is asking the impossible, because a common unit of measurement is lacking. It is, he quipped, like asking "whether a particular line is longer than a particular rock is heavy." *Bendix Autolite Corp. v. Midwesco Enterprises, Inc.*, 486 U.S. 888, 897 (1988) (Scalia, J., dissenting).

Costs are often easy enough to compute: Simply calculate the loss to the interstate commercial actor caused by the regulation. "Putative local benefits," however, might be much more difficult to compute. Even if there is a cost associated with, say, a particular safety rule, how can a court compare that to the loss to interstate commerce? To illustrate, assume that a nondiscriminatory regulation R imposes costs on out-of-state commerce equal to $100,000. Assume as well that R is a safety regulation that saves one life per year. It is going to be difficult for a court to weigh those two things. In some ways, the test, as articulated by the Court, takes care of this: Only those costs shown to "clearly exceed" the local benefits will suffice to invalidate a nondiscriminatory law that incidentally burdens interstate commerce. This is a very deferential test that does not usually result in the invalidation of statutes.

When the Court has invoked *Pike* to strike down state or local laws, either the "putative local benefits" are nil; the Court is suspicious of legislative motives, but it lacks the evidence to prove discriminatory motive or clear discriminatory effects; or both. In *Southern Pacific*, for example, the Court was persuaded by the record of the trial court, which demonstrated no safety benefit in shorter trains. In fact the evidence suggested that insofar as shorter trains meant more trains in railyards and on the tracks, the law might produce more accidents. 325 U.S. at 775–778. The Court also seemed concerned about allowing the state leeway to establish a de facto national standard that imposed costs on interstate commercial actors, potentially hampered commerce itself, and deprived other states of the opportunity to enact and enforce their own regimes because of the likelihood that interstate actors will rationally choose to comply with the strictest extant standard. *Id.* at 773–775.

Or consider *Kassel v. Consolidated Freightways, Inc.*, 450 U.S. 662 (1981). There was plenty of evidence in *Kassel* that something other than mere traffic safety was at work in Iowa's law prohibiting tractor-trailers in excess of 60 feet. However, the plurality felt uncomfortable grounding its decision on the (admittedly scanty) evidence that existed. Instead, Justice Powell and the plurality questioned the extent of the safety gains (the "putative local benefits") and noted the costs, both to truckers (in increased costs and lost time) and to surrounding states (in costs to roads and possibly safety because of increased traffic). Despite the verbal formulation of "clearly excessive," reading *Kassel*, it is clear that formulation leaves judges plenty of wiggle room to reach a desired result. Deprived of *Pike* balancing, one might expect to see the Court find more protectionism in purpose or effect lurking behind the facial neutrality of laws like Iowa's.

It is important to stress, however, that seeking to strike down a facially neutral statute when there is no strong evidence of protectionist purpose or effects is a tough row to hoe. It will, at a minimum, require the compilation of an extensive factual record and convincing a trial court to adopt those facts in its findings.

QUESTION 3. Up in smoke. Concerned about the health risks associated with smoking, and the attendant costs to the state providing care to smokers, Connecticut has taken the extraordinary step of prohibiting the sale of all tobacco products in the state. Connecticut has a tiny cigar industry, but otherwise produces no tobacco products. Out-of-state tobacco companies sue, claiming the law violates the DCCD. They note that, as a result of the law, they potentially stand to lose "millions" of dollars in revenue each year from tobacco sales. The state argues that it spends $1.2 million per year on "tobacco-caused" health care. Other costs include losses in productivity and absenteeism caused by smoking and smoking-related illnesses, which the state estimates at $1.5 million per year. What should a reviewing court do?

A. Invalidate the law, because the burden on interstate commerce exceeds the putative local benefits.
B. Sustain the law, because it is facially neutral.
C. Invalidate the law, because it discriminates against interstate commerce.
D. Sustain the law, because the burden on interstate commerce does not clearly exceed the benefits to the state.

ANALYSIS.   Unlike the laws in the preceding questions, Connecticut's law does not differentiate between in-state and out-of-state tobacco. Sales of all tobacco products are prohibited. Moreover, unlike some questions that follow, it is not the case that, although facially neutral, the effects of the law fall entirely or nearly entirely on out-of-state commerce. There is some in-state cigar-making. Therefore, **C** is incorrect.

However, **B** is not a sufficient condition for upholding a state or local law under the DCCD. Even-handed statutes—even those lacking discriminatory purposes or effects (discussed later)—can be invalidated if they do not satisfy *Pike* balancing. The facts do indicate the possibility that out-of-state tobacco companies will lose as much or more than Connecticut might save by avoiding smoking-related costs (assuming that no one will buy tobacco products out of state and use them in Connecticut), so you might have found yourself attracted to **A**, but the inquiry is not whether the burdens *exceed* the local benefits, it is whether the benefits are *clearly exceeded* by the burden on interstate commerce.

Therefore, **D** is the better answer. The benefits to Connecticut are not zero; the state will likely save money by banning the sale of tobacco products. The companies argue they stand to lose "millions," but they don't specify an amount. *Pike* balancing is a deferential test. The benefit of the doubt will go to the state where there is ambiguity. Because the facts do not give evidence suggesting that costs "clearly exceed" the (real) benefits to Connecticut, a reviewing court would likely uphold the law.

––––––––––––––

The Supreme Court has repeatedly held that facially neutral statutes that have discriminatory effects or are passed with the purpose of discriminating against interstate commerce are subject to the same scrutiny as a facially discriminatory statute. *Bacchus Imports, Ltd. v. Dias*, 468 U.S. 268, 270 (1984); *Minnesota v. Clover Leaf Creamery Co.*, 449 U.S. 456, 471, n.15 (1981). The difficulty is that the Court has not been clear what effects are discriminatory or how one ascertains a discriminatory purpose. Thus, with a facially neutral statute, it is often difficult to predict when a reviewing court will employ *Pike* balancing as opposed to strict scrutiny. Some generalizations are possible, however.[2]

b. Facially neutral statutes motivated by a discriminatory purpose. If you can demonstrate that a state or local law was passed with the intent to disadvantage out-of-state goods or economic actors, or was designed to benefit in-state goods and actors (usually at the expense of those from out of state), that should be enough to trigger strict scrutiny. I say "should," because the Supreme Court is sometimes reluctant to rely solely on legislative purpose to

––––––––––––––

2. The following discussion borrows from Brannon P. Denning & Rachel M. Lary, *Retail Store Size-Capping Ordinances and the Dormant Commerce Clause Doctrine*, 37 Urban Law. 907, 922–925, 933–936 (2005).

strike down a suspect state law, as are some lower courts. Nevertheless, cases like *H.P. Hood & Sons v. DuMond*, 336 U.S. 525 (1949) (invalidating decision to deny license to milk producer on ground it would promote "destructive competition"), and *Bacchus Imports v. Dias*, 468 U.S. 268 (1984) (striking down tax exemption for locally produced alcohol where purpose was to encourage production and consumption of that alcohol), show that this is still a viable branch of the DCCD.

The Court has never been clear how one proves purpose. Many of the Court's purpose cases involve laws or ordinances that, although facially neutral, were drafted with protectionist purposes stated in the body of the law itself. Assume that the legislature was not that maladroit. Where might you look to prove the presence of protectionist purpose? One possibility is that the statute itself might recite what could be construed as a protectionist or discriminatory purpose, or that such a purpose might be offered by the state as a justification. But this would likely be as rare as a state drafting a facially discriminatory statute. Lower courts, therefore, have drawn on the Court's doctrine in other areas to supply an answer.

After *Washington v. Davis*, 426 U.S. 229 (1976), held that disparate impact without evidence of discriminatory intent was insufficient to establish a racial discrimination claim under the Fourteenth Amendment, the Court offered some guidance on proving discriminatory purpose. "[W]ithout purporting to be exhaustive," the Court summarized "subjects of proper inquiry in determining whether racially discriminatory intent existed": (1) effects on a particular group; (2) the historical background of the decision, "particularly if it reveals a series of official actions taken for invidious purposes"; (3) the "specific sequence of events leading up to the challenged decision"; (4) procedural or substantive departures from the "normal . . . sequence" especially if substantive "factors usually considered important by the decisionmaker strongly favor a decision contrary to the one reached"; and (5) "[t]he legislative or administrative history . . . especially where there are contemporary statements by members of the decisionmaking body, minutes of its meetings, or reports." *Village of Arlington Heights v. Metropolitan Housing Development Corp.*, 429 U.S. 252, 265–268 (1977).

A number of lower courts have urged adopting these criteria in DCCD cases. For example, the Eighth Circuit has approved the use of

> direct and indirect evidence to determine whether a state adopted a statute with a discriminatory purpose. This evidence includes (1) statements by lawmakers . . . (2) the sequence of events leading up to the statute's adoption, including irregularities in the procedures used to adopt the law . . . (3) the State's consistent pattern of "disparately impacting members of a particular class of persons," . . . (4) the statute's historical background, including "any history of discrimination by the [state]," and (5) the statute's use of highly ineffective means to promote the legitimate interest asserted by the state. . . .

The Fourth Circuit has similarly endorsed

[s]everal factors . . . as probative of whether a decisionmaking body was motivated by a discriminatory intent, including: (1) evidence of a "consistent pat-
tern" of actions by the decisionmaking body disparately impacting members
of a particular class of persons; (2) historical background of the decision,
which may take into account any history of discrimination by the decisionmaking body or the jurisdiction it represents; (3) the specific sequence of
events leading up to the particular decision being challenged, including any
significant departures from normal procedures; and (4) contemporary statements by decisionmakers on the record or in minutes of their meetings.

Smithfield Foods, Inc. v. Miller, 367 F.3d 1061, 1065 (8th Cir. 2004); *Waste
Management Holdings, Inc. v. Gilmore*, 252 F.3d 316, 336 (4th Cir. 2001).

It stands to reason that, at a minimum, plaintiffs should be able to intro-
duce, as evidence of purpose, (1) the historical background of the decision to
enact the law; (2) the sequence of events leading up to the passage of a law or
ordinance that is suggestive of impermissible protectionism, like the timing of
the law or the use of irregular procedures; (3) the legislative or administrative
history of the law or ordinance, including statements of purpose appearing on
the face of the statute or that are offered in support of the law; and (4) any gap
between means and ends, evidenced by, for example, exemptions that dispro-
portionately benefit existing, in-state commercial interests.

The background and the sequence of an ordinance's enactment are helpful to establish the context in which the bill was being considered. Further, if
the ordinance was enacted using extraordinary measures, or without the usual
debate accompanying legislation, that should be admissible to show that the
legislative body might have been trying to hide something.

Without a doubt, the most useful information will come from the legislative history (including statements from supporters and opponents — especially those who are voting on the law) — and from the apparent (or actual)
operation of the bill itself. The more difficult problem comes in evaluating the
comments of supporters (possibly members of the public) who express impermissible motives in urging passage. These, too, should be admissible, especially
if no one voting for the measure contradicts or challenges those impermissible
motives; however, such statements should carry less weight than those made
by legislators.

Finally, if legitimate purposes are behind a law, then the law should not
contain particular exemptions of persons or entities that would otherwise be
covered by it. Such exemptions should lead a court to question the legitimacy
of the putative purpose, especially (in the DCCD context) if the exemptions
manage to carve out most or all of the local businesses that would otherwise
be affected, thus possibly rendering the regulated class merely a proxy for out-
of-state commercial actors or goods.

In *Kassel v. Consolidated Freightways, Inc.*, 450 U.S. 662 (1981), for example, the Court invalidated an Iowa law prohibiting tractor-trailers in excess of
60 feet. Although the plurality ultimately decided the case under a balancing

analysis, it referred to numerous parochial exceptions in the statute that seemed to call into question the sincerity of the state's asserted interest in safety. The Iowa statute permitted 60-foot doubles (common nowhere but in Iowa), farm equipment, mobile homes, and trucks hauling livestock. The law also permitted border cities in Iowa to adopt the length standards of adjoining states. *Id.* at 665–666. The law also allowed Iowa truck manufacturers to ship 70-foot trucks and permitted oversized mobile homes to be moved through the state if they were being moved from a point in Iowa or delivered to an Iowa buyer. *Id.* at 666. The governor had also vetoed a bill that would have permitted 65-foot doubles, stating that it would primarily benefit out-of-state trucking firms whose trucks passed through Iowa. *Id.* at 666 n.6.

QUESTION 4. How do you like them apples?   The North Carolina Department of Agriculture issued a regulation banning the use of state grades on closed containers of apples sold in the state. The regulation specified that the only grade that could be used was the grade approved by the United States Department of Agriculture. Apple growers in Washington objected to this regulation, noting that they had spent a considerable amount of money developing a grading system acknowledged by those in the industry as being superior to the federal grading system. North Carolina, which also produces apples for sale, has no state grading system. In their lawsuit, the Washington apple growers allege the regulation was motivated by a discriminatory purpose. Which of the following would *not* be helpful in demonstrating discriminatory purpose?

A. A preamble to the legislation reciting that the purpose of the bill was to ensure consumers were not confused by a proliferation of grading systems.

B. A letter from a member of the North Carolina apple growers' association to the state agriculture commissioner complaining of competition from out-of-state apples, specifically mentioning Washington, and asking for "help."

C. The fact that the law does not impact North Carolina apples because the state has no state grading system.

D. The regulation was issued as an "emergency" regulation without the usual notice-and-comment period required by the state's administrative procedure act.

ANALYSIS.   To the extent that purpose makes a difference in constitutional doctrine, the Court usually permits evidence from which one might infer an improper purpose, as it is often difficult to demonstrate directly. In the DCCD, the improper purpose would be anything that smacked of protectionism or discrimination against out-of-state commerce. Thus, **B** would be useful information, because it suggests that the regulation was prompted by concerns of local apple growers that they were having difficulty competing against their out-of-state competitors.

C would be useful as well. Although a facially neutral regulation whose impact is felt by out-of-state commerce only is often regarded as proof of the discriminatory effects of the law, the effects can also raise questions about the purpose as well. A similar situation might arise if the law was facially neutral, covering in-state and out-of-state products alike, but containing numerous exemptions that coincidently shielded local products from the impact of the law. Similarly, short-circuiting the ordinary means of passing laws might raise suspicions that something untoward was motivating the departure from normal procedures. Therefore, **D** would be helpful as well.

That leaves **A**, which is not helpful in establishing a discriminatory purpose, because the purpose stated on the face of the law—consumer protection—is a valid exercise of the state's police power and does not suggest unconstitutional economic protectionism or discrimination against interstate commerce.

c. Facially neutral statutes with discriminatory effects. A statute might be facially neutral, but nevertheless violate the DCCD because of the way in which the statute operates in fact—its effects can discriminate against out-of-state commerce or commercial actors. If that is shown, then strict scrutiny applies: The law will be upheld only if states can demonstrate a legitimate purpose unrelated to protectionism or discrimination, and demonstrate that to effectuate that purpose no less discriminatory means are available. Here is another doctrine puzzle, though: Which effects count when assessing a discriminatory-effects claim under the DCCD? The Supreme Court has not provided a clear answer.

The Court's leading discriminatory-effects cases lend themselves to some generalizations, however. The clearest cases involve statutes with effects that insulate one locality's economic actors from competition by out-of-state economic actors. Protectionism, however, can take many forms, including, but not limited to: (1) effectively barring the import of out-of-state goods, or barring their sale once imported; (2) acting to raise the cost of doing business in a state for out-of-state competitors, which costs are not also borne by in-state actors; (3) stripping competitive advantages from out-of-state competitors; (4) otherwise leveling the playing field to the benefit of in-state economic actors; or (5) subsidizing in-state actors through mechanisms that are funded entirely (or largely) by out-of-state economic actors.

In the leading discriminatory effects case, *Hunt v. Washington State Apple Advertisers Commission,* 432 U.S. 333 (1977), the Court struck down a North Carolina regulation prohibiting the use of state grades on closed containers of apples sold in the state. Because North Carolina had no grading system similar to the Washington grading system regarded as superior even to that of the

USDA, the impact of the regulation fell exclusively on out-of-state apples in general and Washington apples in particular. Because the containers in which apples were shipped were preprinted, Washington growers were subject to costs that local growers did not have to bear. Although facially neutral, the Court had little trouble concluding that the "practical effect" of the regulation was to discriminate against Washington apples. *Id.* at 350.

"The first, and most obvious, [effect]," the Court wrote, "is the statute's consequence of raising the costs of doing business in the North Carolina market for Washington apple growers and dealers while leaving those of their North Carolina counterparts unaffected. . . . " *Id.* at 350–351. Second, the Court concluded that the regulation tended to "strip[] away from the Washington apple industry the competitive and economic advantages it has earned for itself through its expensive inspection and grading system," thus having "a leveling effect which insidiously operates to the advantage of the local apple producers." *Id.* at 351. At best, the Court concluded, Washington apples are deprived of a hard-earned "market premium," and at worst, the regulation functioned as an "embargo" against the apples. *Id.* at 352. *See also Dean Milk Co. v. Madison,* 340 U.S. 349 (1951) (invalidating local ordinance prohibiting sale of milk not pasteurized within five miles of city square; "practical effect" of ordinance was to "exclude[] from distribution . . . wholesome milk produced and pasteurized in Illinois" for purely geographic reasons when less discriminatory means available to safeguard city's interests).

The year after *Hunt,* however, the Court decided *Exxon Corp. v. Governor of Maryland,* 437 U.S. 117 (1978), and upheld a Maryland statute prohibiting oil producers and refiners from owning and operating retail gas stations. Maryland had no in-state petroleum producers or refiners, so the impact of the law fell entirely on out-of-state interests. Meanwhile the beneficiaries of the law were independent gas stations, owned largely by Maryland citizens who had complained they were unable to secure access to gasoline during times of shortage. Nevertheless, the Court rejected Exxon's discriminatory effects claim. The Court noted that nothing barred out-of-state residents from opening up independent gas stations to compete with those run by in-state residents. *Id.* at 126. Further, it concluded that because the statute had no likely effect on the volume of goods coming into the state, it was not likely to enable the independent retailers to assume a larger market share than they would have absent the regulation. In a cryptic, but much-quoted, line later in the opinion, the Court wrote that the DCCD "protects the interstate market, not particular interstate firms, from prohibitive or burdensome regulations." *Id.* at 127–128.

Exxon has puzzled judges and scholars alike, because instead of a straightforward application of *Hunt,* it seems to create additional requirements. For example, in *Hunt,* there was no discussion of whether the regulation in North Carolina altered or disrupted the flow of apples into the state. Out-of-state residents were free to sell apples in North Carolina, as long as they marketed them using the federal grade or no grade at all.

For some commentators, *Exxon* can be explained on the ground that the Court was satisfied that no protectionist purpose motivated the passage of the statute. According to these scholars, because the Court is concerned only with smoking out and eliminating protectionist purpose, any law lacking such a purpose will be upheld. This assumes, contrary to what the Court has said, that discriminatory effects alone are not sufficient to invalidate a state law.

Another explanation is that the Court saw no reason to get involved because of the presence of powerful interests (oil companies in *Exxon*) that could be counted on to vigorously oppose any sort of other in-state interest group rent-seeking. This is possible, but there is no hint of it in the Court's opinion.

A third possibility is that *Exxon* means that discriminatory effects claims can only be brought successfully where the burdens on the out-of-state economic actor are not borne by an in-state competitor, or where the market share lost as a result of the regulation inures to the benefit of the in-state competitor. This is probably the best reading of *Exxon*. The Court seemed to focus on the lack of harm to similarly situated out-of-state entities in upholding the state laws. The Maryland law in *Exxon* might have disadvantaged or discriminated against gas stations owned by oil producers and refiners in favor of independently owned gas stations, owned primarily by in-staters, but it did not keep out-of-state independently owned gas stations from competing with existing stations in Maryland. Nor did it shrink the market for out-of-state goods, leaving a larger share of the market for in-state goods. *Exxon* serves as a sort of "wild card" in discriminatory effects cases, making their outcomes difficult to predict. The ambiguity, however, makes this fertile exam material! Lucky you.

Finally, constitutionally unobjectionable laws can be combined, or "linked" in a way that violates the DCCD. Consider the case of *West Lynn Creamery v. Healy*, 512 U.S. 186 (1994), in which Massachusetts passed a series of measures to bolster the state's troubled dairy farmers. One measure imposed a tax on sales of milk by milk dealers. The tax was facially neutral, applying regardless of the origin of the milk. The revenue from that tax went into a special fund created by the state to subsidize dairy farmers in the state. The combination of the measures meant that in-state dairy farmers would often get a rebate (and then some) on the taxes paid on the milk sales; out-of-state milk dealers, however, were not eligible for the cash subsidies. The Court concluded that the "undisputed effect [is] to enable higher cost Massachusetts dairy farmers to compete with lower cost dairy farmers in other States. . . . " *Id.* at 194.

QUESTION 5. Car wars. Texas requires car dealers to be licensed by the state. Under the state licensing statute, "automobile manufacturers" are not eligible to become licensed car dealers in the state. Texas has no automobile manufacturers located in the state. Car manufacturers located in Michigan have begun to experiment with selling certified used cars over the Internet. Under this sales model, leased automobiles that have been turned back in, fleet cars, and other quality, low-mileage cars are put through a series of factory-approved checks and then resold as used, but with extended warranties. Customers could shop online, then have a car they selected delivered to a local dealer in their area. The dealer would be paid a fee by the manufacturer for service and handling, but the customer would otherwise not have to visit the local dealership until the car was delivered, because financing, too, would be handled online. Texas law, though, prohibits such sales from being made to Texas residents because the manufacturers do not—and cannot—possess a car dealer's license. Car manufacturers sue, alleging that the law has discriminatory effects. Which of the following would be the strongest argument in support of their claim?

A. That Texas has no automobile manufacturers located in the state.
B. That the effects of the statute fall solely on out-of-state manufacturers.
C. That the effect of the law would be to increase market share in used cars for in-state used car dealers.
D. That it reduces competition among used car dealers in Texas, resulting in higher prices for consumers.

ANALYSIS. *Exxon* seems to hold that discriminatory effects are not present merely because a state law's regulatory burden falls on out-of-state firms. Therefore, **B** is not going to be enough to sustain a discriminatory effects challenge. Moreover, although the fact that the state has no automobile manufacturers of its own might make it seem as if the intent is to benefit in-state businesses (Texas used car dealers) at the expense of the out-of-state manufacturers, *Exxon* rejected an analogous argument that Maryland's law benefited in-state independent retail gas station operators at the expense of out-of-state petroleum producers and refiners. So **A** is not going to be helpful to their claim, either.

Because the DCCD is sometimes described in terms of creating or preserving a "free trade" zone free among the states, you might have been tempted to answer **D**. But whether a state's regulations result in higher prices or reduced competition among its own citizens is of no consequence to the DCCD, unless those come about as a result of discrimination against interstate commerce. That leaves **C**, which is the best answer. If the automobile manufacturers could demonstrate that, as a result of their being excluded from selling cars in the state, the market share for cars claimed by in-state dealers would increase, that would be helpful in establishing their claim because it appears that the in-state competitors are benefiting to the detriment of the out-of-state manufacturers as a result of the law. On the other hand, the same might have been said about the independent retail gas stations in *Exxon*.

4. Exceptions to the DCCD

a. Congressional consent The DCCD is different from other doctrines in constitutional law because Congress retains the power (through its affirmative commerce power, discussed in Chapter 4) to overrule the Court and declare a state law or practice permissible despite the DCCD. Thus, the Court's DCCD decisions are provisional; loser states can lobby Congress to permit regulation — even discriminatory legislation — in a particular area free from the strictures of the DCCD. Congress has even done this on occasion. *See, e.g., Prudential Ins. Co. v. Benjamin,* 328 U.S. 408 (1946) (upholding the McCarran–Ferguson Act, which disabled the DCCD as to state regulation of the "business of insurance").

The provisional nature of DCCD decisions might, in small measure, redeem the "super-legislature" aspect of balancing benefits and burdens in the absence of evidence of discrimination or protectionism. The Court has indicated, however, that Congress must clearly and unambiguously indicate its intention to disable the DCCD, although it says that Congress need not do so according to any particular verbal formula. *See, e.g., South-Central Timber Development Co. v. Wunnicke,* 467 U.S. 82, 91–92 (1984). Congressional consent, or "redelegation" as it is sometimes called, is the flip side of Congress's power to preempt conflicting state legislation, discussed later.

b. The market-participant exception. The market-participant exception (MPE) operates as an exception to the DCCD for state activity that mimics the actions of private economic actors in a particular market. When the state is buying or selling goods or services using the money of its taxpayer-citizens, the MPE permits the state to favor in-state goods or actors in ways that the DCCD would otherwise prohibit. The rationale is that states ought to have some leeway to make choices that private market participants would be free to make when deciding how to spend their own money. For example, if a state wishes to provide cash subsidies to struggling in-state industries only, it may do so notwithstanding the DCCD. The theory is that, like a private market participant, a state is free to spend its own money to buy what it wishes (or to sell what it makes at whatever price it chooses). When it spends its money, the state does not have to favor in-state and out-of-state residents equally, because the bulk of the money likely came from the tax revenues of the former.

In *Reeves v. Stake,* 447 U.S. 429 (1980), for example, South Dakota had built, at state expense, a cement factory. Its policy had been to sell the cement to anyone willing to buy it. During a cement shortage, however, the state decided to supply in-state buyers first, leaving the remainder (if any) for out-of-state purchase on a first-come, first-served basis. Several out-of-state companies that relied on the South Dakota cement sued, claiming that the regulation was facially discriminatory.

The Court held that South Dakota could choose to sell cement from the state-owned cement plant only to South Dakotans because it is functioning as a participant in the market for cement, as opposed to a "market regulator";

that is, it was not telling privately owned cement companies to sell only to South Dakotans during times of shortage. Perhaps a more familiar example is that of in-state tuition. All state-run universities have lower tuition for in-state students than for those who come from out of state. States could be said to be participating in the market for students,[3] and in doing so have decided to subsidize the education of their own students to a greater degree than those coming from out of state.

Note, too, that to take advantage of the MPE, the state must actually be mimicking a private market participant. The state may not, for example, participate in a particular market by offering discriminatory tax credits to in-state businesses, even where the tax credits are economically identical to a cash subsidy. Using the tax code in this way, the Court has held, is a "primeval government activity" and is not available to private market participants. *New Energy Co. v. Limbach,* 486 U.S. 269, 277 (1988).

Although defining "participation" as opposed to "regulation" is relatively easy, a more difficult question concerns defining the "market" in which the state is participating. In *South-Central Timber v. Wunnicke,* 467 U.S. 82 (1984), for example, the State of Alaska, which conditioned the sale of state-owned timber on its being processed in the state prior to export, argued that it was participating not in the market for timber per se, but in the market for processed timber. The problem with the state's argument was that it was not involved in actual timber processing in any way. *Id.* at 98. The Court accepted South-Central Timber's argument that the state was a participant in the timber market only and was using its position there to try to benefit the local processing market through what amounted to regulation.

South-Central Timber thus gave birth to an "exception" to the MPE. The Court labeled the local-processing requirement Alaska tried to impose on the sale of its timber an impermissible "downstream" restriction. As Justice White's plurality opinion put it: "The limit of the [MPE] must be that it allows the State to impose burdens on interstate commerce within the market in which it is a participant, but allows it to go no further. The State may not impose conditions, whether by statute, regulation, or contract, that have a substantial regulatory effect outside of that particular market." *Id.* at 97. If not limited in this way, White argued, "the doctrine has the potential of swallowing up the rule." *Id.* at 97–98. The Court went on to explain that its drawing the line at downstream restrictions makes sense because "downstream restrictions have a greater regulatory effect than do limitations on the immediate transaction. Instead of merely choosing its own trading partners, the State is attempting to govern the private, separate economic relationships of its trading partners; . . . it restricts the post-purchase activity of the purchaser, rather than merely the purchasing activity." *Id.* at 99.

---

3. Assume that tuition charged out-of-state students by state colleges and universities "substantially affects" interstate commerce, thus implicating the DCCD at all.

In *White v. Massachusetts Council of Construction Employees,* 460 U.S. 204 (1983), the Court suggested an "exception" to the downstream restrictions exception in public contracting cases. The Mayor of Boston issued an order requiring that half of crews working on public works projects funded with city money be residents of the city. The order applied not only to contractors who were in privity of contract with the city, but to their subcontractors as well. The Court brushed aside a DCCD challenge holding that the MPE applied, even to the subcontractors, because everyone was, in a sense, "working for the city."

QUESTION 6. Bookmaking. Alabama passed a statute mandating that all printing contracts paid for by state money be bid competitively. A year later, the act is amended; the amendment creates an exception to the prior year's act. If an in-state printing company's bid is within 20 percent of the lowest bidder's bid, and the low bidder is an out-of-state company, the Alabama printer is automatically awarded the contract, despite not being the low bidder. When the University of Alabama's yearbook printing contract comes up for a bid, LaGrange Printing Co., a Georgia company, is the lowest bidder. However, Phenix City Printing, an Alabama company, enters a bid that is only 18 percent higher than LaGrange Printing Co., thus winning the contract. LaGrange Printing sues, alleging that the Alabama law violates the DCCD. What should a reviewing trial court do?

A. Uphold the law, because Alabama is not acting as a market regulator.
B. Strike down the law, unless Alabama can demonstrate a nonprotectionist governmental interest and the lack of less discriminatory means to achieve its interest.
C. Strike down the law, because Alabama's statute imposes an impermissible downstream regulation.
D. Uphold the law, because conditions imposed on a government contract are insulated from DCCD review.

ANALYSIS.   First, if you spotted that the amendment to the Alabama law was facially discriminatory, you're getting the hang of the DCCD. Therefore, you might have been tempted to apply strict or heightened scrutiny, and choose **B**. However, remember that the MPE is an exception to the DCCD. Therefore, you have to consider carefully the other choices.

If you read closely, you would not choose **D**, because *South-Central Timber* stands for the proposition that certain conditions on government contracts are not covered by the MPE. "Downstream" restrictions that attempt to exert control outside the market in which the state is participating, the Court has held, are not covered by the MPE. Here, however, Alabama has not attempted to impose any restrictions beyond the market—printing services—in which it has chosen to participate. The state is only requiring that any state money used to buy services in that market go to in-state printing companies when it is not dramatically more expensive to do so. The statute is discriminatory to be sure, but it does not attempt to impose any restrictions beyond that particular market. Therefore **C** is not correct. This leaves **A**, which is the best answer, because Alabama is simply exercising its discretion in its choice of vendors, and is willing to pay a little more to support local businesses, as any consumer would be entitled to do.

QUESTION 7. A hard(ened) bargain.   Assume that in addition to the "South Dakotans-first" policy on the part of the state cement plant in *Reeves v. Stake,* it also forbade the resale of cement by South Dakotans to out-of-state residents. Would this State's actions still be covered by the MPE?

A. Yes, because the state is simply imposing conditions as an incident to the sale.

B. Yes, because it does not impose restrictions outside the market.

C. No, because it represents an impediment to interstate commerce.

D. No, because the ban on resale is a downstream restriction.

ANALYSIS.   This is a tougher question. Remember, the key rationale for the MPE is the Court's feeling that when spending their (or their taxpayers') money, states ought to be free to act in ways private purchasers may act when buying or selling goods. Therefore, behavior that doesn't look like something a private person could or would do should make you take a second look. **A** is incorrect, because *South-Central Timber* made clear that states were not free under the MPE to impose any conditions they wished on transactions in which it was the buyer or seller of goods or services. **C** is a bit of a red herring: All laws to which the MPE might apply represent impediments to interstate commerce — in fact, they are often facially discriminatory laws that would almost certainly be struck down absent the availability of the MPE.

That leaves **B** and **D**. Here, it is important to define the market or markets, as the case may be. South Dakota is seeking to participate in one market — the sale of cement. As with many products, there is often a secondary market or an aftermarket — the resale of cement to persons ineligible to buy it from the state-owned plant. It is this secondary market that South Dakota is seeking to stifle. The problem is that private sellers generally don't care what happens to the goods once they are sold to the buyer. If the buyer wishes to turn around and sell them to a third party (usually at a profit), that usually means little to the initial seller. Here, however, South Dakota is trying to prevent that secondary market from emerging. As in *South-Central Timber,* the ban on resale looks less like market participation and more like market regulation. Therefore, of the two remaining answers, **D** is the best. Incidentally, the Court in *Reeves* specifically mentioned the lack of any ban on resale in support of its decision. *Reeves,* 447 U.S. at 777 n.17.

c. Discrimination in favor of public entities. The Court may be in the process of creating another exception to the DCCD (or at least a portion of it), although the precise rationale for and scope of the exception remains unclear as of this writing. In 1994, the Court invalidated a law requiring that all garbage collected in Clarkstown, New York, be disposed of at a processing facility built by a private company that had agreed to sell it to the city for a nominal price after the company had recouped its costs plus a profit. A majority of the Court viewed this "flow control" ordinance no differently than any other facially discriminatory law requiring local processing of some good (here, garbage) to benefit local interests (here, the local garbage processing facility), and struck it down. *C&A Carbone, Inc. v. Clarkstown,* 511 U.S. 383 (1994).

In *United Haulers Association, Inc. v. Oneida-Herkimer Solid Waste Management Authority,* 127 S. Ct. 1786 (2007), the Court was presented with a similar set of facts, but with one important difference: Instead of being privately owned, the waste processing facility in *United Haulers* was publicly owned.

Chief Justice Roberts first noted that the significance of the private–public distinction was left open by the *Carbone* Court. 127 S. Ct. at 1793. The Court then cited "[c]ompelling reasons" for its holding that flow control ordinances, like the Authority's "do not discriminate against interstate commerce for purpose of the dormant Commerce Clause": (1) that private and public entities were not similarly situated, (2) that waste collection and disposal was a traditional governmental function, and (3) that the effect of the flow control ordinance "is likely to fall upon the very people who voted for the laws." 127 S. Ct. at 1795, 1796, 1797.

The Court noted that "States and municipalities are not private businesses—far from it. Unlike private enterprise, government is vested with the responsibility of protecting the health, safety, and welfare of its citizens." Thus, "it does not make sense to regard laws favoring local government and laws favoring private industry with equal skepticism" because the former are not likely to be motivated by "simple economic protectionism." The Chief Justice noted that the motive here was not to enrich local business, but rather to force residents to internalize the cost of the waste they generated. State and local governments ought to be able to act without "federal courts . . . decid[ing] what activities are appropriate for [them] to undertake, and what activities must be the province of private market competition." 127 S. Ct. at 1795–1796.

Further, the Chief Justice wrote that the Court "should be particularly hesitant to interfere with the Counties' efforts under the guide of the Commerce Clause" because waste disposal has been traditionally handled by local governments. Finally, he argued that the need for judicial intervention here is reduced because of the availability of political safeguards: "Here, the citizens and businesses of the Counties bear the costs of the ordinances. There is no reason to step in and hand local businesses a victory they could not obtain through the political process." 127 S. Ct. at 1795–1796.

The Court then applied *Pike* balancing. Even assuming that there was a burden on interstate commerce, the Court concluded the ordinance did not "clearly exceed" the health and environmental benefits that it produced for the counties' citizens. 127 S. Ct. at 1798.

The next term, the Court extended *United Haulers,* holding that a Kentucky income tax exemption for income derived from in-state, but not out-of-state bonds, was not "discrimination" for DCCD purposes. *Dept. Rev. v. Davis,* 128 S. Ct. 1801 (2008). Because issuing bonds to fund public works was as much a traditional governmental function as garbage collection, the majority concluded that "[i]t follows *a fortiori* from *United Haulers* that Kentucky must prevail." 128 S. Ct. at 1810. "Just like the ordinances in [*United Haulers*]," the Court wrote, "Kentucky's tax exemption favors a traditional governmental function without any differential treatment favoring local entities over substantially similar out-of-state interests." *Id.* at 1811. Because proceeds from the state's bonds were used to fund projects in Kentucky, and other states' bonds and those issued by private entities were not, the two groups of bonds (Kentucky and non-Kentucky) were fundamentally different.

One thing to note about the public entities exception, as opposed to the market-participant exception (MPE) is that the former seems to be an exception from the antidiscrimination principle only. Note that the Court in both *United Haulers* and *Davis* applied *Pike* balancing to the challenged laws. The *Pike* analysis was rather perfunctory, however, and the *Davis* Court openly questioned whether it was appropriate given that the Court does not apply *Pike* if it determines the MPE applies.

QUESTION 8. I would gladly pay you Tuesday for a hamburger today. Delighted with the success of the Oneida-Herkimer Solid Waste Authority, Herkimer County decides to create a number of county-owned hamburger stands called "Herki-burger Hamburger Heaven." To ensure their success, the county then requires that all hamburgers be purchased at these county-owned stands. No other hamburger restaurants are permitted in Herkimer County. An out-of-state owner of a competing private hamburger franchise wishes to challenge the ordinance. Which of the following would be the strongest argument against the constitutionality of the hamburger stand?

A. The ordinance is facially discriminatory.
B. Herkimer County is not engaged in a traditional governmental function.
C. Herkimer County is not a market participant.
D. The ordinance affects in-state and out-of-state hamburger stands equally.

ANALYSIS.   As strange as these facts might seem, they come from a question put by one of the Justices at oral argument! Here we have the same facts as *United Haulers,* but with hamburgers instead of garbage collection and disposal. Although **A** is true, it is not helpful here, because the point is that some exceptions—the market-participant exception and *United Haulers'* "public entities" exception—*permit* state and local governments to enact discriminatory laws.

The exception created by *United Haulers* is separate from, and different than the market-participant exception, so **C** is not correct. (In any event, Herkimer is doing more than simply *participating* in the market for hamburgers; it is monopolizing it. The use of governmental power to exclude competitors is not the sort of power ordinarily available to private market participants.) Further, although **D** is true, that actually functions here as an argument in favor of the ordinance's constitutionality, according to *United Haulers,* which pointed out that the flow control ordinance in that case made no distinction between in-state and out-of-state *private* waste haulers. Here, too, no distinction is made between in-state and out-of-state private hamburger stands.

That leaves **B**. It's not clear how much of *United Haulers* hinges on the Court's characterization of garbage hauling as a traditional governmental function. And as we saw in Chapter 4's discussion of *Usery,* the Court has in the past abandoned attempts to define such activities. But one might argue that establishing monopolies to supply things like hamburgers (as opposed to supplying electricity or even garbage collection) is not "traditional" and should therefore be limited. In any event, it is the strongest argument among the choices.

5.   DCCD limits on state and local taxation

Special rules apply to state and local taxes on interstate and foreign commerce. Not so long ago, a good deal of the required constitutional law class was devoted to this issue. In recent years, however, coverage of the DCCD's limits on state and local taxing power has all but disappeared from casebooks and from most constitutional law courses in favor of specialized classes on state and local taxation. Without going into too much detail, I did want to include a few words about the DCCD in this area for the sake of completeness.

After years of confused and confusing opinions, the Court in *Complete Auto Transit v. Brady,* 430 U.S. 274 (1977), listed a few features that would render a tax vulnerable under the DCCD. In very short order, this was recast as a "test," which the Court has largely followed ever since. In a recent case, the Court described the *Complete Auto* test in the following way:

> In *Complete Auto* . . . we explicitly returned to our prior decisions that have sustained a tax against Commerce Clause challenge when [1] the tax is applied to an activity with a substantial nexus with the taxing State, [2] is fairly apportioned, [3] does not discriminate against interstate commerce, and [4] is fairly related to the services provided by the State.

Oklahoma Tax Comm'n v. Jefferson Lines, Inc., 514 U.S. 175, 183 (1995) (quoting *Complete Auto*).

The antidiscrimination prong of *Complete Auto* works as it does in nontax DCCD cases. Discrimination can be on the face of the tax, or in its purposes or effects. *See, e.g., South Central Bell Tel. Co. v. Alabama*, 526 U.S. 160 (1999). The other requirements have, though, no precise counterparts in nontax cases.

a. Nexus. You probably remember from civil procedure that to exercise jurisdiction over those residing outside of a state, the Due Process Clause of the Fourteenth Amendment requires there to be certain "minimum contacts" between the state and the person or thing over which the state is attempting to exercise its power. Similarly, the DCCD requires that states satisfy a certain standard before they are able to exercise their power to tax over someone or something that exists outside the taxing state's physical boundaries. However, the Court has stated that the DCCD demands a higher standard than "minimum contacts"; in some cases the Court requires a physical presence in the taxing state before it can exercise power. *See Quill Corp. v. North Dakota*, 504 U.S. 298 (1992).

b. Fair apportionment. At one point in our history, the Court interpreted the DCCD to prohibit states from taxing interstate commerce altogether. *See, e.g., Leloup v. Mobile*, 127 U.S. 640, 468 (1888) ("[N]o state has the right to lay a tax on interstate commerce in any form"). Eventually the Court concluded that interstate commerce ought to "pay its own way," but also acknowledged that where commerce traveled among various states, or where a multistate business was subject to tax on its activities in each state, double or triple taxation was a danger. To guard against this, the Court began to require that states tax only that portion of economic activity attributable to activity within its jurisdiction. For example, if a corporation has gross receipts of $1,000, and derives half of its revenue from State A and half from State B, and if both states require corporations to pay 25 percent of their gross receipts for the privilege of doing business as a corporation within the jurisdiction, the corporation's tax bill in each state will be $125 (25 percent × (50 percent × $1,000)).

c. Fairly related. This prong does not do much work in tax cases, for the obvious reason that courts are not very well suited for judging whether the tax is fairly related to the services corporations receive from the state. Many taxpayers would probably say that their taxes were rarely, if ever, fairly related. As a result, courts have wisely declined to open up that particular can of worms.

d. Taxation of foreign commerce. There is an additional inquiry when state and local governments tax foreign commerce: whether there is an increased risk of multiple taxation and whether the tax would "impair uniformity in an area where federal uniformity is essential." *Japan Line, Ltd. v. Los Angeles*, 441 U.S. 434, 445 (1979); *see also Container Corp. v. Franchise Tax Bd.*, 463 U.S. 159 (1983).

This is only the most superficial of summaries; there are numerous types of taxes and several of the *Complete Auto* prongs are analyzed differently depending on the type of tax at issue. Any serious research on these issues should begin with Jerome Hellerstein, Walter Hellerstein & John A. Swain, *State Taxation* (3d ed. 1998 & Ann. Supp.).

C.   The Privileges and Immunities Clause of Article IV, § 2

Whereas the DCCD is an implied restriction on state power over interstate commerce, the Constitution does contain several explicit restrictions as well.[4] This section covers one of the most important, the Privileges and Immunities Clause of Article IV, § 2,[5] which reads that "[t]he Citizens of each State shall be entitled to all Privileges and Immunities of Citizens in the Several States." The Clause had a wordier counterpart in the Articles of Confederation; although it was shortened somewhat when carried over to the new constitution, the intent was the same: to prevent states from discriminating against those from other states in favor of their own citizens. As you might guess, there is a high degree of overlap between the Privileges and Immunities Clause and the DCCD. But there are also important differences, too, which make the Privilege and Immunities Clause more helpful in some circumstances than the DCCD. In other cases, these differences will render the Privileges and Immunities Clause decidedly *less* helpful in policing state discrimination.

The Court's contemporary test can be easily stated. Where there is discrimination by a state against the citizen of another state—particularly when the discrimination prevents the out-of-state citizen from plying a trade, conducting business, or paying taxes on the same terms as in-state citizens—the state must demonstrate (1) a substantial reason for the discrimination and (2) that the discrimination itself bears a substantial relationship to the reason for discriminating in the first place. *See, e.g., Lunding v. N.Y. Tax Appeals*

---

4.   Article I, § 10 prohibits states from imposing duties or imposts on imports or exports without congressional consent. The Court has interpreted "imports and exports" to mean *foreign* imports and exports. *See Woodruff v. Parham*, 75 U.S. 123 (1869); *but see Camps Newfound/Owatonna v. Harrison*, 520 U.S. 564 (1997) (Thomas, J., dissenting) (arguing that the Framers intended the Import-Export Clause to apply to foreign and domestic imports and exports; concluding that it ought to be used instead of the nontextual DCCD); Brannon P. Denning, *Justice Thomas, the Import-Export Clause, and* Camps Newfound/Owatonna v. Harrison, 70 U. Colo. L. Rev. 155 (1998) (concluding that Justice Thomas was correct on the intent of the Import-Export Clause, but arguing against wholesale substitution of the Clause for the DCCD). Other restrictions include bans on treatymaking, coining money, impairing contracts, laying duties of tonnage, and entering into agreements or compacts with other states. U.S. Const. art. I, § 10.

5.   Don't confuse the Privileges *and* Immunities Clause of Article IV with the Privileges *or* Immunities Clause of the Fourteenth Amendment. For more on the latter, see Brannon Padgett Denning, The Glannon Guide to Constitutional Law: Individual Rights and Liberties 37-38 (2012).

Tribunal, 522 U.S. 287 (1998); *Supreme Court v. Piper,* 470 U.S. 274 (1985); *Toomer v. Witsell,* 334 U.S. 385 (1948).[6]

A "substantial reason," much like the "legitimate end" prong of strict scrutiny under the DCCD, requires proof that the government is not pursuing the forbidden end of protectionism. To satisfy the substantial reason requirement, the Court has sometimes said that the state must demonstrate that the out-of-state citizens pose a "peculiar source of the evil at which the statute is aimed," which can be remedied only by treating them differently than in-state citizens. *Toomer v. Witsell,* 334 U.S. 385, 398 (1948). Courts often inquire whether the state's objective can be achieved in a manner that does not require geographical distinctions to be drawn as part of the substantial relationship inquiry.

So far, the Privileges and Immunities Clause sounds like it tracks the DCCD, but there are several important differences between the two that you should keep in mind. First, the Court has concluded that the Privileges and Immunities Clause applies only to "natural" citizens,[7] which means that corporations may not invoke its protections. *See Paul v. Virginia,* 75 U.S. 168 (1868).

Second, the Privileges and Immunities Clause protects only fundamental rights;[8] not every distinction made by a state between its citizens and those from other states will run afoul of the Privileges and Immunities Clause. In *Baldwin v. Fish & Game Comm'n,* 436 U.S. 371 (1978), the Court rejected a claim that Montana's higher hunting license fees for out-of-state hunters violated the Clause. The Court concluded that elk hunting was "recreation" and not a fundamental right. By contrast, competing economically with in-state citizens and not being taxed at a higher rate than in-state citizens—the areas of obvious overlap with the DCCD—are deemed fundamental rights to which the Privileges and Immunities Clause's protections apply. *See, e.g., Lunding v. N.Y. Tax Appeals Tribunal,* 522 U.S. 287 (1998) (striking down New York commuter tax); *Supreme Court v. Piper,* 470 U.S. 274 (1985) (striking down state residency requirement for admission to state bar).

Third, the Court has refused to apply the market-participant exception (MPE) to the Privileges and Immunities Clause of Article IV. *United Building & Construction Trades Council v. Mayor of Camden,* 465 U.S. 208 (1984). Unlike the DCCD, which provides a default rule in the absence of congressional action, the Privileges and Immunities Clause "imposes a direct restraint on state action in the interests of interstate harmony." *Id.* at 220. For this reason,

---

6. Other rights protected by the Privileges and Immunities Clause include the right of out-of-state residents' access to courts, *Canadian Northern Ry. Co. v. Eggen,* 252 U.S. 553 (1920), and the right to own and dispose of property, *Blake v. McClung,* 172 U.S. 239 (1898). *Doe v. Bolton,* 410 U.S. 179 (1973), held that states could not limit the right of out-of-staters to obtain abortions in the state, if such abortions were available to in-state residents. Although these cases were decided prior to *Baldwin's* limitation of the Clause to "fundamental" rights, that case did not repudiate any of the Court's earlier holdings.

7. While the Clause itself says "citizen," the Court has held that discrimination based on *residency* is also covered by the Clause. *See United Building and Construction Trades Council v. Camden,* 465 U.S. 208, 216 (1984).

8. Again, one should not confuse these fundamental rights with the fundamental rights protected by the Due Process and Equal Protection Clauses of the Fourteenth Amendment. Denning, *supra* note 5, at Chs. 3, 5.

it is likely that Congress may not authorize violations of the Clause, as it can authorize violations of the DCCD, a fourth difference between the two.

The differences between the Privileges and Immunities Clause and the DCCD are summarized in the following chart:

Differences between the Privileges and Immunities Clause and the DCCD

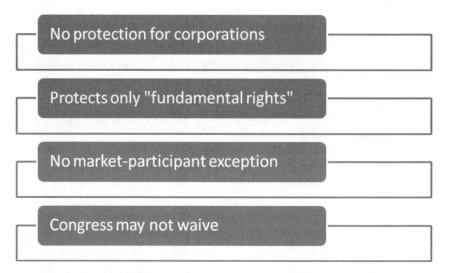

No protection for corporations

Protects only "fundamental rights"

No market-participant exception

Congress may not waive

QUESTION 9. The deer hunter. The State of Montana has passed a law requiring all persons who offer themselves as hunting guides for hire to be licensed by the state. According to the statute, licensed guides must be Montana residents. The justification for this is that only those residing in the state will be sufficiently familiar with the terrain to guide safely. Residency, the state further claims, ensures familiarity with Montana's game laws and can aid the state in preventing unlicensed hunting, the exceeding of bag limits, and the preservation of native game stocks. An out-of-state hunter who used to guide in Montana sues, claiming that Montana's law violates the Privileges and Immunities Clause of Article IV. A reviewing court should hold the law:

A. Constitutional, because hunting is not a fundamental right.

B. Constitutional, because out-of-state guides constitute a "peculiar source of evil."

C. Unconstitutional, because the law deprives out-of-state guides of the ability to pursue employment on terms equal with Montana residents without substantial reasons for the discrimination.

D. Unconstitutional, unless Montana can demonstrate that it is pursuing a legitimate, nonprotectionist interest and that there are no less discriminatory means for pursuing its interest.

ANALYSIS. Given the result in *Baldwin,* you were probably immediately drawn to **A** because the facts above involve a hunting guide. But if you were, reread the facts carefully. *Baldwin* involved fees charged in-state and out-of-state residents for hunting licenses. The facts here involve hunting, but more important, they involve the attempt to prevent out-of-state guides from working in the state and competing against those in-state who wish to be guides. **B** is not really accurate; it seems that the problem (to the extent one exists) is not posed by out-of-state guides per se, but rather by inexperienced guides or those unfamiliar with the state and its terrain. Even if it could be shown that only out-of-state guides posed this problem, there are other ways — testing, training, and so on — that could remedy the problem without excluding them completely. **D** recites the standard of review not for the Privileges and Immunities Clause, but for the DCCD.

That leaves **C** as the best answer: The law strikes at the heart of the Privileges and Immunities Clause's purpose — requiring states to permit out-of-state residents to compete economically with those in-state on equal footing, unless good reasons, unique to out-of-state persons, exist for differential treatment.

QUESTION 10. Bookmaking redux. In Question 6, Alabama had passed a law making an exception to the state's competitive bidding statute in which any bid by an Alabama printing company for state printing jobs that is within 20 percent of the lowest bidder's bid automatically is awarded the contract if the lowest bidder is an out-of-state printing company. Three out-of-state printing companies challenge the constitutionality of the law: PrintCo, Inc., a Georgia printing firm; Jeb Smith and Sons, a sole proprietorship in South Carolina that does printing work; and MidWesCo Printing, Inc., a large printing firm located in Iowa. Which, if any, could bring a Privileges and Immunities Clause claim?

A. Jeb Smith and Sons only.
B. None, because the market-participant exception applies.
C. All three.
D. None, because there is no fundamental right involved.

ANALYSIS. Remember that two important differences between the DCCD and the Privileges and Immunities Clause of Article IV are the inability of corporations to bring claims under the Privileges and Immunities Clause and the lack of any market-participant exception to the Clause. Therefore **B** and **C** are incorrect. Further, **D** is not the best answer, because the issue is whether out-of-state residents can bid for work from the state on equal terms with in-state citizens. The Court has never held that there is no "fundamental right" to a state contract, as some scholars have argued.

The only clearly correct answer is **A**. According to the facts, Jeb Smith and Sons is a sole proprietorship, as opposed to the other entities, which are corporations. Smith alone can bring the Privileges and Immunities Clause claim. Whenever you find yourself answering an exam question that has an individual plaintiff and what looks like a DCCD claim, don't forget to address the possibility that the plaintiff might be able to bring a claim under the Privileges and Immunities Clause—particularly if the facts indicate that the MPE will bar the plaintiff's DCCD claim.

D. Preemption

1. Introduction

Article VI makes clear that constitutional federal laws trump conflicting state laws or constitutional provisions. In the parlance, state law is said to be preempted by federal law. Unlike the DCCD, however, preemption occurs only where Congress has affirmatively acted by passing legislation. Simply stating that federal law preempts conflicting state laws says nothing about the scope of the preemption doctrine; over the years, the Court has created categories of preemption. Preemption may be express or implied. The Court has also further subdivided implied preemption. Each category and subdivision is discussed later. What binds the categories—and all preemption cases generally—is the focus on the intent of Congress. Another thing to remember is that, like its DCCD cases, the Court's decisions here are provisional—if it has misread congressional intent, Congress is always free to pass a law correcting the Court's interpretation. Finally, because preemption turns on the express or implied intent of Congress, much depends on the words of the statute and other facts. Preemption cases are fact-intensive; thus what follows is, of necessity, a very general introduction.

2. Express preemption

Congress can include language in its statute delineating the scope of its preemptive power. When it explicitly includes language indicating its intent to displace state law in a particular area, Congress is said to have expressly preempted state law. On the other hand, Congress may also include a so-called savings clause, which indicates the extent to which state law is not preempted. If Congress included more express preemption clauses or savings clauses in legislation, preemption cases would not be so difficult. However, for a variety of reasons—inattentiveness, inability to agree on the scope of preemption, and so on—Congress often neglects this, leaving the Court to guess at what Congress intended. To aid it, the Court has created doctrines of implied preemption.

3.   *Implied preemption*

As the name suggests, implied preemption doctrines are used when the legislation is silent as to its preemptive effects. There are two types of implied
preemption: conflict preemption and field preemption.

a. Field preemption.   Taking them in reverse order, field preemption occurs
when the Court determines that Congress intended to "occupy the field" by
comprehensively regulating a particular subject, leaving no room for state law.
See Gade v. Nat'l Solid Waste Mgmt. Ass'n, 505 U.S. 96, 98 (1992) (defining
field preemption as "where the scheme of federal regulation is so pervasive
as to make reasonable the inference that Congress left no room for the States
to supplement it"). For an example, see *Burbank v. Lockeed Air Terminal, Inc.,*
411 U.S. 624 (1973), in which the Court concluded that federal regulation of
nighttime flights of jets was so pervasive as to preclude room "for local curfews
or other local controls." Note that in field preemption, there need not be any
actual conflict between the state and federal regimes. The two systems of regulation could be entirely complementary. The theory is, though, that Congress
intended to regulate completely, and its choices reflect an intent to regulate to
the point that it did in the particular field, and no further.

b. Conflict preemption.   Even if Congress has left no indication that its regulation is to be comprehensive—even if it is completely silent as to the preemptive intent of a law—the Court has understood the Supremacy Clause to
require federal law to trump state law in case of a conflict. But when, exactly,
do state and federal laws "conflict"? The Court has two answers, only one of
which might seem intuitive to you.

Impossibility preemption. When you think of a conflict between two laws,
you probably have in mind what the Court has come to call "impossibility"
preemption. If one subject to both a federal and state regulatory regime cannot
comply with one without violating the other, you have impossibility preemption. As it does in all preemption cases, federal law trumps. For an early case,
see *McDermott v. Wisconsin,* 228 U.S. 115 (1913), in which state laws regarding
the labeling of corn syrup were inconsistent with federal laws.

Obstacle preemption. Even where literal compliance with both regimes is
possible, the Court will still preempt a state law that "'stands as an obstacle to the
accomplishment and execution of the full purposes and objectives of Congress.'
. . . What is a sufficient obstacle is a matter of judgment, to be informed by examining the federal statute as a whole and identifying its purpose and intended
effects. . . ." *Crosby v. National Foreign Trade Council,* 520 U.S. 363, 372 (2000)
(citations omitted) (alterations in the original). If, for example, federal law prescribed certain actions to be taken, but not others, and a state law in the same
area authorized those actions that Congress considered and rejected, then the
Court might reasonably conclude that state law poses an "obstacle" to congressional goals by employing the very means of regulation Congress considered and
rejected (assuming, of course, that Congress did not indicate an intent to permit
parallel state regulations that went further than federal law).

QUESTION 11. Burma shave. During the late 1990s, a number of states and municipalities passed laws and ordinances aimed at putting economic pressure on certain rogue regimes around the world. In many cases, Congress, too, had imposed sanctions on these same countries. In 1998 both Congress and the State of Massachusetts passed laws relating to the country of Burma. Congress authorized the President to take certain actions to ensure a peaceful transition to democracy in Burma, but it stopped short of prohibiting U.S. companies from doing business in the country or with that country's military government. The U.S. law was otherwise silent on the extent to which states could impose sanctions as well. Massachusetts, on the other hand, barred companies that did business in that country from bidding on contracts with state or local governments. The Supreme Court struck down the Massachusetts law. Based on what you read above, what would you guess was the basis for its conclusion?

A. Massachusetts had violated the DCCD by discriminating against foreign commerce.
B. Congress had expressly preempted Massachusetts's law.
C. It was impossible for companies subject to federal and state law to comply.
D. Massachusetts's law posed an obstacle to Congress's legislative aims.

ANALYSIS.   I wanted to see how well you'd been paying attention. First, the facts given help you eliminate three answers right off the bat, leaving you with the correct one. Because Congress has acted, the DCCD is not at issue here (although, as an alternative ground for its decisions, lower courts found that the Massachusetts law did violate the DCCD as well as being preempted). Therefore **A** can be eliminated.

Moreover, the facts tell you that the federal law was silent as to its preemptive intent. Because express preemption will involve explicit language in the statute barring complementary state laws, the lack of such language here means you can strike **B** as well. Moreover, nothing in the facts indicates that companies subject to both laws couldn't comply. Federal law prescribed some sanctions; Massachusetts's law went further. But it was not impossible to comply with both regimes according to the facts, so **C** can be eliminated, too.

Congress had stopped short of banning companies from doing business in Burma because it didn't want to disadvantage existing U.S. companies who had contracts and investments in place in the country. Moreover, Congress hoped to provide the President with a combination of diplomatic carrots and sticks that he could employ as the facts warranted. Because the state law here prohibited business or investment if one wished to do business with the state, the Court concluded that Massachusetts had chosen obduracy and inflexibility where Congress had opted for more room to maneuver. The state's law, the Court concluded, posed an obstacle to congressional aims and was thus preempted. *See Crosby v. National Foreign Trade Council,* 520 U.S. 363, 372 (2000). **D,** therefore, would be the correct answer.

> **QUESTION 12. Busted for standin' on a corner in Winslow,**
> **Arizona.** Arizona passed a controversial immigration bill. One of its
> provisions, section 5(C), made it illegal for an illegal immigrant to apply
> for work, solicit work in a public place, or perform work as an employee
> or an independent contractor. Federal law had no comparable federal
> penalties, owing to Congress's decision not to impose criminal penalties
> on those—even those in the country illegally—who were looking for
> work. Which of the following statements is true?
>
> A. The state law is an obstacle to congressional aims.
> B. Federal law occupies the field, leaving no room for supplemental state
>   regulation.
> C. One could not comply with both state and federal law.
> D. The state law is valid.

ANALYSIS.   This question is based on the law invalidated in part in *Arizona v. United States*, 132 S. Ct. 2492 (2012). In the case, the Supreme Court invalidated section 5(C), along with another provision, Section 6, which authorized state officers to arrest, without a warrant, any person the officer has a probable cause to believe has committed a public offense that would make him removable from the country. *Arizona*, 132 S. Ct. at 2506.

Examining the federal immigration law, the Court concluded that § 5(C), which "enacts a state criminal prohibition where no federal counterpart exists," was preempted because "Congress made a deliberate choice not to impose criminal penalties on aliens who seek, or engage in, unauthorized employment." *Id.* at 2503, 2504. Permitting that provision to stand "would interfere with the careful balance struck by Congress with respect to unauthorized employment of aliens" therefore the law "is an obstacle to the regulatory system Congress chose." *Id.* at 2505.

But you need not have known about the case, or the Court's holding, to reason to the correct decision. The facts tell you that the state is regulating where there is no comparable federal law. Therefore, **B** could not have been correct, because "field preemption" occurs only when the federal government has regulated in an area comprehensively, leaving no room for supplementary regulation by states. Nor is **C** correct: If there is no federal law, it is possible to comply with one regime without violating another. Between the remaining answers, **A** is a better answer than **D**. Recall that the facts state the decision *not* to criminalize the act of looking for or securing employment, even by those in the country illegally, reflected a choice on Congress's part. As the Court pointed out, to uphold the state law would upset the balance Congress struck; therefore, state law had to give way.

You might be interested to know that Section 6 was likewise preempted in the *Arizona* case. It, the Court pointed out, "attempts to provide state officers even greater authority to arrest aliens on the basis of possible removability than Congress has given to trained federal immigration officers." *Id.* at 2506. That it could be exercised without input from the Federal Government, in the Court's opinion, "would allow the State to achieve its own immigration policy." *Id.* Allowing it to stand "violates the principle that the removal process is entrusted to the discretion of the Federal Government." *Id.*

There are two final notes about preemption. First, the examples have presupposed a conflict between a federal statute and a state or local statute or ordinance. However, the Court has also held that federal law can preempt state common law tort remedies as well. *See, e.g., Geier v. American Honda Motor Co., Inc.,* 529 U.S. 861 (2000). Second, the Court has sometimes said that there is a "presumption against preemption" when Congress regulates in an area traditionally regulated by states as part of their police power. When this is the case, the Court has said that its analysis "start[s] with the assumption that the historic powers of the States [are] not to be superseded by . . . Federal Act unless that [is] the clear and manifest purpose of Congress." *Rice v. Santa Fe Elevator Corp.,* 331 U.S. 218, 230 (1947). Although the Court had seemed to deemphasize this presumption, especially in cases in which the interest in uniformity of policy is high, *see, e.g., Geier v. American Honda Motor Co., Inc.,* 529 U.S. 861 (2000), the presumption against preemption may be due for a renaissance. *See Wyeth v. Levine,* 129 S. Ct. 1187 (2009) (refusing to preempt state tort claim for failure to warn about side effects of drug where drug complied with federal labeling rules).

E.   The Closer: Putting it All Together

We've ended where you should really begin your analysis of restrictions on state regulation of commerce—by looking for preemption issues. A constitutional exercise of any congressional power can preempt state law, but preemption issues often lurk where state law regulates an area that Congress enters by dint of its commerce power. And Congress's footprint is often quite large! Remember, too, that Congress cannot only preempt state law, it can permit what would otherwise be violations of the DCCD. Check for both.

After checking for congressional action, if a state or local law regulates interstate commerce, you should ask whether the law is facially discriminatory or facially neutral. You also want to remember that even if facially neutral, a law can still discriminate in purpose or effect. Again, you'll want to check the facts and see if there are signals that discriminatory effects or discriminatory purposes are masked by the facial neutrality of the law. If so, then heightened or strict scrutiny will apply and the law will likely be invalidated. If not, then *Pike* balancing would apply, and the law will probably be upheld, given that test's deference.

But don't forget the exceptions—congressional consent, which I've already mentioned, the market-participant exception, and *United Haulers/Davis*'s "public entities" exception should be looked for. Even if the MPE applies to save a facially discriminatory law, you might have a Privileges and Immunities Clause issue to discuss, but only if a "fundamental right" is at issue and the claimant is not a corporation. I've tried to summarize this in the following flowchart:

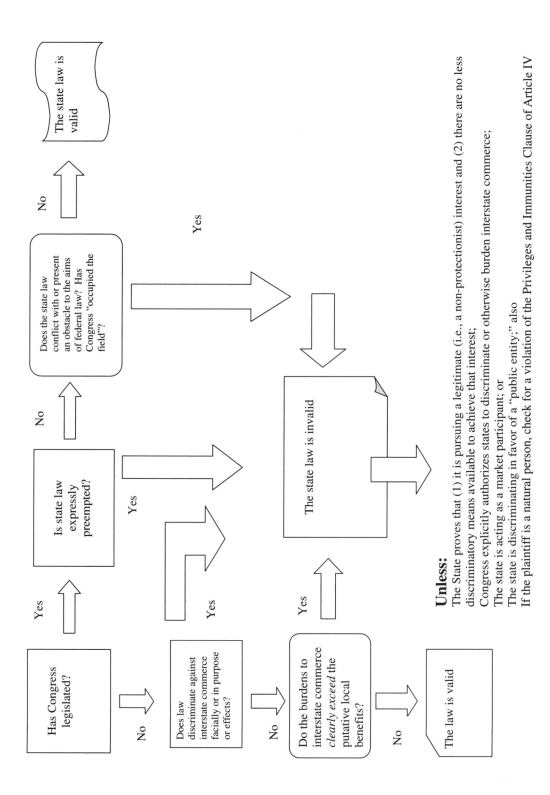

Has Congress legislated?

Yes → Is state law expressly preempted?

No → Does the state law conflict with or present an obstacle to the aims of federal law? Has Congress "occupied the field"?

No → The state law is valid

Yes → The state law is invalid

No → Does law discriminate against interstate commerce facially or in purpose or effects?

Yes → The state law is invalid

No → Do the burdens to interstate commerce *clearly exceed* the putative local benefits?

Yes → The state law is invalid

No → The law is valid

Unless:
The State proves that (1) it is pursuing a legitimate (i.e., a non-protectionist) interest and (2) there are no less discriminatory means available to achieve that interest;
Congress explicitly authorizes states to discriminate or otherwise burden interstate commerce;
The state is acting as a market participant; or
The state is discriminating in favor of a "public entity;" also
If the plaintiff is a natural person, check for a violation of the Privileges and Immunities Clause of Article IV

QUESTION 13. **The deer hunter II.** Montana has a law on the books prohibiting any person to act as a hunting guide for hire without a license. The law further reads that except as provided for in the statute, "no person not a resident of this state may obtain a license to act as a hunting or fishing guide for hire." The only way that a nonresident may obtain a license, according to the next section is if "(i) the nonresident owns land in this state on which he or she guides; and (ii) pays an annual fee of $2,500." The annual fee for a resident license is $20 per year. Will is a guide who lives in Wyoming. Before the new law, Will brought dozens of hunters per month into Montana from Wyoming and other surrounding states. Each paid between $200 and $500 a day to have Will guide them, and his clients spent hundreds or thousands of dollars apiece on licenses, equipment, food, and lodging in Montana. Will wants to challenge the law in court. While researching the issue, you find a federal statute, "Reaffirmation of State Regulation of Resident and Nonresident Hunting and Fishing Act of 2005," which provides in relevant part that the Commerce Clause "shall not be construed to impose any barrier . . . to the regulation of hunting or fishing by a State or Indian tribe." Will files a DCCD challenge and a challenge under the Privileges and Immunities Clause of Article IV, § 2. What is the likely outcome?

A. He will prevail on either the DCCD or the Privileges and Immunities Clause claim, because the law is facially discriminatory and he is not a corporation.

B. He will prevail on the DCCD, but not the Privileges and Immunities Clause claim, because the law is facially discriminatory but hunting is recreation and not a "fundamental right."

C. He will prevail on neither the DCCD nor the Privileges and Immunities Clause claim, because Congress consented to the Montana law and because hunting is recreation and not a "fundamental right."

D. None of the above.

ANALYSIS. This was a tricky question. You should have been immediately on guard because of the facial discrimination in the statute and because of the fact that Will seems to be an individual. That means that he potentially has both a DCCD as well as a Privileges and Immunities Clause claim. But there's that federal statute, which consents to all state regulation of hunting and fishing. The statute is broad, but seems clear; thus, that federal statute knocks out Will's DCCD claims. **A** and **B** can be discarded on that basis alone.

If you got this question wrong, my bet is that you chose **C**. It is true that *Baldwin* held that hunting is not a fundamental right, but Will isn't trying to hunt on equal terms with Montanans, he's trying to *guide* on equal terms, because guiding is what he does for a living. Here the Court's cases are clear that the right to pursue a common calling on equal terms is a fundamental right that implicates the Privileges and Immunities Clause. Because there's no indication that Congress can "consent" to a state violation of Article IV, § 2, any more than it can "consent" to violations of any other explicit constitutional restrictions on states, the federal statute wouldn't doom a Privileges and Immunities Clause claim. That leaves **D** as the best answer. I told you it was tricky!

Denning's Picks

1.	Clean hands	**B**
2.	Something fishy	**D**
3.	Up in smoke	**D**
4.	How do you like them apples?	**A**
5.	Car wars	**C**
6.	Bookmaking	**A**
7.	A hard(ened) bargain	**D**
8.	I would gladly pay you Tuesday for a hamburger today	**B**
9.	The deer hunter	**C**
10.	Bookmaking redux	**A**
11.	Burma shave	**D**
12.	Busted for standin' on a corner in Winslow, Arizona	**A**
13.	The deer hunter II	**D**

6

Separation of Powers

A.   Overview

The previous chapters discussed the extent to which the Constitution separates power "vertically," between the federal and state governments. This chapter, however, covers what might be described as "horizontal" separation of powers among the three branches of the federal government, encompassing in particular those controversies between the legislative and executive branches. Separation of powers cases also tend to be those in which the Constitution's familiar "checks and balances" come into play.

Following a survey of some broad themes in separation of powers cases, this chapter discusses the scope and limits of presidential power in both domestic and foreign affairs. It covers the power of the President to appoint and remove executive branch officials, and the ability of Congress to limit those appointments or removals. The chapter then discusses the role of the executive and legislative branches in the creation and control of the administrative state. Finally, it discusses constitutional immunities for legislative and executive branch officials.

1.   Introduction

The received political wisdom of the framing era held that power should be separated among legislative, executive, and judicial branches. Early state constitutions—and many modern state constitutions—contain explicit statements to that effect. No such statement is found in the U.S. Constitution. The Constitution, instead, attempted to achieve separation of powers through structure: The Constitution is designed to prevent concentration of power into a single branch of government.

But the various powers—legislative, executive, and judicial—are not hermetically sealed off from one another. Instead, the Framers also sought to restrain each branch by enabling the other branches to exercise checks on each other. For example, Congress has the power to pass legislation, but both the executive and the judicial branches are involved in lawmaking to some extent. The President must sign or veto a bill before it becomes law, for example. The judiciary has the power to review acts of Congress and assess their constitutionality. At the same time, separation of powers doctrine holds that one branch may not attempt to "aggrandize" power at the expense of another branch, or inhibit other branches in the execution of their constitutionally assigned powers. Each branch must be able to exercise its power independent of undue influence from the others. These broad principles—that power may not be concentrated in one branch and that the branches may not attempt to inhibit the ability of the others to exercise power given to them by the Constitution—exist alongside the specific separation of powers "rules" (like those in Article I, § 7, or in the Appointments Clause) in the Constitution itself.

2. *"Formalism" vs. "functionalism" in separation of powers*

If you read a treatise or scholarly discussion of separation of powers cases, you'll often run across a distinction between formalism and functionalism. Understanding the difference between the formalist and functionalist approaches to separation of powers cases will help you understand the different positions taken by majority opinions, and the dissenting opinions' criticism in separation of powers cases. Whether one adopts a "formalist" or a "functionalist" position in separation of powers cases (and the cases themselves provide numerous examples of both approaches—as do individual Justices in different cases) depends largely on the extent to which one regards both the structural separation of powers principles and the explicit constitutional provisions as hard-and-fast rules that may not be violated (the formalist position), or views experimentation with the boundaries among the branches as acceptable as long as there is no concentration of power that comes at the expense of other branches (the functionalist position).

Simply put, a formalist regards the separation of powers provisions in the Constitution as rules to be followed to the letter. In addition, formalists also tend to assume that there are well-defined categories of "legislative," "executive," and "judicial" power; when one branch attempts to exercise the powers of another, that action is unconstitutional.

By contrast, functionalists tend to consider the ultimate ends of particular actions, and the likely effect of such actions on separation of powers principles. As long as the act does not aggrandize power to a single branch or seek to diminish the power of a coordinate branch, the functionalist will argue for staying the judicial hand, as long as no specific prohibition in the Constitution is violated. Functionalists regard the division of powers among the branches as less defined and more fluid than formalists. Further, they are less likely to regard the separation of powers provisions in the Constitution as rules and treat them more like standards.

B.   The Powers of the President in Domestic Affairs

The President's powers are defined in Article II, which deals with the executive branch in general. Unlike Article I, the enumeration of executive powers in Article II is not as detailed; nor does the "vesting clause" in Article II limit the President to executive powers "herein granted." *See* U.S. Const. art. II, § 1 ("The executive power shall be vested in a President of the United States of America."). Article II, § 2 does, however, enumerate several powers — as commander-in-chief, the power to make treaties, to make certain appointments, just to name a few. The relatively spare description of the executive quickly gave rise to a debate that continues to the present between "presidentialists" and "congressionalists."

Presidentialists, like Alexander Hamilton and Theodore Roosevelt, claimed that Article II's vesting clause confers in bulk all those powers understood by the Framers to be "executive" in nature. The roles specifically described in Article II, § 2, they argue, represent instances in which other branches share in the exercise of certain executive powers. For example, treatymaking was understood to be an executive power at the time of the Framing, but the Constitution requires that treaties negotiated by the President be approved by two thirds of the Senate.

Congressionalists, like James Madison and William Howard Taft (as President), argue that it would be inconceivable that the Framers, having recently thrown off the yoke of a monarchy and bearing a healthy suspicion of executive authority from clashes with royal governors, would have modeled the office of the presidency on those very executive officers against whom they had rebelled. Congressionalists argue that the enumeration of powers in Article II, § 2 would be superfluous if the vesting clause had the broad sweep claimed for it by presidentalists. As their name suggests, congressionalists believe that except for the few constitutionally assigned roles and powers, the executive branch can be checked by Congress.

As we will see in the following section, the President has traditionally been regarded as having more latitude in the conduct of foreign affairs than in exclusively domestic affairs, but as the leading presidential powers cases demonstrate, the line between the two is not always easy to discern.

As a result of a nationwide strike in the steel industry that President Harry S. Truman feared posed a threat to forces in Korea, he ordered the Secretary of Commerce to seize control of steel mills and continue operating them. The owners of the mills sued, and the Supreme Court eventually ruled against the President. *Youngstown Sheet & Tube Co. v. Sawyer*, 343 U.S. 579 (1952). There were a number of opinions; we focus on two — Justice Hugo Black's majority opinion, and the influential concurring opinion by Justice Robert Jackson.

Justice Black's opinion is a good example of the separation of powers formalism described earlier. For him, deciding the separation of powers question began with a characterization of the President's action — was it authorized by Congress or by the Constitution? He concluded that if the President's action was to be upheld, it was because it was undertaken pursuant to constitutional authority. "There is no statute that expressly authorizes the President to take possession of property as he did here. Nor is there any act of Congress . . . from which such a power can be fairly implied," Justice Black wrote. *Youngstown Sheet & Tube*, 343 U.S. at 585. Although there were statutes on the books that permitted the seizure of private property under certain conditions, the Truman administration disclaimed reliance on those statutes. Moreover, Black pointed out, Congress declined to grant the President the power he was now claiming when it passed the Taft–Hartley Act in 1947.

Black then rejected the constitutional bases for the President's action. The commander-in-chief power was no help. Requisitioning private property, even for the war effort, "was a job for the Nation's lawmakers, not for its military authorities." 343 U.S. at 587. Nor could the President rely on the vesting clause or on Article II's injunction that the President "take care that the laws be faithfully executed. . . ." U.S. Const. art. II, § 3. As Justice Black pointed out, "In the framework of our Constitution, the President's power to see that the laws are faithfully executed refutes the idea that he is a lawmaker. The Constitution limits his functions . . . to the recommending of laws he thinks wise and the vetoing of laws he thinks bad." 343 U.S. at 587.

Justice Black's opinion was syllogistic. The major premise was that only Congress may make laws. The minor premise was that the President's seizure was the equivalent of congressional lawmaking. The conclusion was that the President's actions, having not been undertaken by Congress, were therefore unconstitutional. Justice Black's approach depends in large part on the ability to correctly classify the action being taken, and assumes fixed categories of legislative and executive action. If it was "executive," then the President might do it, without Congress; but if it was "legislative," then if he did it on his own authority, he was violating the Constitution's allocation of responsibility.

Justice Robert Jackson's opinion, by contrast, is regarded as the quintessential functional opinion. It, and not Black's opinion, has become the accepted starting point for analyses of executive power questions. Despairing of answering separation of powers questions by resort to text and history, Jackson posited an influential tripartite schema where judicial scrutiny of executive action waxed and waned to the degree the action was expressly or impliedly authorized by Congress. *Id* at 635–639 (Jackson, J., concurring). Where Congress had explicitly or implicitly delegated power to the President, his power was said to be at its apex; to conclude he lacked authority meant that neither the President nor Congress had the ability to do whatever it was he was doing. *Id.* at 635–637. At the other end of the spectrum was presidential action that defied the express or implied will of Congress. Here the President's power was "at its lowest ebb," and to survive judicial review, the President had to rely on his independent constitutional power minus whatever power over the subject he shared with Congress. *Id.* at 637. When the President acted without either express or implied approval or disapproval, Jackson wrote, "there is a zone of twilight in which he and Congress may have concurrent authority, or in which its distribution is uncertain. Therefore, congressional inertia, indifference or quiescence may . . . at least as a practical matter, enable, if not invite, measures on independent presidential responsibility." *Id.* This chart might help you visualize Jackson's schema:

Presidential Action	*Presidential Power*	*Level of Court Scrutiny*
Acts pursuant to express or implicit authorization from Congress	At its maximum; "personf[ies] the federal sovereignty"	Presumption in favor of presidential action; heavy burden to invalidate; invalidation means that "Federal Government as an undivided whole lacks power"
Congressional grant or denial of power absent	Can only rely on his independent power, *plus* on the "zone of twilight" in which Congress and the President have concurrent authority, or where distribution is uncertain	Says that "congressional inertia, indifference or quiescence may sometimes, *at least as a practical matter,* enable, if not invite measures on independent presidential responsibility"
Measures incompatible with the express or implied will of Congress	Power "at its lowest ebb"; may rely only on independent power *minus* constitutional powers of Congress over the matter	"Must be scrutinized with caution, for what is at stake is the equilibrium established by our constitutional system"

Jackson concluded that the President's power was at its low ebb, as Congress had considered, but rejected, granting the President the authority he exercised here. The seizure was unconstitutional, because none of the President's independent powers—the commander-in-chief power, the "take care" clause, the vesting clause—furnished power to seize private property. Jackson also resisted appeals to exigency, writing that Congress could easily grant such powers, if it thought wise. *Id.* at 646–647. He ended with a warning to Congress, cautioning it that "power to legislate for emergencies belongs in the hands of Congress, but only Congress itself can prevent power from slipping through its fingers." *Id.* at 654.

QUESTION 1. Senatorial discourtesy. Frustrated by a lack of cooperation from the Senate, which seems intent on denying him most of his nominees for important cabinet and judicial posts by not holding hearings and not scheduling votes on them, the President has decided to take matters into his own hands. Claiming authority under his constitutional duty to "take care that the laws be faithfully executed," the President begins handing out "temporary" commissions to scores of persons whose offices require the Senate to advise and consent to their nominations. The President had considered making numerous "recess appointments" under the authority given to him in Article II, § 2, clause 3, but decided against it because (1) he would have to wait until the Senate went into recess, which it is unlikely to do in anticipation of such a move on the part of the President; and (2) he is afraid that if the Senate does recess and he makes a massive number of recess appointments, the Senate will retaliate by not considering any of the President's pending legislation. There is an act on the books (the Vacancies Act) that limits the tenure of temporary appointees who have not been confirmed by the Senate. The President, however, makes it clear that his acting appointees will occupy their positions in excess of the limit set in the Vacancies Act, and will remain until the Senate takes action on the nominees he has sent to it. If challenged, what should a reviewing court do?

A. Uphold his appointments, because the Senate has frustrated the President's ability to ensure the laws are faithfully executed, and because the President has an independent power to appoint.

B. Invalidate his appointments, because he is acting contrary to the express will of Congress, expressed in the Vacancies Act.

(C.) Invalidate his appointments, because he is acting contrary to the Vacancies Act and because the Senate must otherwise confirm all nominees.

D. Uphold his appointments, because the appointments are similar to the recess appointments the Constitution empowers the President to make.

ANALYSIS.   This question called for the application of Justice Jackson's test for presidential action from *Youngstown Sheet & Tube v. Sawyer*. The Vacancies Act represents Congress's express opinion that temporary appointees should serve for a limited amount of time; the President's stated intention to violate that puts him at odds with Congress. Ascertaining whether he can or cannot make these appointments requires you, under *Youngstown*, to assess the President's power *minus* that of Congress over the matter. The Constitution gives the President power to appoint, but only with Senate "advice and consent." Thus the Constitution requires the branches to share power. Thus, **A** misstates the role of the President. The "take care" clause would be of no help, because he is violating an act of Congress, not executing it, by having temporary appointees stay in excess of the time permitted under the Vacancies Act. The President's only ability to appoint unilaterally occurs with recess appointments, which the facts indicate the President was not inclined to make. It hardly matters that the President's actions were "like" those provided for in the Constitution. Therefore, **D** does not help much; the fact that there were seizure provisions on the books that were "like" the one President Truman used did not cut any ice with the *Youngstown* Court.

Although **B** correctly notes the President is opposing Congress here, it is incomplete. Acting contrary to the will of Congress doesn't *automatically* result in the presidential action's invalidation. Rather, a reviewing Court has to consider the President's independent power *minus* that power Congress possesses over the same subject matter. Here, the President is not only acting contrary to the Vacancies Act, but his unilateral appointments violate Article II's assignment of a confirmation role to the Senate as well. Therefore, **C** is the best answer.

QUESTION 2. Dis-appointment.   Concerned that the "advice" part of the Senate's advice and consent power has atrophied, Congress passes a law requiring the President to notify the Senate of all vacancies requiring Senate confirmation and prohibiting the President from naming any person to one of those vacancies until the President, or the President's representative, has consulted with the Senate majority leader and the Chair of the Senate committee with jurisdiction over the nominee's department. When the President acts to fill a recent vacancy on the Supreme Court without the consultation required by the Act, Senators sue, seeking an injunction requiring presidential compliance. A reviewing court would probably do what?

A. Deny the injunction, because Congress has usurped the President's constitutional power to appoint, granted in Article II, § 2.
B. Grant the injunction, because the President is acting contrary to the express wishes of Congress.
C. Grant the injunction, because the Senate has the power to offer "advice and consent" to presidential nominees.
D. Deny the injunction, if the Senate has acquiesced over time to presidential appointments without consultation.

ANALYSIS.   At first, this might look a lot like the facts in *Youngstown*. So you might have immediately been drawn to **B**. But remember that Jackson's opinion actually says that when the President bucks Congress, and his power is at its lowest ebb, he can rely only on his independent power *minus* constitutional powers of Congress over the matter. Clearly the President has the power to nominate various officials. U.S. Const., art. II, § 2. The Senate has the power to offer "advice and consent" to such nominees, but Congress as a whole doesn't have any role to play in *appointments*, which is a presidential prerogative. Its role (actually, the Senate's role) is limited to offering "advice," which by definition is precatory not mandatory, and consenting—or not—to those nominees. Therefore **C** does not furnish a sufficient reason for a court to grant an injunction. If Congress *has* little or no constitutional power, and the President is assigned that role by the Constitution, then the President has a good argument that Congress is attempting to usurp his authority. As between **A** and **D**, then, **A** is the better answer. Congressional acquiescence becomes relevant only in the "zone of twilight" where the challenged act does not fall solely within the presidential authority and where Congress is silent.

C.   The President's Foreign Affairs Powers

1.   *Introduction*

Few areas of constitutional law have been more disputed over the last half-century than the proper demarcation of Presidential and Congressional authority in foreign affairs—war powers in particular. In this section, we examine general cases involving presidential power and foreign affairs, including cases involving the use of so-called executive agreements (which are not approved by the Senate) in lieu of treaties (which require assent by two thirds of the Senate), as well as controversies over presidential war powers.

Presidentialists often cite *United States v. Curtiss-Wright Export Co.*, 299 U.S. 304 (1936), to support broad (some say extravagant) claims for executive primacy in foreign affairs matters. To understand *Curtiss-Wright's* import, some background is required. At the time the case was decided, the Court had invalidated, under the nondelegation doctrine, certain delegations of power by Congress to executive agencies to regulate the economy (see *infra* E.1).[1] In *Curtiss-Wright*, Congress had similarly delegated power to the executive branch: The President was empowered by statute to proclaim an arms embargo in a conflict involving Paraguay and Bolivia. The Curtiss-Wright Export Corp.

---

1.   *See Schechter Poultry Co. v. United States*, 295 U.S. 495 (1935); *Panama Refining Co. v. Ryan*, 293 U.S. 388 (1935).

was convicted of violating the embargo by shipping arms to Bolivia. A lower court found this delegation of power to be unconstitutional.

The Supreme Court, however, drew a distinction between domestic and foreign affairs. In the latter, not only might Congress have more authority to delegate to the executive branch, but the President himself had considerable power to exercise unilaterally. "The broad statement," the Court wrote, "that the federal government can exercise no powers except those specifically enumerated in the Constitution, and such implied powers as are necessary and proper to carry into effect the enumerated powers, is categorically true only in respect of our internal [i.e., domestic] affairs." *Curtiss-Wright,* 299 U.S. at 315–316. The Court's theory was that federalism concerns did not apply when it came to foreign affairs because all power to conduct foreign affairs had passed *in toto* to "the United States" at the moment independence was declared.

The Court went on to opine that in addition to federal supremacy in foreign affairs, the Constitution also prescribed *executive* supremacy: "In this vast external realm, with its important, complicated, delicate and manifold problems, the President alone has the power to speak or listen as the representative of the nation." *Id.* at 319. Quoting John Marshall's speech in the House of Representatives, the Court proclaimed the President to be "the sole organ of the nation in its external relations." *Id.* at 320. Describing the President's power as "the very delicate, *plenary and exclusive power*" in foreign relations, the Court added that the power did not require congressional authorization for its exercise. *Id.*

Although not necessarily going as far as the *Curtiss-Wright* opinion, the Court continues to give the President some leeway when it comes to foreign relations matters. In *Dames & Moore v. Regan,* 453 U.S. 654 (1981), for example, the Court upheld some extraordinary measures the President undertook by executive order to settle the Iranian hostage crisis.

In response to the taking of the American Embassy in 1979, then-President Carter froze Iranian assets in the United States pursuant to a congressional statute. To end the crisis, President Reagan agreed to unfreeze those assets, and transfer a portion of them into an escrow account to settle outstanding claims United States citizens had maintained against the government of Iran, which had nationalized assets and canceled contracts following the Iranian Revolution. In addition, the President's order canceled liens and attachments of Iranian assets prior to transferring those assets out of the country; the order also transferred the claims themselves to a special U.S.–Iran claims tribunal for resolution.

Rejecting a challenge by companies that objected to having their claims transferred from federal court to the arbitral tribunal, and to the removal of liens against property needed to satisfy any judgments from those court cases, the Supreme Court upheld the executive order, concluding that it was "a necessary incident to the resolution of a major foreign policy dispute between our country and another" and that Congress had "acquiesced in the President's action. . . ." *Id.* at 688.

In upholding the President's power to settle the claims with the executive order, the Court referred to Justice Jackson's *Youngstown* concurrence as the appropriate analytical framework. It concluded that unfreezing the assets and canceling the liens and attachments were explicitly authorized by congressional statute. The Court declined to hold, however, there was statutory authority for the suspension of the court claims and transfer of those claims to the tribunal. Neither the International Emergency Economic Powers Act (IEEPA) nor the "Hostage Act" authorized the suspension and transfer, the Court held. *Id.* at 678. Nevertheless, the Court took notice of those as evidence of actions similar to the one undertaken by the President of which Congress approved. "We think both statutes highly relevant in the looser sense of indicating congressional acceptance of a broad scope for executive action in circumstances such as those presented in this case." *Id.* at 677. In addition, the Court described as "[c]rucial to our decision," the fact that "Congress has implicitly approved the practice of claims settlement by executive agreement" and that it had not objected to the President's actions in this particular case. *Id.* at 680, 687 (noting that "Congress has not disapproved of the action taken here").

Some scholars have argued that *Dames & Moore* reverses the presumptions of Jackson's *Youngstown* concurrence and that it now favors executive action instead of closely scrutinizing it. After all, they point out, the numerous statutes that permitted the President to seize private property under certain conditions could have easily been interpreted as evidence of "congressional acceptance of a broad scope for executive action in circumstances such as those presented in" *Youngstown*. A possible difference is the fact that Congress had not, in *Dames & Moore*, recently and clearly rejected granting presidential power to settle claims in the manner the President did, unlike the rejection of presidential seizure power in *Youngstown*. In addition, as the *Dames & Moore* Court was quick to point out, no one in Congress was objecting to the executive branch's actions. That they were undertaken in service of settling a foreign relations dispute with another country undoubtedly influenced the Court's decision.

2.   *Treatymaking and executive agreements*

It might come as a surprise that the settlement of the Iranian hostage crisis was effected through an executive agreement, as opposed to a treaty. Recall, however, that although the President has the authority to *make* treaties, they must be agreed to by two thirds of the Senate. U.S. Const. art. II, § 2, cl. 2. The text of the Constitution, however, suggests that treaties are not the only international agreements it recognizes. *Compare* U.S. Const. art. I, § 10, cl. 1 (prohibiting states from entering into "any Treaty, Alliance, or Confederation") *with id.* cl. 3 ("No State shall, without the consent of Congress . . . enter into any Agreement or Compact with . . . a foreign Power. . . ."). In fact, Presidents have entered into so-called executive agreements from the beginning of the Republic. Since the New Deal, the executive agreement has nearly replaced the treaty as the primary way to commit the United States internationally.

Executive agreements generally come in two forms: the sole executive agreement and the congressional-executive agreement. The first is, as its name suggests, an agreement negotiated by the executive branch without any involvement by the legislature. The second, by contrast, is negotiated by the President, but is then implemented through the normal legislative process by simple majority vote in both houses of Congress. The North American Free Trade Agreement, for example, was a congressional-executive agreement, negotiated by President Clinton and then implemented through legislation passed by Congress.

Supreme Court cases in the 1930s approved the President's use of executive agreements to settle claims with foreign nations. *United States v. Belmont,* 301 U.S. 324 (1937), and *United States v. Pink,* 315 U.S. 203 (1942), concerned the effects of the Roosevelt administration's decision to extend diplomatic recognition to the Soviet Union. As part of the recognition, the U.S. government agreed to aid the Soviets in reclaiming assets in the United States owned by persons and entities who had their property seized by the Soviet government. In both cases, the Court reversed lower court decisions holding that state law prohibited the state aiding and abetting confiscation of private property. The Court held that executive agreements constituted "the law of the land" and, pursuant to the Supremacy Clause, trumped contrary state law.

In recent years, questions have arisen regarding the preemptive effect of executive branch policy statements that aren't formal executive agreements. Recent Supreme Court pronouncements have produced some confusion. For example, in *American Insurance Association v. Garamendi,* 539 U.S. 396 (2003), the Court held that an executive branch policy seeking to settle claims against German companies through a foundation established by the United States, Germany, and Austria preempted a California state law requiring, as a condition of doing business in the state, that insurance companies disclose information about insurance policies issued in Europe between 1920 and 1945. Despite the fact that the agreement establishing the forum for settling the Holocaust-era disputes specifically disclaimed any preemptive effect, the Court held that "[t]he principal argument for preemption . . . is that the [California law] interferes with the foreign policy of the Executive Branch, as expressed principally in the executive agreements with Germany, Austria, and France." *Garamendi,* 539 U.S. at 413.

Critics noted that the Court's position was in tension with the Supremacy Clause itself (which speaks only of the Constitution and laws made pursuant to it, as well as treaties, having preemptive effect) and that if mere statements of executive foreign policy preempted contrary state law, that might mean that executive opposition to, say, application of the death penalty to foreign nationals might preempt state law to the contrary. *Cf. Breard v. Greene,* 523 U.S. 371 (1998) (refusing to stay execution of foreign national where defendant was not advised of his right under the Vienna Convention on Consular Relations to request a meeting with his consul despite State Department request that Virginia halt the execution pending appeal).

In *Medellin v. Texas,* 128 S. Ct. 1346 (2008), however, the Court retreated from the broad statements in *Garamendi,* and seemed to limit *Pink, Belmont,* and *Garamendi* to executive branch settlement of claims with foreign nations. *Medellin* arose out of protracted international litigation on behalf of Mexican nationals sentenced to death in the United States without the opportunity to contact the Mexican consul, as the Vienna Convention requires of its signatories. In 2004, the International Court of Justice (ICJ)—to whose jurisdiction the United States had submitted to settle disputes under the Vienna Convention—held that the United States had violated the Convention and that the nationals were entitled to have their state court convictions reconsidered. In response, the President issued an executive memorandum ordering the state courts to give effect to the ICJ's ruling. When Texas appealed, the U.S. Supreme Court held that the Vienna Convention was not binding on domestic courts because no legislation implementing the convention had been passed in Congress.[2]

The Court further rejected the Bush administration's attempt to enforce the ICJ's judgment through its executive memorandum. Although acknowledging that a systematic practice of the executive branch that has not been objected to can serve as a source of executive branch power, the Court found that the memorandum in this case went far beyond the settlement of claims recognized and approved in cases like *Pink* and even in *Garamendi.*

> The claims-settlement cases involve a narrow set of circumstances: the making of executive agreements to settle civil claims between American citizens and foreign governments or foreign nationals. . . . They are based on the view that "a systematic, unbroken, executive practice, long pursued to the knowledge of the Congress and never before questioned," can "raise a presumption that the [action] had been [taken] in pursuance of its consent." . . .
>
> The President's Memorandum is not supported by a "particularly long-standing practice" of congressional acquiescence . . . but rather is what the United States itself has described as "unprecedented action." . . . Indeed, the Government has not identified a single instance in which the President has attempted (or Congress has acquiesced in) a Presidential directive issued to state courts, much less one that reaches deep into the heart of the State's police powers and compels state courts to reopen final criminal judgments and set aside neutrally applicable state laws. . . . The Executive's narrow and strictly limited authority to settle international claims disputes pursuant to an executive agreement cannot stretch so far as to support the current Presidential Memorandum.

128 S. Ct. at 1371–1372.

---

2. Such treaties are called "non-self-executing," in contrast to "self-executing" treaties that are binding without implementing legislation by Congress.

QUESTION 3. **Claim jumpers.**   The President has entered into an executive agreement with the Government of Venelivia, settling claims between that government and several companies whose assets were seized by Venelivia when their operations were nationalized. As part of the agreement, the President agrees to order the transfer of property held in U.S. banks, which had previously been frozen. The State of Ames, in which some Venelivian property is held, refuses, citing a state law prohibiting the transfer of foreign assets to countries who seize property of Ames corporations without paying fair market value. (One of the businesses nationalized by the Venelivian government was based in Ames.) The Ames Attorney General sues to prevent the transfer of assets in federal court, alleging that the executive agreement is unconstitutional. What should the judge do?

A. Dismiss the case, because the President has broad powers in foreign affairs matters.

B. Dismiss the case, because the President may enter into agreements settling foreign claims that trump state law.

C. Enjoin the transfer because claim settlement must occur through a treaty approved by two thirds of the Senate.

D. Enjoin the transfer unless the President was authorized by statute to settle the claims with Venelivia.

ANALYSIS.   The facts here recall those in *Pink* and *Belmont*, where the U.S. government assisted the Soviet Union in recovering property held in the United States pursuant to an executive agreement extending diplomatic recognition to the Soviets. In the face of the conflict between the executive agreement and the Ames statute—at least where the President is attempting to settle claims between private citizens and a foreign state—the executive agreement will trump state law. The President may do this via an executive agreement, as opposed to a formal treaty, so **C** is incorrect. Moreover, the President need not be specifically authorized by Congress to enter into such agreements; therefore **D** is incorrect as well. And although the President does indeed have broad powers in foreign affairs matters, **A** is not the best answer, at least as compared to **B**, which correctly states the rule of *Belmont* and *Pink*.

QUESTION 4. **Arbitrary arbitration.**   As part of the United States' settlement of outstanding claims with Venelivia, the President enters into another executive agreement establishing an arbitral panel for the resolution of future claims between American citizens and the Venelivian government. The agreement recites that it is the policy of the U.S. government that all claims be settled through the panel, as opposed to ordinary litigation in state or federal courts. After Venelivia nationalizes BigOilCo, a corporation with its principal place of business in the State of Ames, BigOilCo files suit, taking advantage of a new Ames statute enabling citizens who have property nationalized overseas to receive treble damages if they can prove they received less than fair market value for their property. The United States intervenes, arguing that the executive agreement preempts the Ames law as applied to disputes with Venelivia. Which of the following statements is true?

A. The executive agreement does not preempt the Ames statute because it does not explicitly preempt state law.

B. The executive agreement cannot preempt state law, because it is not authorized by Congress.

C. The statement of policy is sufficient to preempt state law.

D. All state laws contrary to foreign policy articulated by the executive branch are preempted.

ANALYSIS.   The twist here is that although the executive agreement itself does not expressly preempt contrary state law, an accompanying "policy statement" included in the agreement does. Again, though, at least where claims settlement is involved, the *Garamendi* case teaches that such a statement will suffice to preempt state law. Therefore **C** is the correct answer.

A is an incorrect statement of the law—the agreement doesn't have to specifically preempt state law. The executive agreement in *Garamendi* explicitly *disclaimed* preemptive effect. **B**, too, is incorrect because the President can enter into executive agreements without congressional authorization. **D**, however, goes too far: It is clear after *Medellin* that not *all* state laws can be preempted as a matter of presidential prerogative, even where foreign affairs are involved.

QUESTION 5. Gun shy.   Concerned about growing violence among drug gangs in Mexico, the United States and the government of Mexico enter into a series of executive agreements intended to reduce violence along the border, including measures to prevent guns from making their way from the United States across the border into Mexico. In connection with the executive agreement, the President sends a memorandum to the Governor of Texas ordering him to confiscate weapons in certain border towns where violence has escalated. Those who are lawfully possessing arms will have the opportunity to demonstrate that and will have their weapons returned. Assume for purposes of this question that Texas generally permits law-abiding citizens to possess guns and even carry them concealed on their person if they have a license to do so, which is available as a matter of right to citizens 21 or older who have passed a safety course and have not been convicted of certain violent crimes. The Governor sues to prevent enforcement of this executive policy. What should a reviewing court do?

A. Side with the President because his actions, taken in conjunction with an executive agreement, preempt contrary state law.

B. Side with the President because considerations of federalism do not restrain executive branch action in foreign affairs.

C. Side with the Governor because the President's actions were not ratified by Congress.

D. Side with the Governor because the policy embodied in the memorandum cannot preempt state law.

ANALYSIS. This question furnishes a good illustration of the point made earlier — not every state law is vulnerable to preemption by a mere statement of executive policy. Although some broad language in *Garamendi* suggested otherwise, the Court made clear in *Medellin* that executive branch power, even in foreign affairs, did not extend that far. *Medellin* seemed to limit *Garamendi* to the settlement of private claims between countries and American citizens. Here, however, the executive branch is attempting to override Texas's gun laws on the strength of an executive policy statement. Thus, **A** doesn't state the law here accurately.

Likewise, **B** is inaccurate. The Court has never held that federalism is absolutely irrelevant in foreign affairs disputes. But **C** is incorrect, too: Presidents don't need the explicit approval of Congress to enter into executive agreements. That leaves **D**, which is the correct answer after *Medellin*.

3. *Congressional and Presidential war powers*

The Constitution's allocation of military power between the President and Congress is a subject of perennial debate. Owing to judicial unwillingness to get involved in war powers disputes, moreover, it is a debate that is unlikely to ever be settled definitively. The Constitution gives Congress the power "to declare war," but the President is designated the "commander-in-chief." *Compare* U.S. Const. art. I, § 8, cl. 11 *with* U.S. Const. art. II, § 2, cl. 1.

Most recent controversies have concerned the ability of the President to commit combat troops to hostilities abroad without congressional authority. Presidents of both parties have argued that the War Powers Resolution, 50 U.S.C. §§ 1541–1548, passed in the wake of the Vietnam War, is unconstitutional. The War Powers Resolution requires consultation with and notification of Congress when troops are committed to combat. It also authorizes Congress to require withdrawal after joint resolution. For reasons discussed later, this provision of the Act is almost surely unconstitutional.

Although there exists considerable disagreement about the ability of Congress to limit the President's war-making powers, presidentialists and congressionalists agree that one of Congress's most effective checks would be a refusal to fund military operations. The perception that by doing so Congress would be stranding soldiers in the field — even though Congress could appropriate funds for their withdrawal — has limited that check's utility. Although disclaiming the obligation to do so, Presidents in recent years have found it expedient to obtain congressional authorization before committing American troops to major conflicts.

In the wake of the attacks of September 11, 2001, the Supreme Court has heard a number of cases involving the scope of executive power to detain persons suspected of being terrorists and the power to try them before military commissions, as opposed to indicting them for violations of federal criminal law and trying them in civilian courts. A related issue is the extent to which executive and legislative branches can alter the habeas corpus rights of such persons, short of suspending the writ entirely as the Constitution permits under certain circumstances. *See* U.S. Const. art. I, § 9, cl. 3.

Early cases suggested wide-ranging powers for the President and interpreted the rights of enemy combatants fairly narrowly. Civilians, though, were treated differently. In a case arising out of the Civil War, *Ex Parte Milligan,* 71 U.S. 2 (1866), the Court held unconstitutional the use of military tribunals to try civilians where civilian courts were open and operating.

But in *Ex Parte Quirin,* 317 U.S. 1 (1942), the Supreme Court upheld the use of military commissions to try eight Nazi saboteurs sent ashore to engage in espionage and sabotage against the United States during World War II. In *Johnson v. Eisentrager,* 339 U.S. 763 (1950), the Court rejected the argument that Germans arrested and imprisoned in China while working for the Japanese during World War II were entitled to habeas relief following their trial by military commissions. The Court found that the federal district court lacked jurisdiction over noncitizens captured overseas and tried before military commissions. The Bush administration relied heavily on both cases, on congressional statutes passed in the wake of the September 11 attacks, and on its claims of inherent executive power in justifying broad powers to detain suspected terrorists and try them before military commissions.

The Court heard a trio of cases in 2004 on the status of so-called enemy combatants. In *Rasul v. Bush,* 542 U.S. 466 (2004), a majority of the Court concluded that those held at Guantanamo Bay, Cuba, could invoke the federal habeas corpus statute because the statute's scope extended to the military base there, which, although in a foreign country, was considered sovereign territory.

In *Hamdi v. Rumsfeld,* 542 U.S. 507 (2004), an American citizen captured in Afghanistan was transferred from Guantanamo Bay to the naval brig in Charleston, South Carolina. Hamdi challenged the factual basis for his detention and sought habeas review of his continued imprisonment. A plurality of the Court held that the President had congressional authority to detain sus-pected terrorists without trial under the Authorization of the Use of Military Force passed on September 14, 2001. Nevertheless, the plurality did hold that Hamdi was entitled to certain procedural due process rights without speci-fying, precisely, what those might be beyond notice and an opportunity to be heard, long understood to be the irreducible minimum of constitutional due process.[3] In a similar case, *Rumsfeld v. Padilla,* 542 U.S. 426 (2004), an American citizen arrested in the United States and detained on suspicion of planning an attack with a radioactive "dirty bomb" sued over his detention without charges at the same military prison where Hamdi was held. The Court did not address the merits, finding that Padilla had filed his habeas corpus petition in the wrong place, and had not named the proper defendant in his suit.

Following those cases, Congress enacted legislation limiting the habeas corpus rights of detainees to contest the validity of their detention. The administration then designed a plan for trying detainees before military com-missions. In *Hamdan v. Rumsfeld,* 548 U.S. 557 (2006), however, the Court con-strued the legislation to preserve detainees' habeas corpus rights, as Congress had not affirmatively undertaken to suspend those rights. Further, the Court concluded the executive branch had no authority to establish military com-missions, they were barred by the Geneva Convention, and that the author-ity to establish them—and thus override the treaty obligations—could not be inferred from various acts of Congress. "[A]t most," the Court wrote, the legislation "acknowledge[d] a general Presidential authority to convene mili-tary commissions in circumstances where justified under the 'Constitution and laws,' including the laws of war." 548 U.S. at 594–595. The Court was also influenced by the degree to which the Uniform Code of Military Justice both limited the use of military commissions and incorporated some protections of the Geneva Convention, in contrast to the administration's plan.

When Congress responded with the Military Commissions Act, which explicitly authorized the use of military commissions and suspended habeas corpus for detainees at Guantanamo Bay, the Court held that Congress could not limit habeas corpus rights without invoking its power under the Suspension Clause, which permits suspension "in cases of Rebellion or Invasion [where] the public Safety may require it." U.S. Const. art. I, § 9, cl. 2; *Boumedienne v. Bush,* 128 S. Ct. 2229 (2008). The Court held that habeas relief extended to aliens held at Guantanamo Bay, Cuba, because the base there was de facto U.S. territory. In so holding, the Court was able to distinguish *Eisentrager,* rather than overrule it. The Court further found that commissions established by Congress to review the status of those declared to be enemy combatants were an inadequate substitute for habeas corpus. It remains to be seen whether

---

3. The requirements of procedural due process are covered in Brannon Padgett Denning, The Glannon Guide to Constitutional Law: Individual Rights and Liberties, Ch. 3.B. (2012).

Boumedienne applies to detainees held outside the United States in places like Iraq and Afghanistan.

It is difficult to assess the long-term impact of the cases arising out of the so-called War on Terror, but a few observations are possible. First, it appears from the preceding cases that the Court will continue to insist on its right to review actions undertaken by the executive and legislative branches regarding individual detainees, including the right to challenge their status as "enemy combatants." Second, the Court's cases evince a rejection of the most sweeping claims of executive power advanced by the Bush administration. Third, the cases seem to reflect a disinclination to permit the creation of zones, like Guantanamo Bay, that are under the effective control of the United States, but are beyond the jurisdiction of its courts. At the same time, the Court's decisions seemed to avoid including too much detail, lest the Court completely tie the hands of national security officials.

D.   The Appointment and Removal of Executive Branch Officials

1.   Introduction

The Constitution's allocation of power over the appointment and removal of executive branch officials has also produced a number of conflicts between Congress and the President, especially when the executive and legislative branches are controlled by different parties. This section reviews the source and scope of the President's appointment and removal powers, as well as the extent to which Congress may limit or check either power.

2.   Appointment powers

Article II, § 2 gives the President the power to appoint "ambassadors, other public ministers and consuls, judges of the Supreme Court, and all other Officers of the United States, whose Appointments are not herein otherwise provided for and which shall be established by law." U.S. Const. art. II, § 2, cl. 2. The Senate is required to give its "advice and consent" to such officers.

Congress, however, may invest the appointment of "inferior Officers" in one of three places: (1) the President alone (i.e., without Senate confirmation); (2) in courts of law; or (3) in the heads of executive departments. *Id.* By negative implication, however, Congress may not attempt to reserve to itself the power to appoint executive branch officials. *See, e.g., Buckley v. Valeo,* 424 U.S. 1 (1976).

The distinction between principal officers of the United States, who must be appointed by the President and confirmed by the Senate, and inferior officers whose appointments can be made without Senate confirmation, is thus an important one. Unfortunately, the Constitution itself contains no criteria for distinguishing one from the other. The Court addressed this question in *Morrison v. Olson*, 487 U.S. 654 (1988), in which it held (among other things) that the Independent Counsel established by Congress was an inferior officer whose appointment could be vested by Congress other than in the President.

At issue in *Morrison* was the creation of the position of Independent Counsel, whose appointment could be requested by the Attorney General to investigate wrongdoing by certain high-level executive branch officials. The position was created in the wake of the Watergate investigation; Congress felt that one of the lessons of that scandal was that the Department of Justice's investigation of the President and other high-level officials could be compromised by presidential interference. In an incident known to history as the "Saturday Night Massacre," President Nixon ordered the Attorney General to fire Harvard law professor and former Solicitor General Archibald Cox, who was investigating the circumstances surrounding the Watergate break-in. Attorney General Elliott Richardson resigned rather than comply, as did Deputy Attorney General William Ruckelshaus. It fell to then-Solicitor General Robert Bork, who was later nominated by President Ronald Reagan to the U.S. Supreme Court, but rejected by the Senate, to carry out Nixon's wishes.

Under the Independent Counsel statute, the Attorney General's request was made to a special panel of the Court of Appeals for the D.C. Circuit. Once appointed, the Independent Counsel would conduct an investigation using all the powers of the Justice Department and the Attorney General. The Independent Counsel, further, could be removed only for cause, and only by the Attorney General.

Morrison presented several separation of powers issues for the Court to resolve. First, the Court had to decide whether the Independent Counsel was an inferior officer or not. As discussed later, the Court also had to decide whether the restrictions on the President's ability to remove the Independent Counsel were constitutional, and whether the office as a whole impermissibly intruded on executive branch power. These questions are discussed later.

If the Independent Counsel was an "officer of the United States" then the appointment mechanism was unconstitutional, as such officers are to be nominated by the President and confirmed by the Senate. If the Independent Counsel was an inferior officer, on the other hand, then Senate confirmation would not be required, and the appointment could be vested elsewhere (just not in Congress itself).

Concluding that the Independent Counsel was indeed an inferior officer, the Court looked at several factors: (1) whether the officer "is subject to removal by a higher Executive Branch official"; (2) whether the officer "is empowered ... to perform only certain, limited duties"; (3) whether the "office is limited in jurisdiction"; and (4) whether "the office is limited in tenure." 487 U.S. at 671–672.

The Court wrote that "[a]lthough the [Independent Counsel] may not be 'subordinate' to the Attorney General (and the President) insofar as she possesses a degree of independent discretion to exercise the powers delegated to her . . . the fact that she can be removed by the Attorney General indicates that she is to some degree 'inferior' in rank and authority." 482 U.S. at 671. As to the scope of office and the jurisdiction of the Independent Counsel, the Court noted that the counsel "is empowered to perform only certain limited duties," namely, investigation and prosecution of certain federal crimes. *Id.* Further, not only is the Independent Counsel statute "itself restricted . . . to certain federal officials suspected of certain serious federal crimes, but an independent counsel can only act within the scope of the jurisdiction that has been granted by the Special Division pursuant to a request by the Attorney General." *Id.* Finally, although the Court conceded that there was no time limit on the appointment, "[n]onetheless, the office . . . is 'temporary' in the sense that an independent counsel is appointed essentially to accomplish a single task, and when that task is over the office is terminated, either by the counsel herself or by action of the Special Division." *Id.* at 672.

The Court also concluded that the appointment of inferior officials, like the Independent Counsel, could be vested in a special division of the Court of Appeals for the D.C. Circuit because there was no "incongruity" between the discharge of the judges' judicial function and their power to appoint the Independent Counsel and define the Counsel's jurisdiction. *Id.* at 676. It noted specifically that the duties to appoint and define jurisdiction were "temporary," that there was no power to supervise the investigation on the part of the judges, and that safeguards were present to ensure that the judges on the special division would not hear cases involving the Independent Counsel. *Id.* at 677. This was an interesting extra step, as the text of the Constitution itself seems to permit appointment of inferior officials by the President, courts, or heads of departments without any regard for whether the appointment was "incongruous" with those officials' other duties or not.

QUESTION 6. Bank shot. Outraged by executives' pay by companies—especially banks—receiving federal loans, Congress passed, and the President signed, the Compensation Reform Act, which created a "Comptroller of Executive Compensation"—inevitably referred to in the press as the "Compensation Czar." The Compensation Czar is required to approve compensation plans of companies receiving federal money. The Compensation Czar reports to the Secretary of the Treasury and is appointed by a panel consisting of the Secretary, and three members chosen from the House of Representatives, and three members of the Senate. Business executives challenge the constitutionality of the Compensation Czar in federal court. What should the judge hearing the case do?

A. Reject the executives' challenge, because the Compensation Czar is subordinate to the Secretary of the Treasury and an inferior officer.

B. Reject the executives' challenge, because the appointment of inferior officers may be vested in other officials and branches.

C. Sustain the executives' challenge, because members of Congress are involved in the selection of an executive branch official.

D. Sustain the executives' challenge, because executive branch officials must be nominated by the President and confirmed by the Senate.

ANALYSIS. Because not all executive officials must be nominated by the President and confirmed by the Senate, **D** is an incorrect statement of law. Only "Officers of the United States" are required to be appointed and confirmed in that manner. Because the Constitution permits inferior officers' appointments to be vested in heads of departments, or the President, or courts of law, **A** and **B** are possible answers, assuming that the Compensation Czar *is* an inferior officer. But there's really not enough information given in the facts to know for sure whether the *Morrison* factors are met. Moreover, whether the Compensation Czar is an inferior official or not is somewhat beside the point because under the statute, members of Congress are involved in the selection of an executive branch official. The Constitution doesn't mention anything about Congress being able to delegate to itself or its members a role in selecting executive branch officials; therefore, **C** is the correct answer.

QUESTION 7. Intelligence test. Eager to avoid intelligence that is "cooked" to suit the policy preferences of the executive branch, Congress passes the "Intelligence Integrity Act of 2009" (the Act). The Act creates an Independent National Intelligence Official (INIO), who is responsible for evaluating the work product of the intelligence community. If the INIO receives "substantial and credible evidence" that members of the executive branch are manipulating intelligence that might lead to military action anywhere in the world, the INIO is required to transmit a report to that effect, including recommendations for responding to intelligence politicization, to Congress, which then would hold hearings. The INIO is selected by the Director of National Intelligence, an executive branch official who is appointed by the President and subject to Senate confirmation, and who oversees the nation's intelligence community. The INIO is removable only by the Director of National Intelligence and then only for cause. The President vetoed the Act, but his veto was overridden by two thirds of both houses and the Act became law. Which of the following would furnish the strongest argument for the unconstitutionality of the Office of the INIO?

A. The INIO is neither appointed by the President nor confirmed by the Senate.
B. The INIO cannot be removed by the President.
C. The scope of the INIO's jurisdiction is wide-ranging, involving the review of any and all intelligence collected by the federal government.
D. Congress has no role in the appointment of the INIO.

ANALYSIS. According to *Morrison,* factors such as degree of subordination, scope of jurisdiction, duties, and tenure in office control when the question arises regarding an executive branch office's inferiority. If an officer is *not* an "inferior" officer, then under the Constitution, that position may be filled only by a presidential nomination followed by Senate confirmation. Because it is the Director of National Intelligence, and not the President, making the nomination, and because the position does *not* require Senate confirmation, the INIO must be "inferior" to withstand a challenge. Without more, however, one cannot conclude that the INIO is unconstitutional simply because there is no presidential nomination and Senate confirmation, as **A** suggests.

Nor does it matter that *the President* alone cannot remove the INIO, as stated in **B**. Recall that the Attorney General was the only official empowered to remove the Independent Counsel; the Court concluded that because there was still someone in the executive branch at least nominally superior to the Independent Counsel, she was still subordinate to someone. **D** is an incorrect statement of the law: Congress may *not* have any role in the appointment of executive branch officials.

That leaves **C**, which is the best answer. The *Morrison* Court stressed the limited scope and jurisdiction of the Independent Counsel, as well as the lack of policymaking function in its conclusion that the office is an inferior one. By contrast, the brief given to the INIO is fairly wide-ranging. The intelligence community in the United States is made up of a number of different departments and agencies; the INIO is given authority to evaluate *all* work product from the agencies. Further, decisions about the degree of "politicization" of intelligence requires judgments not only about where the baseline for "nonpoliticized" intelligence lies, but also at what point intelligence deviates far enough from that baseline to be deemed politicized. These seem removed from the Court's description of the limited duties of the Independent Counsel.

3. Removal power

The Constitution itself is silent as to whether the power to remove an officer who received Senate confirmation must also be ratified by the Senate. This question was at the heart of one of the earliest constitutional debates in the

First Congress.[4] Although its members concluded that the President should be free to remove his subordinates without Senate permission, the question was left open: Could Congress expressly *limit* the President's power to remove certain officials? Congress thought so, and impeached President Andrew Johnson for dismissing Secretary of War Edwin Stanton without Senate approval, in violation of the Tenure in Office Act. Johnson was spared removal from office by a single vote following his Senate trial.

In *Myers v. United States,* 272 U.S. 52 (1926), however, the Court, per Chief Justice William Howard Taft, invalidated a law prohibiting the removal of certain postmasters without Senate consent. In an exhaustive opinion, Chief Justice Taft concluded that the President had the exclusive power to remove executive branch officials and that any congressional limitation of that power was unconstitutional. 272 U.S. at 163–164.

Myers is no longer good law for its strongest proposition — that *no* limits on the removal of executive branch officials are permissible. In fact, less than a decade after *Myers,* the Court held in *Humphrey's Executor v. United States,* 295 U.S. 602 (1935), that President Roosevelt's removal of a commissioner on the "independent" Federal Trade Commission (FTC) was unlawful because the members of the FTC were to be removed only for cause, including "inefficiency, neglect of duty, or malfeasance in office." 295 U.S. at 620. The Court held the *Myers* rule applied to "purely" executive officials, as opposed to those like the commissioners of the FTC and members of other independent boards who performed "quasi-legislative" and "quasi-judicial" functions. *Id.* at 628.

The trend away from *Myers* continued in *Weiner v. United States,* 357 U.S. 349 (1958), in which the Court held that even where a congressional act was *silent* on the question of removal, the President's power could be limited where independence from the President was desirable. 357 U.S. at 354. At issue was the presidential dismissal of a member of the War Claims Commission. The desirability of limits in *Weiner* was based on the Court's determination that Congress intended awards to be made not on political influence, but according to objective criteria. *Id.* at 355–356. The Court also concluded that officials on the Commission were not purely executive officers. *Id.* at 356.

Morrison, too, addressed the limitations on removal of the Independent Counsel. Recall that the statute limited the President's power to remove by first vesting the power to remove in the Attorney General, then requiring that any removal be "for cause." 487 U.S. at 663. The Court rejected the argument that because Presidents need to be able to remove executive officials at will this limitation violated separation of powers. The Court noted that cases like *Humphrey's Executor* and *Weiner* had rejected such sweeping removal powers for the President. Appellees then countered that a prosecutor was the quintessential executive official, and that even under *Humphrey's Executor,* any

---

4. For a description of the controversy, see David P. Currie, *The Constitution in Congress: The Federalist Period,* 1789–1801, at 37–39 (1997).

limitation of the President's power to remove such an official could not stand. *Id.* at 688–689.

Although acknowledging that the Court "did rely on the terms 'quasi-legislative' and 'quasi-judicial' to distinguish those officials involved in *Humphrey's Executor* and *Wiener* from those in *Myers*," the Court declined to employ rigid categories in deciding whether the limitations on the Independent Counsel were permissible. *Id.* at 689–690. According to the Court, "*Myers* was undoubtedly correct in its holding, and in its broader suggestion that there are some 'purely executive' officials who must be removable by the President at will if he is to be able to accomplish his constitutional role." *Id.* at 690. However, the use of the labels "quasi-executive" and "quasi-judicial," argued the Court, "in large part reflected our judgment that it was not essential to the President's proper execution of his Article II powers that these agencies be headed up by individuals who were removable at will." *Id.* at 690–691. In the end, "the real question is whether the removal restrictions are of such a nature that they impede the President's ability to perform his constitutional duty, and the functions of the officials in question must be analyzed in that light." *Id.* at 691. Later, it restated the standard, asking whether the limitation on the President's ability to remove the Independent Counsel "is so central to the functioning of the Executive Branch as to require as a matter of constitutional law that the counsel be terminable at will by the President." *Id.* at 691–692.

The Court then concluded that the removal limitation did not so interfere, without really defining what the President's "constitutionally-appointed function[s]" were. It noted that the Independent Counsel statute was neither (1) an attempt by Congress to gain a role for itself in the removal of executive officials other than by impeachment, nor (2) an attempt by Congress to require the Attorney General to seek congressional approval for the removal. *Id.* at 692–693. Further, the Court again referred to the "inferior" status of the Independent Counsel, noted its lack of policymaking or administrative authority, and concluded that the need to control the Independent Counsel was not "central to the functioning of the Executive Branch." *Id.* at 695–696.

Humphrey's Executor preserved some realm in which the President's power of removal was unfettered, even if it rejected *Myers*'s scope. After *Morrison*, though, and the Court's functional approach to removal, it is unclear whether *any* executive official serves completely at the President's pleasure. As Justice Scalia complained in his lone dissent, the Court neither defined the President's constitutional duties nor gave clues as to how central certain duties had to be before the official performing them had to be removable at will. *See id.* at 726–727 (Scalia, J., dissenting).

Whatever uncertainty remains regarding the scope of congressional power to limit executive removal, this is clear: Congress itself may have no role (outside the impeachment process) for removing executive branch officials. In *Bowsher v. Synar,* 478 U.S. 714 (1986), the Court invalidated provisions of a 1985 Act assigning executive functions to the Comptroller General, an official who could be removed by joint resolution of Congress. "To permit the execution of laws to be vested in an officer answerable only to Congress would, in practical terms, reserve in Congress control over the execution of the laws. The structure of the Constitution does not permit Congress to execute the laws; it follows that Congress cannot grant to an officer under its control what it does not possess." 478 U.S. at 726.

QUESTION 8. Intelligence retest.   Reread the facts in Question 7 ("Intelligence test"). Which of the following facts, if true, would militate against the limitation on the President's ability to remove the INIO?

A. The INIO is a purely executive official with no legislative or judicial functions.
B. The INIO's review of intelligence by other members of the intelligence community has had a substantial impact on foreign, military, and intelligence policy.
C. The INIO is rendered independent from the President as a result of the limitation.
D. The INIO may be removed for cause by the Director of National Intelligence.

ANALYSIS.   Because of *Morrison*'s decision, the *Humphrey's Executor* distinction between "purely" executive officials and those with other duties is no longer the determining factor when it comes to limiting the President's power of removal. Therefore **A** is not the correct answer.

Further, neither the fact that the INIO is independent from the President, as in **C**, nor the fact that the INIO may be removed for cause by the Director of National Intelligence, as in **D**, militates *against* the limitation on presidential removal. Simply because an executive branch official is insulated somewhat from the President does not mean that limitation is unconstitutional—that was the point of *Morrison*. Similarly, the *Morrison* Court cited the fact that the Independent Counsel was subordinate to *someone* in the executive branch as proof that the limitation on removal did not so inhibit or impair the discharge of the President's constitutional abilities as to require the Counsel's removal at will by the President.

Therefore **B** is the best answer: Were an official to have such an impact on policymaking and policy formulation, that fact would suggest that the President *did* need to remove that person without limitation, lest the President's own policies be compromised by the work of a subordinate.

While *Morrison* made clear that some limits on the President's removal power were permissible, the question of how much insulation from direct or indirect executive branch control Congress could build in to independent bodies was the question in *Free Enterprise Fund v. Public Company Accounting*

Oversight Board, 130 S. Ct. 3138 (2010). The Public Company Oversight Board, or "PCAOB" was created by the 2002 Sarbanes-Oxley Act as a reaction to accounting failures that led to the collapse of companies like Enron. "[T]he Board is a Government-created, Government-appointed entity, with expansive powers to govern an entire industry. Every accounting firm — both foreign and domestic — that participates in auditing public companies under the securities laws must register with the Board, pay it an annual fee, and comply with its rules and oversight." *Free Enterprise Fund*, 130 S. Ct. at 3147.

The members of the Board were appointed by the commissioners of the Securities and Exchange Commission, and could be removed only "for good cause shown" in accordance with prescribed procedures. *Id.* at 3148. Commissioners of the SEC, moreover, "cannot themselves be removed by the President except under the *Humphrey's Executor* standard of 'inefficiency, neglect of duty, or malfeasance in office' . . . . " *Id.* The practical effect of the "dual for-cause limitations" was that the President could remove at will no one with significant authority over, or control of, the members of the Board.

The Board's constitutionality was challenged by parties including an accounting firm that was being investigated by the Board after an inspection produced a report critical of the firm's auditing procedures. Despite a number of constitutional challenges levied at the Board and its make-up, a majority of the Court agreed with only one — the argument that the dual for-cause limitation on the President's removal power violated separation of powers principles.

In previous cases, the Court explained, "only one level of protected tenure separated the President from an officer exercising executive power." *Id.* at 3153. Here, however, the act creating the Board "not only protects Board members from removal except for good cause, but withdraws from the President any decision on whether that good cause exists. That decision is vested instead in other tenure officers — the Commissioners — none of whom is subject to the President's direct control." *Id.* The Board, as a result, "is not accountable to the President," nor is the President "responsible for the Board." *Id.* This, for the Court, violated a basic principle of presidential power: that the responsibility of the President for the whole of the executive branch meant that he can neither surrender responsibility for the executive branch nor his obligation to supervise it. *Id.* at 3154. Indeed, Chief Justice Roberts wrote, if dual for-cause limitations were possible, why not three or more? "The officers of such an agency — safely encased within a Matryoshka doll of tenure protections — would be immune from Presidential oversight, even as they exercised power in the people's name." *Id.* This would "subvert[] the President's ability to ensure that the laws are faithfully executed — as well as the public's ability to pass judgment on [the President's] efforts." *Id.* at 3155.

The dissenters emphasized that neither text, history, nor precedent answered the precise question before the Court, and chastised the majority for failing to take context into account. *Id.* at 3165-3167 (Breyer, J., dissenting). In previous cases, Justice Breyer argued, the Court "has looked to function and context, and not to bright-line rules." *Id.* at 3167 (Breyer, J., dissenting). The dissent doubted the dual for-cause provisions hampered presidential authority to any appreciable degree and furthered a valuable goal of insulating experts from political pressure. He feared that the majority's ruling "sweep[s] hundreds, perhaps thousands of high level government officials within the scope of the Court's holding, putting their job security and their administrative actions and decisions constitutionally at risk." *Id.* at 3179 (Breyer, J., dissenting).

———————

To summarize, we know that Congress can neither reserve for itself the power to appoint executive branch officials, nor the power to remove those officials (other than by impeachment). Little else beyond that is clear. According to *Morrison,* inferior officers (who may be appointed by someone other than the President and not subject to Senate confirmation) must (1) be subordinate to someone; (2) have limited duties; (3) have limited jurisdiction, including a lack of policymaking responsibilities; and (4) have a limited tenure. In the absence of clear guidelines, application of these factors will be fact specific.

For removal, we know that Congress cannot prohibit removal of executive branch officials altogether, but it may limit the removal as long as the limitations don't impede the President's ability to discharge his constitutional duties. Further, a court might limit presidential removal, even in the absence of statutory language limiting removal, if the court concludes that independence from the President is desirable. Moreover, after *Free Enterprise Fund*, we know that Congress may not limit the President's removal power by providing additional insulation of executive branch officials through multiple for-cause limitations. Finally, as the debate between Chief Justice Roberts and Justice Breyer in that case demonstrates, where one comes out on the resolution of separation of powers conflicts tends to depend on whether one views such conflicts as better resolved through formal, bright-line rules or more functional criteria.

QUESTION 9. Removing day.　In an effort to combat rising entitlement costs, Congress passes legislation creating a National Budgetary Reform Board. The members of the Board are nominated by the President and confirmed by the Senate. They are charged with developing a plan to reform federal entitlement programs and lower the national debt. They have been given license to look at all aspects of entitlement spending, as well as ways to reform the tax code. By law, Congress must take an up-or-down vote on the Board's plan within 60 days of its being presented to both Houses. Members of the Board may be removed only for cause, and only by the Chairman of the Federal Reserve Board, who himself can be removed for cause by the President. As the Board begins deliberations, word leaks of the wide-ranging reforms contemplated by it, and pressure builds on the President to "do something." Unable to replace either the Board members or the Fed Chairman other than "for cause," he sues in federal district court, claiming that the composition of the Board violates separation of powers principles. A reviewing court should:

A. Find for the Board, because insulation from Presidential removal here is essential to its work.

B. Find for the Board, because Congress has not attempted to aggrandize power to itself at the President's expense.

C. Find for the President because the combination of the for cause provisions violates the Constitution.

D. Find for the President because congressional restrictions on his removal power are unconstitutional.

ANALYSIS.   Under *Free Enterprise Fund*, the Court has held that double for-cause provisions that insulate executive branch officials from presidential responsibility and supervision are unconstitutional. The best answer then is **C**. Neither **A** nor **B** is correct because whether the insulation is "essential" or not is not relevant to the constitutionality of this particular set of removal restrictions. Similarly, though separation of powers questions sometimes turn on functional inquiries into the extent to which one branch is attempting to "aggrandize" power at another's expense, *Free Enterprise Fund* took a more formal approach, at least as it concerned a dual for-cause restriction. **D** is incorrect because not *all* removal restrictions are unconstitutional.

E.   Congress, the President, and the Administrative State

1.   Introduction

This section discusses the Court's treatment of executive–legislative branch conflicts over the establishment and maintenance of administrative agencies, and congressional attempts to exercise oversight of those agencies. The administrative state is a fact of life in modern governance, and although the Court has generally embraced functionalism in dealing with administrative agencies—whose existence admittedly is not necessarily contemplated by the original Constitution—its decisions on congressional attempts to oversee executive agency decision-making adopt formalist readings of some of the Constitution's provisions, especially its lawmaking provisions.

2.   The nondelegation doctrine

Classical separation of powers theory held that power delegated to one branch could not be redelegated to other branches. Obviously, were the Court to adhere to a pure version of this "nondelegation" doctrine, the administrative state would never have gotten off the ground. In practice, though, the Court has only invoked the doctrine to invalidate two laws, both of which were passed as part of the so-called first New Deal—Franklin Roosevelt's attempt to deal quickly with the Great Depression following his inauguration in 1933.

In the first of these cases, *Panama Refining Co. v. Ryan,* 293 U.S. 388 (1935), the Court invalidated a portion of the National Industrial Recovery Act (NIRA), which empowered the President to block shipment of goods produced in excess of certain quotas established at the state level. In the second, *Schechter Poultry Co. v. United States,* 295 U.S. 495 (1935), the Court invalidated a live poultry code approved by the President as part of NIRA's provisions for the establishment of "codes of fair competition." In both cases, the Court concluded, Congress had specified no standards that would guide or limit the President's discretion.

In other cases, however, as long as Congress delegates power in a statute that includes an "intelligible principle"—which may include vague injunctions to regulate "in the public interest"—to guide the exercise of the delegated power by the executive agency, that statute will satisfy the nondelegation doctrine. *See Hampton v. United States,* 276 U.S. 394, 409 (1928) (stating that as long as Congress "shall lay down by legislative act an intelligible principle to which the person or body authorized to" exercise delegated authority "is directed to conform, such legislative action is not a forbidden delegation of legislative power").

The Court reaffirmed this broad reading of the nondelegation doctrine in *Mistretta v. United States,* 488 U.S. 361 (1989), in which the Court rejected a challenge to Congress's delegation of power to the United States Sentencing Commission to promulgate binding sentencing guidelines for federal judges.[5] A defendant subject to mandatory minimums promulgated by the Commission argued that Congress had violated the nondelegation doctrine by establishing the Commission. The Court observed that the Commission had been charged by Congress to (1) assure that sentencing achieved congressional purposes—deterrence, public safety, rehabilitation, and the development of appropriate sentencing ranges—set forth in the act; (2) provide certainty and fairness; and (3) reflect knowledge of human behavior when considering sentences in the context of the criminal justice system. 488 U.S. at 374. The act also referred to a number of factors the Commission was to consider when establishing categories of offenders and gave detailed guidance regarding punishment of certain serious offenses. *Id.* at 374–375. In light of such statutory guidance, the Court had little trouble concluding that the Act met the "intelligible principle" test, especially in light of the general standards the Court had upheld in other cases. *Id.* at 379. *See also Whitman v. American Trucking*

---

5.   The Court later held that the guidelines were not binding, only advisory. *See United States v. Booker,* 540 U.S. 220 (2005).

Association, Inc., 531 U.S. 457, 472–476 (2001) (upholding broad delegation of power to the EPA to regulate air quality).

3. *Bicamerality and presentment*

a. Legislative veto. As previously noted, the Court has tended to interpret some of the Constitution's explicit separation of powers provisions strictly. Article I, § 7, for example, sets forth the Constitution's lawmaking procedures. To become law, legislation must be passed by both houses of Congress ("bicamerality") and then presented to the President for veto or signature ("presentment"). The Court's strict enforcement of bicamerality and presentment has frustrated congressional attempts to reserve a check on executive agencies exercising delegated power through the legislative veto, as well as attempts to empower the President to amend legislation after its passage so that he signs into law something different than that which passed both houses of Congress (the so-called line-item veto).

The legislative veto was a device by which Congress attempted to retain oversight of executive branch implementation or exercise of delegated power whereby particular executive branch decisions could be overridden by resolution of one or both houses of Congress. The resolution was not sent to the President for signature or veto. Supporters argued that the legislative veto was a reasonable compromise between Congress legislating to an impossible level of detail to constrain agency discretion and delegating all of its power away and having to resort to amending underlying legislation if unhappy with executive implementation. The Court, however, invalidated the legislative veto in *INS v. Chadha,* 462 U.S. 919 (1983).

Chadha involved a provision of the Immigration and Nationality Act permitting one house of Congress, by resolution, to reverse the decision of the Attorney General — granted by the same act — to halt deportation proceedings against aliens. 462 U.S. at 925. *Chadha* challenged the one-house veto as being inconsistent with Article I, § 7's lawmaking provisions; the Court agreed.

According to the Court, all actions that were "legislative" in nature must comply with the "single, finely wrought and exhaustively considered, procedure" outlined in Article I, § 7. *Id.* at 951. The Court concluded that the action taken by the House, which "had the purpose and effect of altering the legal rights, duties, and relations of persons, including the Attorney General, Executive Branch officials, and Chadha, all outside the Legislative Branch, constituted lawmaking. "[A]bsent the House action, Chadha would remain in the United States. Congress has *acted* and its action has altered Chadha's status." *Id.* at 951. If Congress wished to alter the ability of the Attorney General to exercise power delegated to him by Congress, it must do so, the Court held, the same way it delegated the power in the first place: by observing the lawmaking procedures in Article I, § 7. *Id.* at 954–955. The majority conceded the expediency of the legislative veto, but argued that "[t]here is no support in the Constitution or decisions of this Court for the proposition that the cumbersomeness and delays often encountered in complying with explicit constitutional standards may be avoided, either by Congress or by the President." *Id.* at 959. After *Chadha,* in summary dispositions, the Court invalidated a two-house legislative veto, *U.S. Senate v. Federal Trade Commission,* 463 U.S. 1216 (1983), and a one-house veto over administrative decision making, *Process Gas Consumers Group v. Consumers Energy Council of America,* 463 U.S. 1216 (1983).

b. Line-item veto.   The Constitution speaks of a President's power to "return" a "Bill" passed by both houses "with his Objections," U.S. Const. art. I, § 7, cl. 2. Although the Constitution does not define a "bill," President Washington established the tradition that a bill must be either accepted or rejected in toto. Long possessed by state governors, Presidents since Ronald Reagan have sought a line-item veto, which permits executives to invalidate parts of bills, instead of having to choose between signing a "must-pass" bill with objectionable provisions in it, or vetoing the entire bill. Appropriations bills, for example, which Presidents often face tremendous pressure to sign, are frequently littered with nongermane "riders" or larded with pork, which some define as appropriations for someone else's district.

In 1996, Congress passed a limited line-item veto that permitted the President to disallow certain spending provisions if certain conditions obtained. Specifically, the act gave the President the ability to cancel three types of spending: (1) "any dollar amount of discretionary budget authority; (2) any item of new direct spending; or (3) any limited tax benefit." *Clinton v. New York,* 524 U.S. 417, 436 (1998). Such cancellation had to be accompanied by findings that the cancellation would reduce the budget deficit, not impair "essential Government function," and "not harm the national interest." *Id.* The President would then notify Congress of the cancellation; Congress could then pass a "disapproval bill" reversing the President's cancellation, but that bill would be subject to a presidential veto. *Id.* at 436–447.

Relying largely on *Chadha,* the Court struck down the line-item veto, finding that its provisions did not comply with Article I, § 7's "finely wrought" lawmaking procedures. *Id.* at 438. "What has emerged in these cases from the President's exercise of his statutory cancellation powers," the Court wrote, "are truncated versions of the two bills that passed both Houses of Congress." *Id.* at 440. In other words, what the President signed following exercise of his cancellation power was not the "law" that was passed in the House and the Senate. The majority distinguished cases, like one involving the Tariff Act,[6] in which the Court had permitted Congress to delegate power to the President to suspend tariff exemptions under particular conditions. *Id.* at 442–443.

---

6.   Under the Tariff Act, Congress gave the President the power to suspend tariff exemptions if other countries' duties on U.S. products were, in the President's opinion, deemed "reciprocally unequal and unreasonable." The Court upheld this delegation in *Field v. Clark,* 143 U.S. 649 (1892).

First, the exercise of the suspension power was contingent upon a condition that did not exist when the Tariff Act was passed: the imposition of "reciprocally unequal and unreasonable" import duties by other countries. In contrast, the exercise of the cancellation power [in the cases before the Court] necessarily was based on the same conditions that Congress evaluated when it passed those statutes. Second, under the Tariff Act, when the President determined that the contingency had arisen, he had a duty to suspend; in contrast, while it is true that the President was required by the Act to make three determinations before he canceled a provision . . . those determinations did not qualify his discretion to cancel or not to cancel. Finally, whenever the President suspended an exemption under the Tariff Act, he was executing the policy that Congress had embodied in the statute. In contrast, whenever the President cancels an item of new direct spending or a limited tax benefit he is rejecting the policy judgment made by Congress and relying on his own policy judgment. Thus, the conclusion in *Field v. Clark* that the suspensions mandated by the Tariff Act were not exercises of legislative power does not undermine our opinion that cancellations pursuant to the Line Item Veto Act are the functional equivalent of partial repeals of Acts of Congress that fail to satisfy Article I, § 7.

Id. at 443–444. Elsewhere, the Court stressed the third point, distinguishing statutes permitting the President to decline to spend certain appropriated monies: "The critical difference between [the Line Item Veto] and all of its predecessors . . . is that . . . this statute gives the President the unilateral power to change the text of duly enacted statutes." *Id.* at 446–447.

QUESTION 10. Doling the dollars.   Congress recently passed an Emergency Economic Stabilization Act that permits the President, through the Secretary of the Treasury, to offer loan guarantees to businesses facing shortfalls due to economic distress. The Act also instructs the President to suspend such guarantees if, in his judgment, the executives of the business are possessed of "unreasonable" salary and benefits packages relative to other employees and executives in the industry. When the President suspends loan guarantees to BigCorp because its executives refused to relinquish their corporate jet, the BigCorp executives sued, claiming that the provision of the Act delegating power to the President to suspend the guarantees violated Article I, § 7. Which of the following statements is true about the Act?

A. The Act is likely constitutional, because Congress may delegate power to the President to exercise according to statutory conditions.

B. The Act is likely constitutional, because the Act was passed by both houses and sent to the President for his signature or veto.

C. The Act is likely unconstitutional, because the President's decision to suspend the guarantees was legislative in nature and required passage by both houses of Congress.

D. The Act is likely unconstitutional, because the President's action negates a policy choice made by Congress when it passed the Act.

ANALYSIS.   As we saw in *Chadha* and in *New York v. Clinton,* just because an act giving the President (or one house of Congress) the power to do *X* passes both houses and is signed by the President doesn't always mean that the act passes constitutional muster. Both the legislative veto and the line-item veto initially complied with the requirements of Article I, § 7. Therefore, **B** is not going to be the correct answer.

On the other hand, we saw in the line-item veto case that the Court had, in the past, approved of delegation of certain power to the President, which he could exercise or not following guidelines laid down by Congress. Therefore, **C** is not correct either. **D** is simply incorrect: Granting the President the ability to suspend the loan guarantees—like the ability to suspend the tariff exemption in *Field v. Clark,* discussed in the line-item veto case—*was* a policy choice made by Congress. In the facts presented here, the President was simply exercising the discretion given him by Congress.

That leaves **A**, which is the best answer. As long as delegations to the executive branch include intelligible principles to guide their exercise, they will be permitted. Even if the guidelines are general or subjective, as they are here, the Court will not disturb those delegations.

QUESTION 11. Use your discretion. "Earmarks" are appropriations that members of Congress insert into the annual budget directing dollars into their district for designated uses. Earmarks can take different forms, including so-called unrequested spending, whereby Congress funds a program at a level higher than that requested in the President's budget. As part of earmark reform, Congress has passed the Earmark Accountability Reform (EAR) Act. Henceforth, the President may reduce unrequested spending to the level originally requested by the President, if, in the President's opinion, the additional spending is "wasteful" or "unnecessary" and that finding is reported to Congress. Unless Congress restores the earmarks by majority vote in a resolution that is sent to the President for a veto or signature, the earmarks do not become law. Ames City, the capital of the State of Ames, is due to receive some unrequested spending for infrastructure development, but the President deems that extra money "wasteful" and so indicates in a message to Congress. A resolution restoring the money fails and the Mayor of Ames City sues, claiming that the EAR Act is unconstitutional. How would a reviewing court likely find?

A. The Act is constitutional, because it simply gives the President the power to decline to spend appropriated funds.

B. The Act is constitutional because it complies with Article I, § 7's bicamerality and presentment requirements.

C. The Act is unconstitutional because it enables the President to exercise delegated power.

D. The Act is unconstitutional because it enables the President to substitute his policy judgment for that of Congress.

ANALYSIS. This was a little more difficult, but if you read the description of *Clinton v. New York* closely, you should have been able to pick the correct answer. Let's start with answers easily discarded. Again, **B** is incorrect, because the question isn't whether the initial Act complied with Article I, § 7, but whether the Act further empowered someone to take action in the future that did *not* comply with Article I, § 7, but should have. Similarly, **C** is wrong because Presidents exercise delegated power all the time; only if the delegation is standardless in the literal sense of the word would the Court consider invalidating the Act.

Between the remaining answers, **A** is incorrect, because the President isn't simply declining to spend funds that are appropriated; rather the Act purports to empower the President to reduce funding in a bill that has been appropriated by Congress. While subtle, the difference is an important one. Had the Act simply given the President the power to decline to spend all unrequested funding over the administration-requested amount, it would likely pass muster, as the ability to suspend the tariff exemptions in *Field v. Clark* did. But the Act did something different: It empowered the President to reduce the actual amount in the bill. This meant that—unless Congress reversed the President's alteration through a resolution that was itself subject to presidential veto—the bill that became law following the reduction would be different than that which was passed by Congress. The President's judgment would replace Congress's and, as in *Clinton v. New York,* that is unconstitutional. Therefore **D** is the best answer.

4.   *Other separation of powers considerations*

In addition to the quite specific challenges lodged against the line-item veto and the legislative veto, or that involve the President's appointment and removal powers, several statutes discussed in other sections of this chapter have faced general separation of powers challenges alleging that one branch was either "encroaching" on another's powers, or seeking to "aggrandize" power. *See, e.g., Mistretta v. United States,* 488 U.S. 361, 382 (1989) (noting that members of the Court "ha[ve] not hesitated to strike down provisions of law that either accrete to a single Branch powers more appropriately diffused among separate Branches or that undermine the authority and independence of one or another coordinate Branch"). Perhaps because the U.S. Constitution—unlike many state constitutions—contains no specific separation of powers clause, these broad challenges have generally failed.

For example, in *Morrison v. Olson,* the Court considered whether the Independent Counsel statute "taken as a whole, violates the principle of separation of powers by unduly interfering with the role of the Executive Branch." 487 U.S. at 693. The Court held that the statute neither "involve[d] an attempt by Congress to increase its own powers at the expense of the Executive Branch" nor "work[ed] any *judicial* usurpation of properly executive functions." *Id.* at 695. The Court noted, for example, that the Special Division of the Court of Appeals for the D.C. Circuit could appoint an independent counsel only at the request of the Attorney General. Courts neither reviewed a decision *not* to appoint an independent counsel nor "supervised or controlled the activities of the counsel." *Id.* Further, the Court found that the statute did not impermissibly undermine the powers of the executive or prevent the executive branch from "accomplishing its constitutionally assigned functions." *Id.* (internal quotation marks omitted). Alluding to its finding that the Independent Counsel was an "inferior" officer subject to executive branch control through the Attorney General, the Court concluded that the "Executive Branch [had] sufficient control over the independent counsel to ensure that the President is able to perform his constitutionally assigned duties." *Id.* at 696.

A similar objection was lodged against the Sentencing Reform Act in *Mistretta.* The Court rejected that challenge as well. While acknowledging that the Sentencing Commission (described earlier on p. 165) was unique, it "is not a court, does not exercise judicial power, and is not controlled by or accountable to members of the Judicial Branch. The Commission, on which members of the Judiciary may be a minority, is an independent agency in every relevant sense." 488 U.S. at 422–423. Further, the judiciary's power was not increased by the location of the Commission in it. "Prior to the passage of the Act, the Judicial Branch, as an aggregate, decided precisely the questions assigned to the Commission: what sentence is appropriate to what criminal conduct under what circumstances." *Id.* at 395.

Nor did the Court find that the judiciary was *weakened* by participation in the Sentencing Commission. The Guidelines did not prevent the judiciary from discharging some essential judicial function, nor did they "involve a degree of political authority inappropriate for a nonpolitical Branch." *Id.* at 396. "They do no more than fetter the discretion [of] judges to do what they have done for generations — impose sentences within the broad limits established by Congress." *Id.*

Finally, the Court found that participation of individual judges in the Sentencing Commission was permissible. Not only did the Constitution not prohibit — as it does for legislators — dual office-holding by judges, but simple participation in the work of the Commission did nothing to undermine judicial integrity. Although appointed by the President, and subject to removal by him, the judges would still be federal judges with lifetime tenure. Therefore, the Court felt the President had comparably little influence over judicial members of the Commission. *Id.* at 410–411.

F. Legislative and Executive Immunities

1. *Introduction*

The Constitution explicitly creates some specific protections for members of the legislative branch, spurred no doubt by the Framers' knowledge of historic incidents in which members of Parliament were harassed by the Crown and, in some instances, by Parliament itself. Interestingly, the executive branch receives no explicit immunities in the Constitution; nevertheless, some have been assumed to exist since the early days of the Republic, and the Court has acknowledged, in theory at least, the existence of "executive privilege." The Court has also granted immunity to certain executive branch officials from suit related to their duties. This section discusses both sets of immunities.

2. *Legislative immunities*

a. The Arrest Clause.   Article I, § 6, clause 1 states that

> The Senators and Representatives . . . shall in all Cases, except Treason, Felony and Breach of the Peace, be privileged from Arrest during their Attendance at the Session of their Respective Houses, and in going to and returning from the same; and for any Speech or Debate in either House, they shall not be questioned in any other Place.

The first of these privileges, the Arrest Clause, has been interpreted by the Court to apply only to civil proceedings — arrest for nonpayment of debt would have been of particular concern to those of the Framing generation — and not to criminal matters. *See Williamson v. United States,* 207 U.S. 425, 446 (1908) (upholding conviction of House member for subornation of perjury; concluding that "the term 'treason, felony, and breach of the peace,' as used in the constitutional provision relied upon, excepts from the operation of the privilege all criminal offenses").

QUESTION 12. Arresting developments.   Cleghorn, a Senator, is served with papers regarding a personal injury suit by a motorist stemming from a wreck in which Cleghorn was involved while Congress was in recess. The motorist, who is from another state, sues in federal court; Cleghorn argues that because Congress is in session, the Arrest Clause means he cannot be served with papers in a civil suit until Congress has adjourned because of the potential interference with official duties posed by being subject to a civil lawsuit while Congress was sitting. How should the judge rule?

A. Dismiss the suit, because the suit is a "civil proceeding."
B. Dismiss the suit, because the Arrest Clause guarantees against arrest-like interference such as service of process.
C. Permit the suit, because Cleghorn was not literally arrested.
D. Permit the suit, because no one is above the law.

ANALYSIS.   Don't feel bad if you didn't get this right, it was a little tricky. You might have been drawn to **A** based on what I wrote earlier, or you might have thought **B** made sense given the fact that civil suits can be as distracting and time-consuming as actual arrest. Although both answers make a certain amount of sense, the Supreme Court has interpreted the Arrest Clause strictly. In *Long v. Ansell,* 293 U.S. 76, 82–83 (1934), the Court rejected the argument that the Arrest Clause exempted a Senator from service of process in a civil matter while Congress was sitting. Arrest, the Court held, meant actual arrest and imprisonment. Therefore **C** is the best answer. **D** is incorrect because, of course, the Arrest Clause does offer some immunity to members of Congress not available to others not serving in Congress.

---

b. The Speech and Debate Clause.   The Speech and Debate Clause, however, has provided somewhat more robust protections for members of Congress. The purpose of the Clause, of course, is to ensure that members of Congress not be harassed for opinions expressed in the course of legislative debate. The privilege extends not only to actual suits based on "legislative acts"—slander suits, for example, for remarks made during debates—but also to subpoenas for grand jury testimony.

As the preceding sentence indicates, not every utterance by a member of Congress will receive protection, only those related to her legislative activities. As the Court has defined them,

> legislative acts are not all-encompassing. [T]hey must be an integral part of the deliberative and communicative processes by which Members participate in committee and House proceedings with respect to the consideration and passage or rejection of proposed legislation or with respect to other matters which the Constitution places within the jurisdiction of either House.

Gravel v. United States, 408 U.S. 606, 625 (1972).

Thus, when Senator William Proxmire was sued for a press release awarding his "Golden Fleece Award" to a scientist who conducted federally funded research on primate aggression, the Court concluded that ridiculing Dr. Hutchinson was not an immunity-conferring legislative act. *Hutchinson v. Proxmire,* 443 U.S. 111 (1979). Although conceding that "[a] speech by Proxmire in the Senate would be wholly immune," it concluded that "neither the newsletters [to constituents that reprinted the press release] nor the press release was 'essential to the deliberations of the Senate' and neither was part of the deliberative process." 443 U.S. at 130. The Court has extended Speech and Debate Clause immunity—but only for legislative acts—to members' aides. *See Gravel,* 408 U.S. at 616 ("for the purpose of construing the privilege [with regard to legislative acts] a Member and his aide are to be 'treated as one'").

The Speech and Debate Clause has not been construed to prohibit a legislator from being prosecuted for crimes that relate to legislative acts, like bribery, but the prosecution cannot be based on the legislative acts themselves, like the member's voting record. *See United States v. Helstoski,* 442 U.S. 477, 487 (1979) (noting that "evidence of a legislative act of a Member may not be introduced by the Government in a prosecution" for bribery); *United States v. Johnson*, 383 U.S. 169, 180 (1966) (holding that the Speech and Debate Clause covered "an allegation that a member of Congress abused his position by conspiring to give a particular speech in return for remuneration from private interests"; "The essence of such a charge in this context is that the Congressman's conduct was improperly motivated, and . . . that is precisely what the Speech or Debate Clause generally forecloses from executive and judicial inquiry.").

QUESTION 13. Are you being served? Senator Cleghorn represents Ames, a state in the United States. The Senator recommends several candidates each year from his state for admission to the U.S. service academies. This year there was particularly fierce competition for admission; Cleghorn instructs his aide, Smithers, to see what he can do about ensuring that Cleghorn's candidate is admitted to the Naval Academy. Smithers finds out that there is another strong candidate endorsed by Ames's junior Senator, and Cleghorn's political rival. In a misguided effort to ingratiate himself with his boss, Smithers spreads word that the rival candidate was the subject of a cheating investigation during his senior year (he wasn't). Cleghorn's favored candidate receives admission over the other young man, who finds out that he had been slandered and sues both Cleghorn and Smithers. Cleghorn moves to dismiss the suit, citing the Speech and Debate Clause. What should the reviewing judge do?

A. Dismiss the suit, because Smithers is protected as the alter ego of the Senator.

B. Dismiss the suit, because Smithers's and Cleghorn's activities are protected by the Speech and Debate Clause.

C. Allow the suit to proceed, because no legislative acts were involved.

D. A and B

ANALYSIS. The question is easy if you keep in mind what, precisely, the Speech and Debate Clause protects. The Court has distinguished between legislative acts relating directly to the business of Congress and everything else. Things like arranging for the commercial publication of the Pentagon Papers are outside the scope of the Clause. Although aides are covered by the Clause, they are, like members of Congress, only covered for legislative acts. *See Gravel v. United States*, 408 U.S. 606 (1972) (Clause does not cover legislative aides' assistance in arranging for publication of the Pentagon Papers). Thus, **A** is true only if the underlying acts themselves are "an integral part of the deliberative and communicative processes by which members participate in . . . the consideration and passage or rejection of proposed legislation," as *Gravel* put it.

Constituent service, like recommending candidates for military academies, would fall outside the Court's definition of legislative acts. Thus **B** is incorrect;

as is **D**. That leaves **C**, which is the best answer. Slandering another candidate for a military academy spot in hopes of getting one's constituent admitted would fall outside legislative acts. Smithers's action is more like Proxmire's presentation of the "Golden Fleece" award than any activity that is directly related to the business of Congress.

2. *Executive immunity*

Although the Constitution is silent on executive branch immunities, the Supreme Court has created (or at least recognized) some. For example, the Court has held that the President is absolutely immune from civil suits arising out of his official actions. *Nixon v. Fitzgerald,* 457 U.S. 731 (1982). The Court felt that impeachment, press scrutiny, the desire for reelection, and the desire to avoid the censure of history were adequate protections against executive wrongdoing. Civil liability for official acts, the Court held, would over-deter, possibly paralyzing the President's ability to make the tough decisions the office often required. Although the Court has refused to extend absolute immunity to presidential aides, high-level executive officials do enjoy qualified immunity, meaning that actions that were reasonable under the clearly established law at the time are immune. *Harlow v. Fitzgerald,* 457 U.S. 800 (1982).

A somewhat more difficult question arose in *Clinton v. Jones,* 520 U.S. 681 (1997): Is the President immune from suit commenced during his term in office alleging misconduct occurring prior to taking office? The *Jones* case involved allegations of sexual misconduct on the part of President Bill Clinton when he was governor of Arkansas. The President argued that the suit ought to be stayed during his term of office, because of concerns that subjecting a sitting President to the jurisdiction of a federal judge during trial violated separation of powers. 520 U.S. at 684. Further, it was argued that all of the reasons that a former President should be immune from suits arising out of official acts—the possibility of frivolous lawsuits that would have to be defended, distraction, and expense—applied as well to suits against a sitting President for pre-presidential actions. *Id.* at 694–695.

The Court distinguished *Fitzgerald,* arguing that the earlier case's concern was with the possibility that potential liability could make a President unduly timorous in the conduct of official duties. No such danger presented itself in the case of a President being sued for events that took place prior to assuming office. *Id.* at 694.

Although it acknowledged the potential separation of powers problems, the Court refused to find immunity as a matter of constitutional law. The Court noted, for example, that the President is subject to judicial review of his official actions all the time.

> If the Judiciary may severely burden the Executive Branch by reviewing the legality of the President's official conduct, and if it may direct appropriate process to the President himself, it must follow that federal courts have power to determine the legality of his unofficial conduct. The burden on the

President's time and energy that is a mere by-product of such review surely cannot be considered as onerous as the direct burden imposed by judicial review and the occasional invalidation of his official actions.

Id. at 705. Suits such as the one filed by Paula Jones were the exception rather than the rule, and the Court was willing to bet that the volume of such litigation would not increase as a result of its ruling. The Court, however, did close with an admonition to lower courts to respect the President's schedule and an invitation to Congress to draft a stronger rule if it thought appropriate. So far, Congress has declined to take the Court up on its invitation.

"Executive privilege" is the ability of the executive branch to keep secret certain conversations between the President and his advisors, as well as information, advice, memoranda, and so on, provided to the President by those advisors. The usual argument is that the President needs to ensure that aides and advisors will offer him candid, frank advice; and that if such information were made public, the President's ability to get such advice would be materially hampered. In addition, the argument runs, some material, if revealed, would harm national security, imperil sensitive diplomatic relations, and the like. Although executive privilege isn't explicitly provided for in the Constitution, Presidents have invoked it since the beginning of the Republic.

In *United States v. Nixon,* 418 U.S. 683 (1974), a majority of the Court recognized the existence of the privilege, although the Court declined to apply it to quash a subpoena for recordings and documents in the President's possession issued by a judge hearing the case of seven aides indicted for conspiracy. The Nixon Tapes Case took place against one of the most serious constitutional crises of the twentieth century. The facts, not as well known to students as they once were, are worth recounting.

In the summer of 1972, several men were arrested breaking into the headquarters of the Democratic Party in the Watergate office building. It emerged that one of the burglars had White House connections. It later also emerged that there was a plan to obstruct any investigation into the connection between the burglary and the White House and a conspiracy to cover it up that involved President Nixon himself. Several of Nixon's aides were indicted—the President himself was named as an unindicted coconspirator—and tried.

During hearings conducted in 1973, it came to light that there was a recording device in the Oval Office and that many of the discussions involving Watergate were recorded. When Nixon's aides were indicted in March 1974, the aides sought those tapes. After initially resisting the subpoena, Nixon agreed to release edited transcripts of the tapes, resisting further disclosure on executive privilege grounds; the district judge rejected his arguments and sought access to the tapes themselves. Unusually, the case bypassed the Court of Appeals, proceeding directly to the Supreme Court, which heard arguments on July 8, 1974; a decision was handed down just over two weeks later, on July 24. President Nixon resigned on August 9, avoiding what was almost certain impeachment by the House of Representatives.

Nixon's lawyers made several arguments, the broadest one being that once the President asserted executive privilege, courts could not review that assertion without violating separation of powers. The Court brushed that claim aside, citing *Marbury v. Madison* for the proposition that the Court's power was to "say what the law is": "Any other conclusion would be contrary to the basic concept of separation of powers and the checks and balances that flow from the scheme of a tripartite government." *Nixon*, 418 U.S. at 704.

Addressing the merits of the administration's argument—that the need for confidentiality and separation of powers supported the assertion of privilege here—the Court conceded the importance of both, but denied that either "can sustain an absolute, unqualified Presidential privilege of immunity from judicial process under all circumstances." *Id.* at 706. "Absent a claim of need to protect military, diplomatic, or sensitive national security secrets," the Court continued, "we find it difficult to accept the argument that even the very important interest in confidentiality of Presidential communications is significantly diminished by production of such material for in camera inspection with all the protection that a district court will be obliged to provide." *Id.*

The Court was particularly worried about enforcing the privilege in a case involving "a subpoena . . . requiring the production of materials for use in a criminal prosecution" because "[t]he right to the production of all evidence at a criminal trial" was one of the protections enshrined in the Sixth Amendment. *Id.* at 711. Weighing the importance of the President's need for confidentiality against the "fair administration of criminal justice," the Court found that the rights of the accused won out. *Id.* at 711–712. The Court did conclude its opinion with instruction to the district court to redact those portions of the conversations that were not relevant to the criminal prosecution. *Id.* at 715–716. It is worth noting that *Nixon* notwithstanding, executive privilege disputes are often hashed out outside the courts, especially when conflicts arise between the executive branch and congressional committees.

G.   The Closer: War by Committee

> **QUESTION 14. War by committee.** Dissatisfied with the conduct of the war in Afghanistan following the deployment of an additional 15,000 combat troops, Congress creates a bipartisan "Committee on the Conduct of the War" to study the situation and make legislative recommendations. As a result of the committee's conclusion that the situation was becoming a Vietnam-like quagmire, it recommends immediate withdrawal of all American troops. Congress responds by passing, over the President's veto, the "Declare Victory and Withdraw Act" ordering the President to withdraw all troops from combat zones no later than 30

days following the Act's passage. At the end of the 30-day deadline, the President has still not withdrawn the troops. Members of Congress sue the President, seeking an injunction forcing the President to begin withdrawal. Which of the following would be the best reason for a reviewing court to *reject* the members' suit?

A. The Act unconstitutionally intrudes on the President's independent powers as commander-in-chief by dictating how that power is to be exercised.

B. The President has the sole power to conduct foreign affairs on behalf of the United States.

C. Congress may only use its spending power to control executive branch conduct.

D. The Act injects Congress into military affairs, which are reserved to the President and the executive branch.

ANALYSIS. This question tests how well you recall Justice Jackson's *Youngstown* analysis. Here Congress is attempting to require the President to do something, and the President has acted against the express will of Congress by not withdrawing the troops. Therefore his power is at the lowest ebb. But that does not mean that the President's refusal to withdraw is *ipso facto* unconstitutional. Justice Jackson said that in such cases the President can rely on whatever independent power he possesses minus the power that he shares with Congress over the same matter. The question, then, is whether the President has independent power here and if he shares that power with Congress. Article II makes the President, and the President alone, "commander-in-chief" of the armed forces.

Contrary to **B** and **D**, however, that does not mean that the President has the "sole" power to conduct foreign affairs or that "military affairs" generally are the exclusive preserve of the executive branch. The Senate confirms ambassadors and approves treaties; Congress regulates foreign commerce, raises and supports armies, and prescribes rules governing their conduct. Thus it does not follow that Congress may restrain the President with its spending power only. Therefore **C** is incorrect. If you were looking for the best reason among those listed to reject the members' suits, it would be **A,** that Congress here is attempting to usurp the President's constitutionally assigned commander-in-chief role by dictating whether and how troops are deployed in the field.

✦ Denning's Picks

1.	Senatorial discourtesy	**C**
2.	Dis-appointment	**A**
3.	Claim jumpers	**B**
4.	Arbitrary arbitration	**C**
5.	Gun shy	**D**
6.	Bank shot	**C**
7.	Intelligence test	**C**
8.	Intelligence retest	**B**
9.	Removing day	**C**
10.	Doling the dollars	**A**
11.	Use your discretion	**D**
12.	Arresting developments	**C**
13.	Are you being served?	**C**
14.	War by committee	**A**

7

Closing Closers

Closing Closers

Here are some final questions to test your comprehension of the material covered in the preceding chapters. The answers are at the end, along with a reference to the chapter and section in which the tested material was covered. Those references are intended to give you a quick and efficient way to identify material you might need to continue studying. Good luck!

QUESTION 1. The taxman cometh. The City of Fair Isle in the State of Ames is home to a number of private and public colleges and universities. As a result of a recent economic downturn, Fair Isle is facing an enormous hole in its city budget. To ameliorate the shortfall, the Mayor of Fair Isle proposes, and the city council adopts, a $300 per year "student impact fee" imposed on all colleges and universities in Fair Isle for each out-of-state student enrolled. The Mayor argues that it is a way for those institutions—whose property is tax exempt—to pay their "fair share" and to ensure that the city is compensated for the city resources the students consume. Braun University, one of the affected institutions, sues over the tax, claiming that, among other things, the tax violates the dormant Commerce Clause doctrine. A reviewing court would likely do what?

A. Dismiss the suit, because no interstate commerce is involved.
B. Invalidate the ordinance, because it is facially discriminatory.
C. Invalidate the ordinance, because the burdens on interstate commerce clearly exceed the local benefits.
D. Dismiss the suit, because Braun University lacks standing.

QUESTION 2. Truckin'. The State of Ames, concerned about both safety and wear and tear on its roads, recently passed a law requiring all trucks whose trips do not either begin or end in the state to use only so-called national network roads, which are defined as interstates and older U.S. highways. The definition *excludes* state, county, and local highways and roads. Trucking companies complain that the law will increase costs because it will lengthen trips, require drivers to burn more fuel, and possibly result in delays as drivers are subject to federal rules requiring them to rest at prescribed intervals. Assuming that "safety" and "reducing wear and tear on state roads" are the interests asserted by Ames, and assuming that the law would reduce accidents by a slight amount, what would be the likely result of a challenge to the truck route law?

A. It would be invalidated, because it has an obvious protectionist purpose.
B. It would be invalidated, because the burdens on interstate commerce clearly exceed the putative local benefits.
C. It would be invalidated, because it facially discriminates against non-local truck traffic.
D. It would be invalidated because the effects would fall on out-of-state trucking companies.

QUESTION 3. Home cooking. The State of Ames has created its own miniature stimulus plan, funneling millions of dollars toward various public works projects like courthouses, schools, and roads. The state has also passed a requirement that at least half of all contractors and their employees be residents of Ames. As a result of the requirement, Marta, a painter who regularly works with a crew in Ames, but commutes in from the adjacent state of Barr, was told that she could not work on state-funded projects in Ames. Now out of a job, Marta has decided to sue Ames. Which of the following constitutional provisions or doctrines would furnish Marta's strongest argument?

A. The Privileges and Immunities Clause of Article IV.
B. The Commerce Clause.
C. The Taxing and Spending Clause.
D. The Dormant Commerce Clause Doctrine.

QUESTION 4. Commerce capers. The federal Partial Birth Abortion Ban states that "[a]ny physician who, in or affecting interstate commerce, knowingly performs a partial-birth abortion" shall be fined and sentenced to up to two years in prison. Dr. Don performs a partial-birth abortion as defined by the statute, is prosecuted, and convicted. He appeals his conviction, arguing that the statute impermissibly exceeds Congress's power under the Commerce Clause. The government argues that the ban is well within congressional power. Which of the following factors would be *least* helpful to the government's argument that the Act is permissible?

A. The ban contained extensive findings from Congress documenting the effects that unwanted pregnancies have on the national economy due to absences and health costs, as well as the harm to the economy resulting from crimes committed by children who grow up neglected.
B. The value of abortion services in the country total roughly $650 million annually.
C. Dr. Don performs the partial-birth abortions entirely within one state, and does so for no compensation.
D. The ban contains no explicit jurisdictional element tying the regulated activity to interstate commerce.

QUESTION 5. Bar-b-quandary. After a report shows global warming to be a significant threat, even after attempts to reduce emissions of carbon dioxide from industry and automobiles, Congress feels it must resort to more radical attempts to reduce emissions. Seizing on reports that charcoal grills produce two to three times more emissions than propane grills, and on reports that standard walk-behind mowers produce 11 times the emissions that automobiles do, Congress decides to ban both. Noting that, worldwide, global warming costs the world's economy $9 trillion, Congress finds in the bill that cutting emissions by any means necessary is a national economic imperative. It therefore outlaws the manufacture, distribution, sale, or possession of either a charcoal grill or gasoline-powered lawnmower "in or affecting interstate commerce."

Dave is prosecuted for possession of both a charcoal grill and a gasoline-powered motor, neither of which he uses as part of a commercial operation. He grills food for his family (and any guests) and uses the mower to mow his yard, and no one else's. He appeals his conviction, claiming that the law, as applied to him, exceeds Congress's power under the Commerce Clause. What should a reviewing court do?

A. Uphold his conviction, because Congress has plenary power over things that affect interstate commerce.
B. Uphold his conviction, because Congress may eliminate a market in a good and reach each part of that market, no matter how local or noncommercial.

C. Reverse his conviction, unless the government can prove that Dave's possession of the grill and mower substantially affected interstate commerce.

D. Reverse his conviction, because Dave's possession of the mower and grill are noncommercial.

QUESTION 6. Bar-b-quandary prequel. Assume for purposes of this question only that instead of enacting a ban on mowers and grills, Congress delegates authority to the Environmental Protection Agency (EPA) to promulgate regulations regarding the use of gasoline-powered motors and grills. According to the legislation authorizing the EPA's actions, the regulations, which Congress finds are necessary to protect the economy and the environment, instruct the EPA to regulate mowers and grills to the extent necessary to cut their emissions by at least 90 percent. Such regulations, the legislation states, may include a total ban if the EPA finds one is warranted. Upon hearing of this Act's passage, Pat, who owns a small commercial lawn service, sues, arguing that a ban would be an unconstitutional exercise of the commerce power. A judge hearing Pat's case would likely do what?

A. Dismiss his suit, because Pat owns a commercial lawn service.
B. Dismiss his suit, because the controversy is moot.
C. Dismiss his suit, because the controversy is not yet ripe.
D. Invalidate the legislation, because it represents an unconstitutional delegation of lawmaking authority to a mere agency.

QUESTION 7. Bar-b-quandary reprise. Assume for purposes of this question only that the Supreme Court invalidated the federal ban on grills and mowers described in Question 5. Congress responds by imposing a $500 tax on the sale of any charcoal grill and a $1,500 tax on the sale of gasoline-powered mowers. Gina and Ted, who own the Mower and Grill Emporium, sue, seeking to have the tax invalidated. Which of the following would be Gina and Ted's strongest argument against the tax?

A. Congress may not regulate indirectly what it may not regulate directly.
B. The tax is so high as to constitute a penalty on the purchase of both goods.
C. Congress may not use its taxing power to achieve a particular social policy.
D. The tax is not primarily intended to raise revenue.

QUESTION 8. **Whinge and a prayer.**   Rick, an avowed atheist, files suit in federal court alleging that the plan to have Joel, a popular television evangelist and self-help author, deliver a prayer at the upcoming presidential inauguration violates the Establishment Clause because the executive branch will reimburse Joel for his expenses. What should a federal judge do?

A. Permit the suit to go forward, because it involves government expenditures for religious purposes.

B. Dismiss the suit as moot.

C. Dismiss the suit, because Rick lacks standing.

D. Permit the suit to go forward, because the controversy is ripe.

QUESTION 9. **With extreme prejudice.**   As part of a global war on terror, a President authorizes strikes against persons living abroad designated as high value terrorist targets. Once authorized by the President, persons so designated may be killed by either remote controlled drones or by special operations teams tasked for the purpose. When the President who authorized that program leaves office, she is sued for wrongful death by the parents of one of the persons targeted and killed under the program. The parents claim that the identification of their child as a terrorist was mistaken. Which of the following is true about their suit?

A. The court would dismiss the suit, unless her actions were unreasonable in light of the established law at the time of her Administration.

B. The court would dismiss the suit, because the President is absolutely immune from civil suit for her official actions.

C. Allow the suit to proceed, unless Congress conferred immunity on the President via statute.

D. Allow the suit to proceed, because a President could be liable for actions undertaken while in office.

QUESTION 10. **A rove-ing we will go.**   Don is the former governor of a Southern state currently serving a prison sentence, having been found guilty of financial misconduct while in office. Don sues Karl, who was the former deputy chief of staff to the President of the United States. Don alleges that his prosecution was initiated at Karl's behest, and that Karl improperly pressured the U.S. Attorney in Don's state to prosecute the case as part of a campaign against members of Don's party all over the United States. May Karl claim immunity from civil suit for actions undertaken while he was in office?

A. Yes, executive branch officials are absolutely immune from civil suit for actions taken while in office.

B. Yes, because suits against executive branch officials for official conduct would violate separation of powers principles.

C. Yes, under the rule in *Clinton v. Jones*.

D. Yes, but only if Karl proves his actions were reasonable under the law at the time.

QUESTION 11. Tuition tiff.   Ames University is the flagship university in the State of Ames. Like many state universities, Ames charges its out-of-state students more for tuition than in-state students. In-state students pay $2,500 per semester, whereas out-of-state students are charged $5,000 per semester. Stewart, a junior attending Ames University, is from the neighboring state of Barr. He sues the State of Ames in federal court, alleging that its tuition policy violates, inter alia, the dormant Commerce Clause doctrine and the Privileges and Immunities Clause of Article IV. Stewart seeks a refund for all monies paid in excess of the in-state tuition amount over the last three years. What should the judge hearing the case do?

A. Dismiss it under the Eleventh Amendment.

B. Dismiss it on standing grounds.

C. Invalidate the law, unless Ames can prove that it is pursuing a legitimate interest and that there are no less discriminatory means open to the state.

D. Dismiss it, because education is not a "fundamental right."

QUESTION 12. Car wars.   In an effort to reduce reliance on imported oil, Congress and the White House announce a new initiative to require all cars built and sold in the United States to meet minimum fuel efficiency standards and to require older cars to be outfitted with new technology that will make them more fuel efficient. Because of the scale of such an undertaking, Congress seeks the help of the states by withholding 10 percent of federal highway funds unless state environmental agencies assist in the inspection of the older vehicles. The chief of the Ames environmental protection agency sues the government in federal court, claiming that the program is unconstitutional. How would a judge likely rule on the chief's suit?

A. Dismiss the suit, because the inspection provision is necessary and proper to a regulation of an instrumentality of interstate commerce.

B. Dismiss the suit, because compliance is conditioned on the receipt of federal money.

C. Invalidate the law, because it commandeers state executive officials.

D. Invalidate the law, because it is coercive.

QUESTION 13. I spy.   The President orders the Secretary of Defense to conduct surveillance on citizens and aliens residing in the United States suspected of being involved in terrorist activities. The Secretary of Defense in turn enlists the help of private telecommunications companies to assist the government. Members of Congress are briefed on the program. When news of the program leaks, civil liberties groups sue the Secretary, claiming, among other things, that the President's surveillance program was an unconstitutional exercise of presidential power. Which of the following, if true, would tend to support the President's right to initiate the surveillance program?

A. The presence of a statute banning domestic surveillance and strictly regulating the conditions under which surveillance of aliens may be conducted.

B. The President's power to ensure that laws are faithfully executed.

C. The lack of objection by members of Congress to the program.

D. B and C.

QUESTION 14. Gun show.   As more states authorize law-abiding citizens to obtain licenses to carry concealed handguns as a matter of right if they satisfy the statutory criteria, newspapers and other organizations have expressed interest in obtaining and publishing the names and addresses of those who have obtained concealed-carry permits. Permit holders and gun rights groups object, claiming that this violates the privacy of permit holders and could make them targets for burglary by those wishing to steal their guns. Others object to being solicited by insurance agencies and gun safety organizations, which buy lists of permit holders and contact them in hopes of drumming up business.

In response to permit holders' complaints, Congress passes a statute prohibiting any "person"—defined to include state and local governments as well as private businesses—from buying or selling in interstate commerce the identities of concealed-carry permit holders. The State of Ames, which had been supplementing its budget selling the lists of those holders to private businesses, sues claiming that the statute is unconstitutional. What should a reviewing court do?

A. Invalidate the law, because the federal statute impermissibly commandeers state officials who must comply with it.
B. Invalidate the law, because it exceeds Congress's power under the Commerce Clause.
C. Invalidate the law because it violates the Tenth Amendment.
D. Uphold the law under the Supremacy Clause.

QUESTION 15. Turning over a new Leaf?   Congress passes a law requiring individuals to purchase an electric car to reduce greenhouse gas emissions or pay a fine based on the amount of pollution one's vehicle emits. Only those who currently own cars are subject to the requirement. Abe, who doesn't drive, and commutes to work by bus, challenges the law in federal district court as a violation of Congress's enumerated powers. A reviewing court would likely:

A. Dismiss Abe's suit as unripe.
B. Dismiss Abe's suit as moot.
C. Invalidate the law because it regulates inactivity.
D. Dismiss Abe's suit because he has suffered no harm.

QUESTION 16. Plug or pay.   Assume for purposes of this question only that those who knowingly refuse to purchase an electric car are fined 10% of their gross income, which is levied and collected by the Environmental Protection Agency (EPA). The strongest argument *against* the validity of the electric car tax would be that:

A. It punishes *in*activity, and thus exceeds Congress's powers under the Commerce Clause.
B. It impermissibly regulates private activity.
C. It is an unconstitutional penalty.
D. It is coercive.

QUESTION 17. Sugar, sugar.   Congress passes a law conditioning receipt of 10% of federal funds for Medicaid on states' banning the sale of oversized sugary drinks, defined as drinks sold in quantities of 16 oz. or more. The State of Ames, which receives federal Medicaid monies, sues in federal district court, claiming that the law is unconstitutional. The judge should:

A. Rule against the state because it lacks standing.
B. Rule against the state because the law is a valid condition on federal spending.

C. Rule for the state because the law penalizes the state for noncompliance.

D. Rule for the state because the law is not a permissible regulation of interstate commerce.

QUESTION 18. A shot in the arm.   To stimulate the production of vaccines and antibiotics, Congress passes a law authorizing the introduction of experimental antibiotics and vaccines to the public. As an additional incentive, manufacturers must comply only with minimum safety and effectiveness standards that are less burdensome than full FDA approval. Several patients sue BigPharm, a company that had released an experimental antibiotic, in state court alleging that the antibiotic was defectively designed and that they were injured as a result. BigPharm successfully removes the action to federal court and seeks to dismiss the suit on the grounds that it is preempted. The federal judge hearing the case should:

A. Allow the suit to proceed, unless the federal law expressly preempts state law causes of action.

B. Allow the suit to go forward because state common law suits are not subject to federal statutory preemption.

C. Dismiss the suit, unless there is an express savings clause.

D. Dismiss the suit, because it conflicts with congressional policy.

QUESTION 19. Go fish.   The President negotiates and signs, and the Senate ratifies by the requisite 2/3 majority, a treaty obligating the United States to preserve native fish stocks from large scale commercial fishing, which threatens to devastate fishing worldwide due to overfishing. To implement the treaty, Congress passes legislation placing state wildlife officials in coastal states in charge of monitoring fish stocks, enforcing fishing quotas, and maintaining fish populations at levels set by the treaty. Quint, a fisherman, is found by his state's wildlife officers to have violated his quota; he is fined and sentenced to serve six months in federal prison. On appeal, Quint alleges that the law is an unconstitutional infringement on state sovereignty. A reviewing court should:

A. Affirm his conviction because he lacks standing to raise a state's defenses.

B. Affirm his conviction because the law was a valid regulation of interstate and foreign commerce.

C. Reverse his conviction because the law violated the Constitution's treatymaking provisions.

D. Reverse his conviction because the law commandeered state officials.

QUESTION 20. Convention hall haul.   Ames City, a city in the State of Ames, enters into a partnership with a private developer to develop a hotel and convention center designed to lure tourists and conventioneers to the city. Under the terms of the agreement, Ames City will invest 40% of the building costs and receive 40% ownership. The private entity will build and manage the facility, collecting fees from the city in return, for ten years. Each year, the city's ownership will increase—and the private entity's ownership will decrease—by 6%, until the city owns a 100% interest in the facility. To ensure the entity's profitability, Ames City passes an ordinance in the second year of the agreement requiring all meetings, concerts, or sporting events to use the hotel and convention center, and prohibiting meetings, concerts, or sporting events from booking into other competing venues in Ames City. The out-of-state owner of one of the competing venues sues Ames City, claiming the ordinance is unconstitutional. Which of the following is *least* helpful to Ames City in defending its ordinance?

A. The claim that Ames City is a market participant.
B. The claim that the ordinance treats all venues other than the publicly owned one equally.
C. The claim that providing funding for public spaces is a traditional governmental activity.
D. The claim that the discrimination is in favor of a publicly owned entity.

QUESTION 21. Goal: No coal.   The federal government would like to curb the use of coal by public and private utility companies in favor of cleaner forms of energy generation. Which of the following would *not* be a permissible way in which to curb coal use?

A. A law requiring states to pass laws banning the burning of coal by power plants in the state.
B. A federal law banning the burning of coal to generate power in or affecting interstate commerce.
C. A federal law requiring states to ban the burning of coal by power plants in the state or suffer the loss of 25% of funds available to states to promote alternative energy.
D. A federal law requiring power companies generating power in or affecting commerce to derive 50% of their power from alternative fuel sources, with waivers available to states presenting plans to reduce the amount of power derived from burning coal by half over ten years.

QUESTION 22. **Credit check.**   Eager to jumpstart its flagging economy, the State of Ames offers a tax credit equal to the amount of any new piece of manufacturing equipment put into operation by a company with its principal place of business in Ames. The credit will offset the tax the state imposes on the gross income of businesses with operations in the state. When a corporation with its principal place of business in Barr, a neighboring state, is denied the credit for a plant it built in Ames after the credit was announced, it sues, claiming the credit is unconstitutional. Which of the following statements about the Ames law is *false*?

A. The tax credit discriminates on its face.
B. The tax credit is constitutional because Ames is a participant in the market for new manufacturing facilities.
C. The tax credit is market regulation, not market participation.
D. The tax credit is subject to a dormant Commerce Clause challenge.

QUESTION 23. **Interlock and load.**   In an effort to combat drunk driving, the legislature in the State of Ames recently passed a law requiring that all new cars sold in the state be equipped with ignition interlock devices that disable an automobile's ignition system if the driver's blood alcohol level exceeds .08%. There are no car manufacturers located in the State. CarCo., a large, out-of-state car manufacturer sues in Ames federal district court, claiming that the regulation is unconstitutional. Which of the following facts would be *most* helpful to CarCo. in its suit?

A. Congress rejected a proposal in recently-passed automobile safety legislation to require interlock devices in new cars.
B. Complying with the Ames regulation will be costly to CarCo.
C. The regulation falls on out-of-state companies only.
D. The regulation directly regulates instrumentalities of interstate commerce.

Denning's Picks

1. THE TAXMAN COMETH.   There's no question but that Braun has standing—following passage, the University is subject to an actual injury (the tax), caused by the City, and which a court could remedy by invalidating the tax. Thus **D** is incorrect. The remaining answers discuss some aspect of the dormant Commerce Clause doctrine, but **A** is incorrect because the students affected have crossed state lines to attend Braun, which brings the activity under the phrase "commerce among the several states."

It's possible that *Pike* balancing would find that the costs to interstate commerce would outweigh the local benefits, as **C** claims, but there's a better answer. Because the ordinance differentiates between in-state and out-of-state residents explicitly, it is facially discriminatory and is, as the Court has said, "virtually per se illegitimate," unless the City meets a high standard—showing that it is pursuing a legitimate (i.e., nondiscriminatory or nonprotectionist) interest and that it lacks less discriminatory means of effectuating that interest. The City of Fair Isle is unlikely to meet that burden; therefore, **B** is the correct answer. **Ch. 5.B.2.**

2. TRUCKIN'. Here's another dormant Commerce Clause doctrine question. The key here is to pay close attention to what, precisely, the Ames statute does and what it does not do. There's nothing inherently protectionist expressed in the dual purpose of promoting safety and preserving state roads, so **A** is not correct. **B** is a possible answer, but the facts give little in the way of concrete costs to the trucking industry, and the benefits, according to the facts, are real, or at least not totally illusory. Whether the benefits would be clearly outweighed by the costs to interstate commerce is really a factual question—one that we don't have enough information to answer. Further, *Exxon* teaches that simply because the effects of a facially neutral statute fall on out-of-state companies does not, *ipso facto*, mean that discriminatory effects are present. So **D** is an incorrect statement of law.

Look again at the law itself, which excepts from its operations those trips that begin or end in Ames. That means that, on the face of the statute, in-state economic activity or activity that ends up or originates in the state is treated more favorably than interstate activity that merely passes through the state. That means the statute is *not* facially neutral, contrary to the implication of the other answers, but is rather facially discriminatory. Therefore **C** is the best answer. **Ch. 5.B.2.**

3. HOME COOKING. At first, you might have thought "Ah! Another dormant Commerce Clause question." If you did, look again. Ames has attached that condition only to those public works projects that it is funding. Recall that the market-participant doctrine is an exception to the DCCD, which allows state and local governments to make decisions regarding the spending of taxpayer money that mimic those decisions that private businesses get to make when they buy and sell goods, including discriminating against out-of-state goods and economic actors. **D**, therefore, is not the correct answer. Nor is **B**; the Commerce Clause (as opposed to the dormant Commerce Clause doctrine) limits the ability of *Congress*, not states, to manage the national economy. **C**, too, would be incorrect, because, again, Article I's Tax and Spend Clause applies to Congress, not to the states.

That leaves **A**, which is the correct answer. Marta is an individual, and even if there is no DCCD claim because of the market-participant exception, there is no analogous exception to the Privileges and Immunities Clause of

Article IV. That Clause gives Marta the right to make a living on terms substantially equal to those from out of state, unless the state can demonstrate a substantial interest and that the discrimination is substantially related to that interest.**Ch. 5.C.**

4. COMMERCE CAPERS. Recall that, after *Morrison* and *Lopez,* the Commerce Clause permits Congress to regulate the channels of interstate commerce, instrumentalities of interstate commerce, and those intrastate activities that substantially affect interstate commerce. Factors relevant to proving the latter are: (1) whether the regulated activity is economic or noneconomic; (2) the presence of findings; (3) the presence of a "jurisdictional element" tying the regulated activity to interstate commerce; (4) whether the regulated activity is considered an area of traditional state concern; (5) whether the intrastate activity is part of a national regulatory scheme, the efficacy of which would be undermined if that activity could not be reached by Congress; and (6) whether permitting an exercise of federal power would render the Commerce Clause limitless. *Raich* made clear that if Congress can eliminate a particular market, then it may reach all instances of that regulated market, no matter how local or noncommercial.

Starting from the bottom, **D** is not the correct answer. There *is* language in the statute itself—the "in or affecting interstate commerce" language—that satisfies the Court's preference for a jurisdictional element. **C** wouldn't be particularly helpful, but after *Raich,* it is largely beside the point. If Congress can ban abortions, then it can ban all abortions, no matter how local or noncommercial. **B** would actually be quite helpful; it makes abortions look like economic activity, as opposed to the regulation of a mere medical procedure. That leaves **A**, which is the correct answer. Although findings from Congress are helpful, the *Morrison* Court said that they weren't helpful if they merely repeated the same kind of attenuated causal chains it rejected in *Lopez,* where the government argued that guns in schools resulted in schools that were not safe, leading in turn to lower educational achievement and reduced competitiveness on a global scale. **Ch. 4.B.**

5. BAR-B-QUANDARY. Substitute "marijuana" for "charcoal grills" and "lawnmowers" and the facts in this question are essentially those of *Raich*. But first, to clear some underbrush, **A** is an incorrect statement of law. Congress may regulate intrastate activities that substantially affect interstate commerce, but that's not quite having "plenary" power over everything that merely "affects" interstate commerce—or at least the Court tells us that the two are not the same thing. **C** is incorrect because, as *Raich* demonstrated, there are no *de minimis* exceptions to Congress's power to regulate, once established. It is sufficient for Congress to have had a rational basis for concluding that, in the aggregate, possession of those things substantially affects interstate commerce.

Similarly, **D** is incorrect, because even pre-*Raich* the Court made it clear that activity didn't necessarily have to be commercial as long as it was, in some sense, "economic." According to *Raich* even simple possession of marijuana for personal, medicinal use was economic, because that "legal" marijuana was indistinguishable from that which the government was trying to eliminate. The Court concluded that the government could outlaw *all* marijuana, instead of trying to differentiate between medicinal and recreational marijuana. Similarly, the continued possession of the grill and the mower "competes" in a sense against propane grills and electric or manual mowers and thus is "economic" in the sense used by the *Raich* Court. That leaves **B**, which is the holding of *Raich* and the best answer. **Ch. 4.B.**

6. BAR-B-QUANDARY PREQUEL. If you read the facts carefully, you will have noticed that no regulations have been forthcoming from the EPA. Congress has merely delegated authority to that agency to promulgate them. That delegation of power is coupled with an "intelligent principle" (to reduce emissions in grills and mowers by 90 percent), so **D** is incorrect. The limiting principle falls well within the broad scope given by the Court to Congress in delegating power to executive agencies. **A** might be relevant to the ultimate disposition of the case on the merits, but because no regulations have actually been issued yet, there is a better answer. **B** is incorrect because whatever else the case is, it isn't moot. Nothing has happened yet.

That leaves **C**, which is the correct answer. Recall that "ripeness" is one of those justiciability doctrines intended to ensure that cases are brought at the right time. Here, Pat has neither "suffered harm," nor been threatened with "specific present objective harm"—as no regulations have been issued—nor is he faced with the "threat of specific future harm." He might be able to bring suit once the regulations are issued by the EPA, but at this stage it appears that any suit would be premature. **Ch. 2.C.3.b.**

7. BAR-B-QUANDARY REPRISE. Luxury and excise taxes are frequently used in national tax policy, because they tend to impact behavior. Higher taxes tend to decrease consumption of the thing taxed, and lower taxes have the opposite effect. **C**, therefore, is incorrect. Further, cases like *Davis* illustrate that **A** is incorrect as well. The Court has long interpreted each of Congress's Article I powers to be independent of each other; simply because it may not pass a law under, say, the Commerce Clause, does not mean that it may not find authority in another enumerated power. **D** is incorrect as well; with the overruling of *Drexel Furniture,* the Court declined to tie a tax's constitutionality to the amount of revenue it did or was intended to raise.

That leaves **B**. Although the Court largely leaves taxes to the political process, it has left open the theoretical possibility that a valid tax could end up being an impermissible penalty and thus beyond the scope of Congress's power. Such an argument, although plausible, would encounter rough sledding in court. **Ch.4.C.2.**

8. WHINGE AND A PRAYER. If you focused on the nature of the claim—that the prayer violated the Establishment Clause—you might have been led astray because of the *Flast v. Cohen* exception to the bar against tax-payer suits for "generalized grievances." Recall that the *Hein* case restricted *Flast* to instances where there was a direct expenditure of money by *Congress*. (Under *Flast,* Rick might have standing if Congress voted an appropriation to reimburse Joel directly.) Therefore **A** is incorrect. The suit isn't moot, because according to the facts the inauguration has not yet occurred; therefore **B** is incorrect as well.

Between **C** and **D**, **C** is the better answer because Rick has not suffered any particularized injury to justify standing. His "injury" is simply one that he shares with thousands of other taxpayers who might wish the government *not* to spend money hiring a preacher to deliver a prayer. Such an injury, how-ever, does not satisfy standing's constitutional core. **D** is not as good an answer because Rick *has* alleged the threat of specific future harm; the harm, though, is not sufficient to satisfy standing doctrine's injury-in-fact requirement. **Ch. 2.C.3.a.**

9. WITH EXTREME PREJUDICE.   The correct answer is **B**, under the rule established in *Nixon v. Fitzgerald*. **A** states the test for "qualified immunity," conferred on presidential aides and other high-level executive branch officials since *Harlow v. Fitzgerald*. Both **C** and **D** are incorrect. In *Clinton v. Jones*, the Court held that a President can be sued for actions taken prior to his taking office and that, as a matter of constitutional law, the President is not entitled to have those claims tolled until he completes his term of office. The Court did say, however, that Congress could prescribe a different rule should it wish to. **Ch. 6.F.2.**

10. A ROVE-ING WE WILL GO.   *Nixon v. Fitzgerald* held that the President is absolutely immune from civil suit for actions undertaken while in office. In *Harlow v. Fitzgerald,* however, the Court declined to extend that immu-nity to other executive branch officials. Therefore **A** is incorrect. **C** is incorrect because *Clinton v. Jones* held that Presidents were not immune, as a matter of constitutional law, for conduct occurring prior to taking office. As between **B** and **D**, **B** is incorrect because, of course, *Harlow v. Fitzgerald* does allow for suit of executive branch officials. Instead of absolute immunity, however, executive branch officials other than the President enjoy qualified immunity, meaning they are immune if their actions were reasonable in light of the state of the law at the time of the actions. **D** therefore is the correct answer. **Ch. 6.F.2.**

11. TUITION TIFF.   This was tricky! You were probably drawn to either **C** or **D** because of the obvious discrimination between in-state and out-of-state students effected by Ames's tuition policy. Neither is quite correct because there is a better answer. **C** is incorrect, because Ames could probably claim successfully that it is a participant in the market for university students, and that because it is, in essence, subsidizing part of the education at Ames University, it is entitled to discriminate between in-state and out-of-state students under the market-participant exception. **D** may be correct on the merits, but there is a better answer. **B** is incorrect, because Stewart has suffered injury as an out-of-state student forced to pay more than in-state students. Notice that in the facts, Stewart has sued the *state*—as opposed to a particular state official—and wants retrospective monetary relief, as opposed to an injunction prohibiting the charging of differential tuition. Both facts implicate the Eleventh Amendment. Because nonconsenting states may not be sued in federal court (or in state court for that matter), the Eleventh Amendment would bar Stewart's claim. **A** is the correct answer. **Ch. 2.C.6.**

12. CAR WARS.   It is true that Congress may not commandeer state legislatures or state executive officials. Thus, it may be true that requiring state and local officials to implement a federal program would be "necessary and proper" to the carrying out of the program, but that isn't sufficient to make it constitutional. Therefore, **A** is incorrect. However, recall that in both *New York v. United States* and in the *Printz* case, the Court went out of its way to distinguish commandeering from the conditions attached to federal spending provisions. The latter is governed by the *Dole* case, and conditional spending constitutes an exception to the anti-commandeering principle. Therefore **C** is incorrect as well. *Dole* required conditions on spending to be made for the general welfare (which Congress decides), unambiguous, related in some way to the federal interest in national programs, not otherwise unconstitutional, and suggested that some conditions might be so onerous as to be impermissibly coercive.

Dole upheld a requirement that states raise their drinking ages to 21, or face the loss of 5 percent of federal highway funds. Here states hazard 10 percent of those funds if they don't assist in the inspection of older cars for fuel efficiency. While the Court didn't suggest a threshold, it is unlikely it would deem 10 percent of highway funds to cross the line and be coercive. Therefore **D** is incorrect. That leaves, **B**, the correct answer. The condition described in the question closely tracks that in *Dole*, and would likely be upheld if challenged. **Ch. 4.C.3 and Ch. 4.D.3.**

13. I SPY.   Starting with Justice Jackson's *Youngstown* opinion, it helps to know whether there is any express or implied congressional approval of or opposition to the President's program. If there is approval, or silence, then the President's power is either at its height or one is in the "zone of twilight" where the President's action might be lawful as a practical matter. If, however, Congress has expressly *dis*approved presidential action, the President may rely only on his power *minus* that of Congress over the same subject matter. The question asks which of the four items would *strengthen* the President's hand.

Obviously **A** is incorrect, because it runs counter to the surveillance program described in the facts. **B** is incorrect because all the opinions in *Youngstown* rejected administration attempts to invoke the "take care" clause in support of his seizure of the steel mills. Justice Black and Justice Jackson together noted that the take care clause presupposed law that the President was charged with executing; it was not, both emphasized, an independent source of power from which the President could draw. If **B** is not the correct answer, then **D** cannot be either. That leaves **C**, the correct answer. If Congress is silent, then Justice Jackson emphasizes that, at least as a practical matter, that inaction might be construed by the President as acquiescence or at least as an invitation to action. The Court also emphasized the lack of congressional objection to the presidential settlement of claims with Iran in *Dames & Moore.* **Ch. 6.B.**

14. GUN SHOW.   Another tricky one! (Well, these are supposed to be the trickiest of the lot.) Did you think this was impermissible commandeering? If you did, go back to Chapter 4 and read the section on *Reno v. Condon.* Recall that in *Condon,* the Court upheld a similar bill barring persons (including states) from selling driver's license data. The Court held (1) that because the data was in interstate commerce, Congress could regulate it, and (2) that forcing states to comply with the ban was not commandeering because the states didn't have to do anything, except stop selling the data. To hold otherwise would have been to effect a repeal of the Supremacy Clause, because states are already under a constitutional obligation to comply with a valid federal law. Thus, **A** and **B** are incorrect. **C** is incorrect as well; if the statute does not impermissibly commandeer the state officials, then it does not offend the Tenth Amendment principles embodied in the anti-commandeering doctrine. That leaves **D**, which is the correct answer. The Act regulates a thing in interstate commerce, as permitted by *Lopez* and *Morrison,* and thus trumps contrary state law under the Supremacy Clause of Article VI. **Ch. 4.B.5 and Ch. 4.D.3.**

15. TURNING OVER A NEW LEAF?   In order to have standing an individual, at a minimum, must have suffered some injury-in-fact that is concrete and particularized to the individual, and is actual or imminent. Here Abe is not subject to the law because he does not drive. The correct answer is **D**. For a plaintiff with standing, the action wouldn't lack ripeness because Congress has already passed the law. Nor do facts suggest that circumstances (say, repeal of the law) have rendered it moot. Therefore neither **A** nor **B** are correct. **C** may or may not be correct—but a court would only reach the merits if it has jurisdiction. Here, Abe has suffered no injury, has no standing, and therefore the court has no jurisdiction to hear the case. **Ch. 2.C.3.a.**

16. PLUG OR PAY.   This is the problem the Court faced in the litigation over the Affordable Care Act. Five justices in that case expressed the opinion that Congress may not regulate inactivity under its commerce power, but we don't know what the precedential value of those opinions are, because the dissenting justices did not join that portion of the Chief Justice's opinion, which may be dicta anyway, because he upheld the payment-in-lieu-of-insurance under the taxing power. That suggests **A** is not the best answer. As it happens, there is a better one. Note that the required payment for noncompliance is quite harsh (10% of gross income), there is a "knowing" requirement, and it is collected by the EPA, not by the IRS. This suggests that this is not a valid tax, but an invalid penalty under the criteria endorsed by the Court in *National Federation of Independent Business*. **C** is the best answer. **B** is irrelevant: Congress can regulate private activity, and frequently does, using its enumerated powers. **D** imports a concept ("coercion") that is relevant to conditions imposed on the receipt of federal funds by *states*. **Chs. 4.B.6 and 4.C.2.**

17. SUGAR, SUGAR. The question here is whether or not Congress's condition on the receipt of its Medicaid funds was "coercive." The state receives Medicaid monies and stands to lose them if it doesn't comply with the condition, which it does not want to do. It satisfies the elements of standing—injury-in-fact, fairly attributable to the government, that can be redressed by a favorable decision—so **A** is incorrect. Moreover, whether Congress could directly ban the intrastate sale of sugary drinks of a certain size using its commerce power is irrelevant. Congress can condition spending on compliance with certain requirements if the conditions satisfy the *Dole* test, enabling it to do indirectly what it might be unable to do directly. So **D** is not correct either. **C** isn't correct either. Any condition presenting states with a choice between receiving 100% of federal money and some percentage less than 100% for not complying with the attached conditions is, in a sense, a "penalty," but that doesn't affect the condition's constitutionality. After *National Federation of Independent Business*, a federal spending condition may be invalidated for being *coercive*, but not for "penalizing" noncompliance (a concept that does matter, however, for distinguishing between proper and improper exercises of the taxing power). Because the condition seems unambiguous, the percentage is relatively modest (i.e., is not so large that it would constitute coercion), and is related to the purpose for which money is distributed in the first place (to take care of the health of lower income persons), **B** is the best answer. **Ch. 4.C.3.**

18. A SHOT IN THE ARM. Congress can of course expressly preempt both positive state law and state common law causes of action—but it rarely does so explicitly. Nevertheless, the Court has held that federal legislation may also impliedly preempt state law, including state common law. Therefore, neither **A** nor **B** is the correct answer. Further, a savings clause in a federal statute can carve out state law, preventing it from being preempted, but neither is this necessary to prevent a court from finding that the law is not preempted. So **C** is not the best answer either. That leaves **D**, which is the best answer on the facts, which indicate that Congress wanted to provide some minimum standards to incentivize vaccine and antibiotic production; state tort suits against manufacturers would likely prove to be an obstacle to Congress's goal—the more rapid production of vaccines and antibiotics—and would therefore be deemed impliedly preempted by a reviewing court. **Ch. 5.D.**

19. GO FISH. Did I trip you up? The standing distractor was mean, I confess. After *United States v. Bond*, it is clear that individuals challenging the constitutionality of their convictions can raise arguments like the one Quint has raised here. The treaty and implementing legislation pose no problems from the perspective of the treatymaking clause; it was negotiated by the President, ratified by 2/3 of the Senate, and then the whole Congress passed implementing legislation. So **C** isn't the correct answer. Though **B** is correct—the legislation imposing fishing quotas and the like could be a valid regulation of interstate and foreign commerce in addition to being "necessary and proper" to implement the treaty—it isn't the right answer either because of the *means* Congress employed. If you read carefully, you saw that *state* officials were tasked with enforcing aspects of the treaty. That commandeers state officials, which is not permitted under cases like *New York v. U.S.* and *Printz v. U.S.* **D** is the correct answer. **Ch. 4.D.3.**

20. CONVENTION HALL HAUL.   I know, I can hear you saying, "But I was told that there would be no math." By the second year of the agreement, Ames City is the majority owner (52%) in the hotel and convention center, making it publicly owned. Recall that the Court recently created an exception to the dormant Commerce Clause doctrine's anti-discrimination prong for discrimination in favor of publicly owned entities providing "traditional governmental functions." The ordinance requires all comers to use the city-owned facilities, meaning that all competing facilities—whether owned by in-state or out-of-state owners—are treated equally. **B** therefore would be helpful to Ames City. **C** would also be useful, since the Court in both the *United Haulers* and *Davis* cases made reference to the fact that trash disposal and bond sales, respectively, were activities that government had traditionally engaged in. Ames City could also claim that insofar as creating public spaces to attract tourists and conventioneers is a form of economic development, building and running the convention and hotel is a traditional governmental activity. That, too, would be helpful to turning back the challenge to the ordinance. Finally, **D** is helpful, too. The Court in *United Haulers* stressed that many things other than simple economic protectionism drove cities to discriminate in favor of publicly owned entities. That leaves **A**, the correct answer. Any claim that Ames City is a market participant would *not* be helpful to it, because its activities in passing the ordinance do not mirror activities that private market participants would be able to engage in. (Private businesses cannot force people to use their products or services to the exclusion of competitors.) Mandating the use of a public facility would be considered market regulation, not market participation. **Chs. 5.B.4.b., 5.B.4.c.**

21. GOAL: NO COAL.   Generally, Congress can regulate directly, using its enumerated powers; it can regulate indirectly by attaching conditions to spending or by using its taxing power; or it can regulate directly, but allow states the choice to regulate on their own with the federal standard as the minimum standard or "floor." What Congress *cannot* do is to command the state legislatures to do the bidding of the federal government either directly or by commandeering their executive branch officials to implement a federal program. With this in mind, you should be able to choose **A** as the correct answer. Congress cannot force state legislatures to pass legislation dictated to it by the federal government. Answers **B** (direct regulation of coal burning in interstate commerce), **C** (conditional spending), and **D** (inviting states to regulate on their own in lieu of direct regulation by the federal government) are all options available to Congress that do not unduly infringe on state sovereignty. **Chs. 4.B, 4.C, 4.D.**

22. CREDIT CHECK.   The dormant Commerce Clause doctrine requires states to bear a heavy burden to justify discrimination against interstate commerce or interstate commercial actors. The tax credit at issue, which is available to businesses whose principal place of business is in the state and not available to those businesses whose principal place of business is located elsewhere, is facially discriminatory. So **A** is true, as is **D**. But there is an exception for "market participants": When states participate in a market, buying or selling goods or services with their taxpayers' money, they can discriminate against out-of-state vendors the same as a private market participant could. You might think that the tax credit is a form of market participation because the State is participating in the market for new industry and using incentives to attract industries, the way that, say, the owner of a piece of land might cut the price in the hopes that someone will buy it. The problem is that Ames is doing this, not by offering a cash subsidy nor by offering something it owns on favorable terms to in-state residents, but through the use of its tax code. Private market participants can't offer tax breaks, deductions, or credits in their dealings with others. In *New Energy Co. v. Limbach*, the Court termed the taxing power "primeval governmental activity" that was market regulation, not market participation. **C**, therefore, is a true statement and the correct answer is **B. Ch. 5.B.4.b.**

23. INTERLOCK AND LOAD.   At first, you might be thinking, "Aha! A dormant Commerce Clause problem." But looking at the facts and your choices, you might think twice. First, the law requires all cars sold in Ames to have interlock devices. It's evenhanded. Moreover, it doesn't appear that this is motivated by a discriminatory purpose. And while the burden falls on out-of-state manufacturers only, it doesn't seem to benefit any possible in-state competitor with the out-of-state car manufacturers the way the regulations in *Hunt* benefitted North Carolina apple growers at the expense of the Washington growers. Moreover, the *Exxon* case tells us that merely because the burdens fall primarily on out-of-state businesses, that fact is insufficient to lead a court to conclude that discriminatory effects are present. That means both that **C** is not the best answer, and that that the regulation would likely be evaluated under the more lenient *Pike* balancing test. That test requires the challenger to prove that the burdens to interstate commerce are *clearly excessive* compared to the putative local benefits. **B** won't be particularly helpful either; compliance with all sorts of state regulations is often costly. But that fact tells you nothing about whether the costs would be clearly excessive in relation to the expected reduction in deaths, injuries, and property damage due to drunk driving accidents. Where the Court has invalidated evenhanded regulations under *Pike* balancing, the "benefits" turn out to be zero or even less than zero. That's not likely the case here. **D** is not correct because analysis under the dormant Commerce Clause doctrine no longer turns on whether state regulations "directly" or "indirectly" regulate interstate commerce. That leaves **A**, which is the best answer. If CarCo. could prove that Congress considered, and rejected interlock devices as a part of legislation prescribing safety devices on automobiles, then CarCo. would have a good argument that the state law is impliedly preempted because it stands as an obstacle to congressional aims in the last round of safety legislation. At the very least, the answer represents the most helpful among the choices given. **Chs. 5.B., 5.C.**

Table of Cases

Index